Individuality

*Human Possibilities and
Personal Choice in the
Psychological Development
of Men and Women*

Leona E. Tyler

Individuality

*Human Possibilities and
Personal Choice in the
Psychological Development
of Men and Women*

 Jossey-Bass Publishers
San Francisco • Washington • London • 1978

INDIVIDUALITY
Human Possibilities and Personal Choice in the Psychological Development of Men and Women
        by Leona E. Tyler

Library of Congress Catalogue Card Number LC 78-50897

International Standard Book Number ISBN 0-87589-365-1

Manufactured in the United States of America

JACKET DESIGN BY WILLI BAUM

FIRST EDITION

Code 7806

A joint publication in
The Jossey-Bass Series
in Social and Behavioral Science
& in Higher Education

Preface

This book has been a long time in the making. The actual writing has consumed the best hours of the past three years, but its roots go back much farther than that. During all of my years as a psychologist, my specialty has been individual differences. Even before I became a psychologist, it was largely the hope of coming to understand individuals in all of their uniqueness that influenced me to embark on this career. However, as I taught courses in individual differences and tried to apply what I knew in my counseling practice, I found myself becoming increasingly dissatisfied with what psychologists were doing to facilitate our understanding of individuals. The insistence on organizing the whole field around linear, measurable traits seemed to be blocking progress in dealing with many aspects of individuality.

My dissatisfaction crystalized first in my presidential address to the Western Psychological Association in 1958, "Toward a Workable Psychology of Individuality" (subsequently published in *American Psychologist*, 1959). The two major underemphasized aspects of individuality I considered important then were *choice* and *organization*. These two concepts have played a large part in the research and theorizing I have done ever since; and, as time has passed, other concepts—especially *competencies, repertoires, systems,* and *possibility-processing structures*—have come to appear equally significant. Linking these concepts is the central proposition that an individual is the result of a continuous developmental process in which a unique fraction of the innumerable possibilities inherent in the human race is selected and organized.

In *Individuality* I have tried to build a philosophical and theoretical framework on the foundation of this proposition and to fill it in with relevant research findings from disparate areas of psychology. The structure of the whole book would have been more elegant and satisfying if decisions about what to include had been made on logical grounds alone, but decisions also had to be based on the availability of research findings. Thus, there are gaps and discontinuities. Many of the most interesting questions about the development of individuality have not even been asked yet, let alone answered.

The book is intended to serve two main purposes. One is to broaden the scope of the branch of psychology that we have labeled *individual differences* by including aspects to which concepts of more or less, higher or lower, and better or worse do not apply. My hope is that new assessment techniques and new applications in counseling and placement may come out of this change of emphasis. The second purpose is to stimulate in psychologists concerned with other specialties—such as experimental, developmental, and social psychology—a heightened awareness of the importance of looking at individuals as well as at group averages. I hope there will be increasing use of idiographic along with nomothetic techniques and that new experimental designs and techniques of data analysis will emerge. In summary, the readers to whom the book is addressed are psychologists from both disciplines of scientific psychology who are not entirely content with the present state of the art. Nonpsychologists interested in individuality but impatient with mental testing may also like to consider some of the approaches discussed here.

If I tried to thank all of the persons whose ideas show up in these pages, the list would be a very long one. I would especially like to thank Alvin Landfield and the other contributors to the *1976 Nebraska Symposium on Motivation: Personal Construct Psychology,* Donald Bannister, Han Bonarius, Miller Mair, James

Mancuso, Seymour Rosenberg, and Theodore Sarbin, for making their papers available to me before publication. I am similarly indebted to Herman Witkin for putting me in touch with current research on field dependence and independence not yet published and to Jack Block, who sent me data from his ongoing longitudinal study of young children to examine. Norman Sundberg, friend, neighbor, and research collaborator, has been a constant source of ideas. I also owe a special debt of gratitude to Doris Boylan for her superb job of typing the final manuscript.

Florence, Oregon   LEONA E. TYLER
December 1977

Contents

The Author

LEONA ELIZABETH TYLER, who served as dean of the graduate school at the University of Oregon from 1965 until her retirement in 1971, began her long association with the university in 1940.

Her degrees were earned at the University of Minnesota: a B.S. in English in 1925, a M.S. in psychometrics in 1939, and a Ph.D. in psychology in 1941. After receiving her bachelor's degree, she taught for thirteen years in junior high schools in Minnesota and Michigan. In the course of this experience, she came to appreciate the unique qualities of individuals, especially as revealed in her students' compositions.

Leona Tyler has served as president of the Oregon Psychological Association (1953–1954), the Western Psychological Association (1957–1958), and the American Psychological Association (1972–1973). She has held guest professorships at the University of California, Berkeley (1957–58), and the University of Amsterdam (1962–63), with summer appointments at Stanford University, the University of British Columbia, and the University of Minnesota.

Her research undertakings have focused mainly on the development of interests and organized choices; counseling has also been one of her professional concerns throughout the years, and she has published a number of papers in these areas. She is the author of *Individual Differences: Abilities and Motivational Directions* (1974), *Tests and Measurements* (1971, 2nd ed.), *The Work of the Counselor* (1969, 3rd ed.), and *The Psychology of Human Differences* (1965, 3rd ed.). She is the editor of *Intelligence: Some Recurring Issues* (1969) and a collaborator with N. Sundberg and J. Taplin on *Clinical Psychology: Expanding Horizons* (1973), with N. Sundberg on *Clinical Psychology: An Introduction to Research and Practice* (1962), and with F. Goodenough on a revision of *Developmental Psychology* (1959).

Leona Tyler now lives and writes at her home at Heceta Beach on the Oregon coast. Since retirement, she has traveled extensively in Europe, Asia, and the South Pacific.

Individuality

*Human Possibilities and
Personal Choice in the
Psychological Development
of Men and Women*

≫ 1 ≪

A Philosophy of Possibilities and Choice

In psychology fresh winds are blowing, sweeping away overly restrictive assumptions, dusting off concepts that had been covered over and neglected, picking up and juxtaposing separate ideas to produce novel combinations. A dynasty of dominant theories has been overthrown. No longer does a rigid hypothetico-deductive model hold exclusive sway in the laboratory. No longer is a rigid adherence to Freudian or Rogerian doctrine required of psychotherapists. Physiological, social, and developmental psychologists are proposing new techniques, new concepts, new theories. Pluralism is the order of the day. Like Mao Tse-tung, psychologists are saying, "Let a thousand flowers bloom."

Underlying these liberating changes are some liberalizing assumptions about what it means to be a scientist. For more than a hundred years, the one value held in high esteem by all sorts of

1

psychologists has been respect for scientific ways of thinking and working. Psychologists are proud to be engaged in building a *science* of human behavior to replace the amorphous collection of philosophical ideas that had accumulated over the centuries. This pride has made them lean over backward to be scientific—to adhere strictly to every canon of scientific method, to guard against every assumption that might be considered questionable. No trace of "softness" must be detectable in the reasoning one applies to beings like oneself, with joys and sorrows, anxieties and ecstasies. In an age dominated by material progress, most psychologists have been materialists. Because positivism was espoused by leading philosophers of science, psychologists became positivists. The words *objectivity, rigor,* and *operational concept* were the good words.

During the 1960s and 1970s, widely held assumptions have been questioned, and new ones are being proposed. This reexamination is having an especially liberating effect on the psychology of individuality, which never has fit comfortably into the self-imposed limits under which psychologists were trying to operate. Let us look, then, at some of the changes in objectives, concepts, and hypotheses that are now claiming the attention of psychologists. Perhaps the most fundamental is a shift from *reaction* to *action* as the phenomenon to be studied. Since the behaviorist revolution early in this century, the basic unit into which behavior has been analyzed is a combination of stimulus and response, the S-R unit. While from time to time other ways of conceptualizing complex behavior, especially cognitive behavior, have been suggested and while it has repeatedly proved necessary to redefine and broaden the terms *stimulus* and *response,* most psychologists have clung to the basic S-R concept because they considered it to be essential to a *science* of human behavior. However, as research findings accumulated, it became increasingly apparent that action is more fundamental than reaction. Action occurs in the absence of any identifiable stimulus; living things are *inherently* active; for organisms at all levels, action is a "given" in the equation. What stimulation does is to modify and transform already existing patterns of activity. Biologists and philosophers as well as psychologists are emphasizing the primacy of action. One of the most comprehensive accounts of what a psychology in which the *act* is the fundamental unit would be like is being formulated by Langer (1967, 1972), some of whose ideas are considered in a later section.

Another significant shift in the thinking psychologists do about human nature is the shift from "human-as-machine" to "machine-simulating-human." Early behaviorists acted on the assumption that a living organism is essentially a complex machine, controlled by mechanical principles. During the middle decades of the twentieth century, *models,* both physical and mathematical, fascinated researchers. Although they were recognized to be oversimplifications, they were still viewed as approximations to more complex models that would ultimately account for human functioning. When computers first came into general use, the goal of explaining complex behavior mechanically appeared to have been brought closer. But as time passed a subtle change occurred in the goal itself. There was less talk about the human chess player being essentially a computer with a complex program and more talk about using both the achievements and the limitations in what computers could be programmed to do, as an aid to understanding what Bobby Fischer does. Using models as analogies helps us to understand both behavior that fits the pattern and behavior that does not. And proceeding in this way does not require an assumption that a human is *nothing but* a complicated machine.

Related to this shift in the objectives of model making is a more pervasive shift in what are seen as the ultimate objectives of psychological research. For decades, psychologists assumed and students were taught that the aim of the whole undertaking is to *predict and control.* This purpose generated a self-contained system that worked reasonably well as long as research efforts were confined within the boundaries of laboratories. The outcome of one experiment enabled one to predict what would happen if stimuli were manipulated in a certain way in the next one. Successful predictions were considered to constitute a validation of the reasoning on which they were based. The more control that could be attained over extraneous stimulation, the more the variability of response was reduced, and the more accurate the predictions became. True, predictions about what any single individual would do never turned out to be very accurate, but statistical techniques, continually refined and rendered more sophisticated, allowed the investigator to

draw conclusions from the general trends shown in groups of subjects without paying much attention to unexplained predictive
failures in individual cases.

Recently, two considerations have tempered our enthusiasm
about the "prediction and control" objective. One is our recognition of the fact that predicting what a person or even a group of
persons will do in life situations is very much more difficult than
predicting the outcome of a laboratory experiment. As scientists
imposed more and more rigorous controls in their experiments, they
found that the generalizations based on these experiments were less
and less relevant to anything in the world outside the laboratory.
Psychologists began to ask themselves embarrassing questions. "Are
we really making any headway in finding out how to predict and
control what goes on in the classroom? The labor negotiation? The
legislature?" Social psychologists in particular have become somewhat
disillusioned with prevailing experimental methods. The other consideration that prompts questioning of the "prediction and control"
objective is the growing concern over the ethical aspects of behavior
control. The more psychologists thought about it, the less sure they
were that it would be good for humanity to be subject to control by
behavioral scientists and the authorities for whom they worked.

While the change in objective is still far from complete,
more and more psychologists are seeing their purpose as that of
understanding some of the reasons people behave as they do, so that
scientists and the people who cooperate with them in research undertakings (it hardly seems appropriate to call them *subjects*) may
be able to manage their individual and collective affairs more adequately. Enabling people to anticipate the consequences of their
own acts is a different and ethically much more attractive aim than
enabling some persons to predict and control the behavior of others.

The changes in the prevailing assumptions make possible
the development of a more adequate psychology of human individuality, the study of unique human individuals in their social settings, a kind of research not common in the past. In the laboratory,
individual uniqueness tended to get lost. One studied general processes rather than particular people and drew conclusions about the
general effects of various kinds of stimulating conditions on aggression, anxiety, achievement motivation, and other things, without

paying much attention to the fact that different individuals might be reacting very differently to the experimental situation.

It is true that from the beginning of scientific psychology there have always been scientists who were more interested in individual differences than in general trends. Out of their efforts grew a second branch of scientific psychology (Cronbach, 1957), usually referred to as *differential* or *correlational psychology*. The strategy adopted in this line of work was to single out *traits* and devise schemes for *measuring* how much of the trait each person manifested. Scores on each of these measuring scales or *tests*, as they came to be called, were correlated with scores on other scales and with quantitative indices of performance in practical situations. The inventor of this procedure was Alfred Binet, and the first trait to be measured was intelligence. As the years passed, dozens, then hundreds, even thousands of tests were constructed to measure intelligence and all sorts of other characteristics. Research on the measurement of individual differences constituted a separate stream of scientific work, more or less detached from the mainstream of experimental investigation. But here too the uniqueness of individuals somehow seemed to get lost. Attempts to account for it in terms of the combination of separate trait measurements obtained for an individual never really accomplished this purpose. It seems wrong somehow, for example, to think of a person as so many units of intelligence plus so many units of mechanical aptitude plus so many units of extraversion.

There was another stream of psychological thinking along which recognition of individual uniqueness was carried, the clinical study of persons who were encountering some sort of difficulty in functioning. For a time, it seemed that the genius of Sigmund Freud had charted a course that would lead to a scientific understanding of individuals. Freud and his followers, like the experimental psychologists, were convinced of the importance of scientific values such as determinism, objectivity, and careful observation. The psychoanalytic theoretical system was hailed as a comprehensive framework within which all of the phenomena of individual personality could be comprehended. The vocabulary of psychologists was enlarged to include words and phrases such as *primary* and *secondary process; id, ego,* and *superego;* and *oral, anal,* and *genital stages.* For many people, such as writers, who needed overall concepts about personality to facilitate their work, psychoanalysis *was* psychology. Other theoretical systems based on clinical observation of individuals were also widely circulated by Freud's dissident followers, such as Jung, Adler, and Sullivan; by spokesmen for existentialism, such as Jaspers, Heidegger, and May; and by humanistic psychologists, such as Rogers and Maslow. But all of these systems, while they were useful in clinical work and did stimulate considerable research on personality, still failed to meet the need for a scientific psychology of individuality. They were too large, too general. It is true that we encounter many expressions of individual personality that make sense when viewed from a Freudian, Adlerian, or Jungian perspective. But how many other perspectives would provide insights just as clear? There is no way of validating a broad system as a whole. Furthermore, the focus on *clinical* evidence saddled the psychology of personality with one handicap it has been very difficult to get rid of—a bias toward the study of maladjusted or unsatisfactory ways of living. We know far more about ways of going wrong than about ways of growing right.

There is one other orientation to personality study, one that is present in both the trait-measurement movement and the psychoanalytic movement but not dominant in either, namely the *developmental* approach. As observations of infants and children have multiplied, particularly those made in longitudinal investigations in which the same individuals are studied at successive periods of their lives, it has become increasingly possible to ask and in some cases to answer questions about the origins of individuality.

Before turning to the facts and concepts about human individuals that differential or developmental psychology has generated, let us look first at some assumptions about the nature of human knowledge and about the place of humanity in the universe. Psychologists inherited from their predecessors in other sciences a philosophy of *substance.* Without going into all of the complexities underlying this commonsense notion, let us now consider an alternative, a philosophy of *process.* The outstanding philosopher of the twentieth century, Alfred North Whitehead, elaborated such a philosophy in his book *Process and Reality* ([1929] 1969), adding further clarification in two later books, *Adventures of Ideas* (1933) and *Modes of Thought* (1938). Psychologists paid remarkably little attention to these epoch-making works. It is tempting to speculate about the reason for this neglect. Probably the most important has to do with the timing of the Whitehead publications. During the period when dogmatic behaviorism was in the saddle, there was simply no place for an alternative to the dominant materialistic and reductionistic views. It seems more urgent now to end this neglect than to analyze the reasons for it, because Whitehead's philosophical system promises to serve well as an undergirding for the new ideas that we are considering.

Besides Whitehead, a number of other philosophers have contributed to the transformation of our ways of looking at man and the world. The two volumes of Suzanne Langer's monumental essay, *Mind: An Essay on Human Feeling* (1967, 1972), fill in part of the picture. The work that greatly influenced Langer, Cassirer's *The Philosophy of Symbolic Form* (1953, 1955, 1957), elaborates in detail one of its important aspects. Popper, especially in his last book, *Objective Knowledge* (1972), presents his own set of principles, not derived from Whitehead's but very compatible with them. Recent systematizations by evolutionary biologists, notably C. H. Waddington (1971), have produced an account of the development of life on earth that fits in well with the general philosophy we are considering. A large number of other writers could be listed and their contributions summarized. But as a foundation for a psychology of individuality, it seems more appropriate to direct our attention to the general themes than to give credit to all of their sources—to produce a synthesis rather than an analysis.

The central insight that pervades all of these philosophical systems is that reality is constantly being *created*. We live in an unfinished, never-to-be-finished universe always undergoing what Whitehead calls the "creative advance into novelty." Creation does not have to be initiated, stimulated, or facilitated; it occurs spontaneously throughout the living and nonliving world. For human beings, the prototype of the process is what artists do in transforming raw materials into meaningful forms. Lowe captures the essence of this idea in a summary sentence about Whitehead's philosophy: "The world consists of individual temporal occasions, becoming and perishing. Each arises from a situation which includes an antecedent world of occasions, a creativity with infinite freedom, and a realm of forms with infinite possibilities" (Lowe, 1962, p. 100). The idea is also cogently expressed in Whitehead's own statement (1933, p. 255): "Thus the future of the universe, though conditioned by the immanence of its past, awaits for its complete determination the spontaneity of the novel individual occasions as in their season they come into being."

Volumes could be (and have been) written about the implications of assuming continuing creativity in the universe. For the purposes of this discussion, we shall single out only a few thoughts. As psychologists, we are concerned mainly with the human participants in the creative constitution of reality rather than with the processes of the inanimate world or the long eons of biological evolution. Looking at the human process and thinking of the artist as its prototype, we see that it involves continuous activity rather than the passive reception of what is "out there." What is "out there" is being made by us, moment after moment, day after day, year after year. Furthermore, this ever-present activity is affective as well as cognitive. It involves valuation, purpose, and satisfaction—or the lack of it. And, perhaps most important for psychologists, the successive entities we create are differentiated and judged according to their quality, not their quantity. My world today is slightly different qualitatively from the world I was struggling to create yesterday. Your world is qualitatively different from mine, and every person's world is qualitatively unique.

Whitehead's basic unit, the "actual occasion," is a happening in time, with a beginning, a middle, and an end. It involves a progression from potentiality to actuality. Potentialities are plural, and in the universe as a whole their number is infinite. Actual occasions are singular. For a psychology of individuality, this is one of the most pregnant concepts of all, this assumption that at the outset of each occasion through which reality is constituted there are multiple possibilities. Only a small part of the possible is actualized, but in the process of creating something new a person adds to the supply of raw materials available to the next creator. Thus the supply of possibilities is inexhaustible. "The world expands through recurrent unifications of itself, each, by the addition of itself, automatically recreating the multiplicity anew. The novel entity is at once the togetherness of the 'many' which it finds, and also it is one among the disjunctive 'many' which it leaves; it is a novel entity disjunctively among the many entities which it synthesizes. The many become one and are increased by one" (Whitehead, [1929] 1969, p. 336).

It is in filling out this concept of the continual transformation and enrichment of the raw materials of human creativity that the work of the other philosophers mentioned is most valuable. The human animal, as Langer has emphasized, is by nature a symbolizer, and the symbols individuals have created out of the raw material of their unique experience constitute a heritage of indescribable richness. Cassirer's major work describes in detail the principal varieties. In the first volume (1953), he takes up language and the aspects of experience its symbols have served to express—emotion, space, number, complex concepts. In the second volume (1955), he discusses the forms embodied in mythology, symbols of space and time, life and consciousness. In the third volume (1957), he considers the symbolization process, from simple perceptions to highly elaborated scientific theories. Langer takes up where Cassirer leaves off in the attempt to clarify the symbolic process. The basic concept for her is *feeling,* understood in its broadest sense to cover such things as awareness, tension, pain, intent, and excitement, as well as cognition. It is their interest in this essentially *mental* phenomenon that distinguishes psychologists from physiologists and other biological scientists. Because an organism feels, it acts, and the distinctive feature of human acts is *symbolization.* Langer considers in some detail what all acts and the impulses that accompany them have in common, from the single-celled animals to humans. She argues, however, that the phenomenon of *mind,* in humans, constitutes a complete break with the animal mentality that preceded it, "such a tremendous novelty in animal evolution that it could not have occurred without a peculiar prehistory of coincidences leading up to special developments in the organism that produced it" (Langer, 1972, p. 215). That such coincidences should occur in the course of evolution is not so marvelous as first appears if one considers, as Langer does, the enormous number of genetic potentialities out of which the phenomena of specialization arise. Nature provides examples of many kinds of specialization, and an organism is not necessarily specialized for only one narrow environmental niche. By its own *acts,* using its biological assets in new ways, it exploits new opportunities and allows dormant potentialities to appear. What happened in the line of evolutionary development leading to humanity is that chance assets combined to produce ever-greater and more-diversified sensibilities; increases in the sensitivity of the hand; forward direction of the eyes, facilitating greater precision through binocular fixation; increases in brain size. The extremely receptive brain, overloaded with stimulation from diversified sense organs, made it necessary for the animal possessing it to process much of the input into mental acts rather than direct physical acts. Thus imagination, visual at first, arose. "The underlying unity of the central nervous organ, the brain, could be expected to carry the function of imagination into other sensory systems, too, and finally establish it apart from any special sense as a critical faculty in its own right. Here it becomes the groundwork of symbolization, conception, and all other peculiarly human forms of celebration; the evolution of mind is on its way" (Langer, 1972, p. 264). Thus the general conception of innumerable possibilities, from which active organisms select when they act, replaces the conception of organisms that, like machines, are completely determined by structure and circumstances. This makes the evolution of complexity and diversity intelligible. As Langer expresses it, "Every discovery makes the living organism look less like a predesigned object and more like an embodied drama of evolving acts, intricately prepared by the past, yet all improvising their moves to consummation" (Langer, 1967, p. 378). The convergence between these ideas and Whitehead's is clear.

Popper (1972), starting from a different vantage point in the philosophy of science and apparently quite independent of Whitehead and of Langer, has filled in another part of the broad picture we are attempting to grasp. His basic idea is that the thinking that human beings do creates a *third world,* an autonomous, objective realm of problems, propositions, and factual knowledge. People discover problems.

> They are in no sense made by us; rather, they are *discovered* by us; and in this sense they exist, undiscovered, before their discovery. . . .

In our attempts to solve these or other problems, we may invent new theories. These theories, again, are produced by us: They are the product of our critical and creative thinking, in which we are greatly helped by other existing third-world theories. Yet the moment we have produced these theories, they create new, unintended, and unexpected problems, autonomous problems, to be discovered.

This explains why the third world, which, in its origin, is our product, is autonomous in what may be called its *ontological status*. It explains why we can act upon it and add to it or help its growth, even though there is no man who can master even a small corner of this world. All of us contribute to its growth, but almost all our individual contributions are vanishingly small. All of us try to grasp it, and none of us could live without being in contact with it, for all of us make use of speech, without which we would hardly be human. Yet the third world has grown far beyond the grasp not only of any man but even of all men. . . . And there will always be the challenging task of discovering new problems, for an infinity of problems will always remain undiscovered. In spite and also because of the autonomy of the third world, there will always be scope for original and creative work [Popper, 1972, pp. 160–161].

Here again we meet Whitehead's central theme—that reality is constantly being created by human acts, acts that select and organize and in the process add to the innumerable possibilities that constitute the raw material for other creative acts. What Popper is most insistent about is the autonomy and permanence of what is created.

Let us look now at the essential features of these creative acts, selection and organization. It is clear from the preceding discussion that a person must select and organize in order to cope with the enormous number of possibilities with which he or she is confronted. This is necessary, first of all, in perception. What psychologists and philosophers for many years accepted without question—that perception is simply a passive registration of the external world—has turned out to be an unsound idea. The sense organs are being constantly bombarded by energies of all sorts, to only a fraction of which the person reacts. To say confidently "This is a chair" and to proceed to sit down on it are actions whose neurological and psychological explanations are far from obvious. To perceive is to construct something, putting together parts of the data delivered by sense organs and some of the information stored in the memory. Whitehead pointed out this fact and went on to distinguish between two kinds of perception, perception by causal efficacy, in which one sees objects in terms of what can be done with them, and perception by presentational immediacy, in which one sees patches of color and hears patterns of sound. The first kind is much more frequent and natural than the second. It requires a special learning process to perceive in terms of presentational immediacy. Impressionist painters, for example, become adept at it, and psychologists in early laboratories, a century ago, cultivated the skill in order to carry out their plan of analyzing all experience into units of pure sensation.

In the psychology of individuality, this account of perception takes on considerable importance. Individuals perceive many things differently, and other aspects of individuality rest on these differences. In trying to understand individual personality, we shall be paying particular attention to the "mental screens" individuals use in processing input from the environment. Such structures designed for screening have been called by various names—*sets, attitudes, interests, values, prejudices,* and many others—by psychologists investigating particular problems. We shall be looking at the results of some of these investigations later. What is important to realize at this point is that they all represent, at different levels of complexity, the individual's creative acts, the person's own inventions to be utilized in meeting life's demands. What comes in from the surrounding environment is too voluminous and too fragmentary to be dealt with. A person must select and organize, and the characteristic means for doing this constitute one of the most fundamental aspects of individual personality.

The crucial significance of time in connection with this process should never be lost sight of. Time flows in one direction only; what is past belongs to the world of Whitehead's *actual entities,* whereas what is in the future belongs to the world of possibilities. At each present moment, the transfer from one world to the other takes place, and the process is irreversible. The actions one has taken, the choices one has made, cannot be erased. They must be accepted as real, solid, determinate parts of the raw material for creative acts of the present, which until the moment of action are not determined. There is another way in which human individuality is affected by time. For each individual, time is *finite*. During this century, the number of years a person in the United States can expect to live has been greatly increased, but the life span is still limited, and there are infinitely more possibilities for experience than any one lifetime can contain. Furthermore, each period or stage of life is of limited duration, and many experiences appropriate for one stage cannot be obtained at another. The games one did not have time to play at ten cannot be played at fifty. The joy of young love, not seized at eighteen, can never be experienced in the later decades, no matter how long one lives. Even the days are limited, as those who burn the candle at both ends discover. Whatever we may say about humanity as a species, a man or a woman as an individual lives only one life that often turns out to be far too short for what one wishes to crowd into it. Again we are brought up against the necessity for selecting and rejecting, closing the door on a large number of possibilities as one does so.

Whitehead had much to say about these inevitable rejections. He called them "negative prehensions" and repeatedly called attention to their persisting influence on the entities from which they have been excluded. "A feeling bears on itself the scars of its birth: It recollects as a subjective emotion its struggles for existence, it retains the impress of what it might have been but is not" (Whitehead, 1969, p. 265). Thus if we are to understand completely a successful businessman, we must take into consideration the poet, the martyr, and the explorer he decided not to be.

For many psychologists, a major obstacle to the adoption of possibility as a fundamental concept in the psychology of individuality is that it seems to undermine the deterministic framework they have been taught is essential to scientific work. If possibilities are real, then one's personality could have been different from the way it is. The rigid link between causes and effects is broken or at least weakened. "Chance" threatens to overwhelm rationality. Phys-

ical scientists, of course, have been living with indeterminism for
fifty years or more, ever since the enunciation of the Heisenberg
principle. In recent years, the chance factor in biology has become
a reality that cannot be ignored. Monod has written a profound
little book about this, entitled *Chance and Necessity* (1971). The
heart of the argument this molecular biologist presents can be found
in the chapter on molecular ontogenesis. He explains that, in the
formation of complex proteins out of simpler subunits, there is a
"random" sequence of combinations, inherently unpredictable.
"From the work on these sequences and after systematically comparing them with the help of modern means of analysis and com-
puting, we are now in a position to deduce the general law: It is
that of chance. To be more specific: These structures are 'random'
in the precise sense that, were we to know the exact order of 199
residues in a protein containing 200, it would be impossible to
formulate any rule, theoretical or empirical, enabling us to predict
the nature of the one residue not yet identified by analysis" (Monod,
1971, p. 96). However, once constituted, the random sequence is
reproduced in an invariant way, "thousands and thousands of times
over, in each organism, by a highly accurate mechanism which
guarantees the invariance of the structure. . . . Randomness caught
on the wing, preserved, reproduced by the machinery of invariance
and thus converted into order, rule, necessity" (Monod, 1971, pp.
97–98). Monod goes on to show how the whole course of the evolution of the "biosphere" manifests this same process, the invariant
perpetuation of what originated in a random happening. "Among
all the occurrences possible in the universe, the a priori probability
of any particular one of them verges upon zero. Yet the universe
exists; particular events must take place in it, the probability of
which (before the event) was infinitesimal. . . . Not only for
scientific reasons do biologists recoil at this idea. It runs counter to
our very human tendency to believe that behind everything real in
the world stands a necessity rooted in the very beginning of things.
Against this notion, this powerful feeling of destiny, we must be
constantly on guard. . . . Destiny is written concurrently with the
event, not prior to it" (Monod, 1971, p. 145).

    The last sentence in the preceding quote could almost stand
alone as a capsule statement of the heart of Whitehead's philosophy,

although there is no evidence in the book that Monod was influenced by Whitehead. Prior to an "actual occasion," there are multiple possibilities; after it, there is an "actual entity," invariant, persistent; at the boundary, there is chance or creativity, depending on how one looks at it.

The great reluctance that many scientists, psychologists among them, feel to accept the fact that there is a chance component at the heart of things may arise from the connotations of the word *chance*. It suggests chaos, anarchy, purposelessness. But it is not necessary to interpret the concept of chance in that way. As early as 1892, Peirce (another philosopher whose ideas were largely ignored for many years) presented quite a different conception of chance. He held that chance represents *spontaneity,* limited and regulated, but not absolutely determined by the laws of nature. "By thus admitting pure spontaneity or life as a character of the universe, acting always and everywhere though restrained within narrow bounds by law, producing infinitesimal departures from law continually, and great ones with infinite infrequency, I account for all the variety and diversity of the universe" (Peirce, [1892] 1958, p. 175). Chance, at the heart of the universe, does not mock human ideals. On the contrary, it is what makes the continuing creation of human values possible.

In a much more recent discussion by a neurologist, James Austin, the interaction between chance and creativity is highlighted. "Why do we still remember men like Fleming? We venerate them not as scientists alone. As men, their total contribution transcends their scientific discoveries. In their lives we see demonstrated how malleable our own futures are. In their work we perceive how many loopholes fate has left us—how much of destiny is still in our hands. In them we find that nothing is predetermined. Chance can be on our side, if we but stir it up with our energies, stay receptive to its every random opportunity, and continually provoke it by individuality in our hobbies and our approach to life" (Austin, 1974, p. 64).

Perhaps the most penetrating analysis of the significance of the possibility-actuality sequence for human freedom is a paper by Popper, "Of Clouds and Clocks," Chapter Six in *Objective Knowledge* (1972). Clouds and clocks are prototypes of two kinds of system—the cluster of elements in irregular motion and the precise mechanism in which the movement of each part is unvarying and predictable. Popper characterizes the Newtonian mechanics on which determinist assumptions rest as the proposition: "All clouds are clocks." He translates then Peirce's idea, cited earlier, into the proposition: "To some degree, all clocks are clouds." He comes out on the side of Peirce, as an indeterminist. However, he goes on to qualify this indeterminism, as Peirce did, so that it does not rule out regularities and a degree of predictability in the universe. It means only "that *not all* events in the physical world are predetermined with absolute precision, in all their infinitesimal details" (Popper, 1972, p. 220). He does not believe "that perfect chance" is the only alternative to perfect indeterminism. What we need for understanding rational human behavior—and indeed, animal behavior—is something *intermediate* in character between perfect clouds and perfect clocks. He goes on to elaborate his own view of the organism as a hierarchical system of "plastic controls" and to apply this in his own field of history and philosophy of science. Like the whole evolutionary process, science is a process of trials and error elimination. The concept of multiple possibilities thus turns up in a new form: There is an infinite number of erroneous hypotheses regarding every scientific problem, but in the process of coping with them a single conclusion emerges. The essential difference between the evolutionary process and the process of scientific advance is that evolution eliminates errors by eliminating the organisms exemplifying them, whereas the scientific process eliminates hypotheses, not scientists. Again, the temporal progression from plural possibilities to a singular actuality through a creative process is in harmony with Whitehead's metaphysics.

What all these thinkers show is that one can be a scientist without being a determinist—that there is room for the postulation of creative acts that produce something new, in science as in art and all of human life. A psychology that rests on these ideas will be much more concerned than were systems of the past with individual uniqueness and its origins, considering how the person deals with multiple possibilities, constantly selecting and organizing throughout his or her existence in finite time. That is what this book is about. We assume that research of the past on human individuality is valid, but limited—that it should be included, but incorporated into a broader framework. The question toward which the dominant trait psychology has been directed is *"How much* of some quality does the individual possess?" Two other questions are equally important: *"Which* characteristics out of the many that might have been developed does this person show—which competencies, which interests, which motives?" and *"What shapes* have these characteristics taken; what psychological structures does this person use to process experience?"

Many writers besides those cited might have been mentioned, and there are undoubtedly many that we have missed. All of the ideas we have been attempting to combine into a coherent pattern have surfaced repeatedly during the short history of psychology as well as during the long history of mankind. In the 1930s, Woodworth, in successive editions of his widely used general psychology text (1944), was stressing the inherent activity of the organism as a factor in behavior. Alfred Adler, breaking with Freud's rigidly deterministic theory, emphasized the individual's inherent creativity and freedom. Gordon Allport (1937) argued for a psychology that would be *idiographic* as well as *nomothetic,* that would study the uniqueness of individuals as well as their common features. Perhaps the time has now come for all of these voices to find a more attentive audience.

This chapter exemplifies the process it postulates. Out of a large number of possible sources, some were selected and organized into a new "actual entity," which in turn becomes part of the raw material toward which the creativity of others can be directed. In psychology, as in life, nobody ever really has the last word.

2

Research Strategies
Old and New

Since the dawn of human history, thinking people have been impressed with the fact of individual uniqueness. In every family, mothers and fathers notice that children are as different in their temperament and behavior as they are in appearance. In every shop and office, individual workers show somewhat different competencies, preferences, and sensitivities. Even in highly authoritarian schoolrooms and totalitarian states, differences in the way individuals react to the same treatment always appear. Artists and writers have been especially fascinated by the qualities that make persons unique. Down through the centuries, they have striven to capture on canvas or the printed page these essential aspects of individuality. Long before there was a science of psychology, psychological studies of great penetration were produced by Sophocles, Rembrandt, and Shakespeare. However, one need not be a genius of this magnitude to set down on paper the things that are significant about an individual. In every mental health clinic, detailed case histories of adults and children to whom help is given involve the same sort of effort to capture individuality in words.

In other situations, less time-consuming techniques have had to be invented to deal with individual differences. The first-grade teacher assigns her pupils to the Bluebirds, Robins, or Swallows according to how far along they are in learning to read. The foreman or supervisor sizes up the workers in his department and gives them particular job responsibilities accordingly. Government agencies use civil service examinations to select new employees. The proprietor of a small machine shop questions each applicant and tries the person out on a sample of the work to be done. There are dozens of practical, down-to-earth techniques for selecting, placing, and handling individuals. The trouble with such informal ways of sizing people up is that a great deal of superstition and prejudice gets mixed in with them. One of the major aims of scientific work on human individuality has been to sort out the sound from the unsound ways. It is only recently that it has been generally recognized, for example, that neither skin color nor sex is a useful indicator of anything related to job competence. In the absence of any real evidence, it was natural for people to assume that blacks and whites were inherently suited for different roles in life, and that males were inherently qualified for positions not suitable for females. Each person, as he or she grows up, seizes on a system for making sense of the world of diverse individuals that must be dealt with. This is why so many false and inadequate classifications continue to circulate and are so difficult to get rid of. The psychological study of how individuals differ has always had a strong practical orientation. Since we all must deal with individual differences, it helps to know something about them.

The oldest systematic way of organizing observations about individual differences is to classify people into types. When we consider the infinite variety of possibilities discussed in Chapter One— possibilities for perception, for action, for learning, and the human variations to which they lead—it is apparent that classification of some sort is an absolute necessity for finite human minds. It has been a first step in the development of all the sciences. In chemistry, the periodic table for classifying the elements facilitated the exploration of properties and relationships of the multitudinous substances and materials in our world. It had many forerunners—the Greek classification of earth, air, fire, and water; the distinction between acids and bases; and the separation of organic from inorganic substances. In botany, Linnaeus, building on many previous efforts, produced the taxonomy based on genus and species concepts that still enables scientists to deal intelligently with the infinitely varied plant world. Psychologists for a long time have seen the need for a similar classification system, but so far none has emerged that is altogether adequate.

The one with the deepest roots in history classifies persons on the basis of anatomical or physiological characteristics. Hippocrates, the father of medicine, distinguished between the *phthisic* type, characterized by long, thin bodies, and the *apoplectic* type, with short, thick bodies. While he was concerned principally with susceptibility to different diseases, others down through the centuries held that there were basic psychological differences as well. For Galen, the next great medical systematizer, there were four constitutional types, with different temperaments based on the predominance of different fluids or "humors" in the body. The four were the sanguine, the choleric, the phlegmatic, and the melancholic. In our own century, Kretschmer (1925) in psychiatry and Sheldon (1940) in psychology have picked up the idea of temperamental types based on physical and physiological differences and have produced some evidence for the validity and utility of such a classification.

Other typologies that have been proposed have been based on qualities of mind and character rather than on physique. A distinction Nietsche made between Dionysian (emotional, expressive) personalities and Apollonian (rational, restrained) personalities has been used for analyzing cultures and historical epochs as well as individuals. William James contributed another influential classification when he distinguished the tough-minded from the tender-minded. A more elaborate typology than either of these is Spranger's (1928) classification on the basis of dominant values —theoretic, economic, esthetic, social, political, and religious. The incorporation of this system into Allport's and Vernon's (1931) *A Study of Values* (in later editions, Allport, Vernon, and Lindzey), a widely used test, brought the system into prominence. The most influential and widely accepted typology proposed so far is that of Carl Jung. The basic distinction is between extraverts and introverts, based on whether the person's primary involvement is with the world outside or with inner experience. Jung's whole system (1923), however, is more complex than this, classifying persons on the basis of other sets of functions that cut across the extraversion-introversion distinction—sensation versus intuition, thinking versus feeling, and judgment versus perception. The combination produces sixteen types rather than two. This typology has also been incorporated into a test, the *Myers-Briggs Type Indicator* (Myers, 1962), and thus made available to psychologists wishing to do research on it.

For a considerable time after quantitative research on individual differences began, twentieth-century psychologists were inclined to disparage typologies and classification systems as a means of conceptualizing individual differences. But during the last half of the century the pendulum has been swinging back, and the utility of such sorting procedures is again being recognized. The typologies now being proposed are based not on armchair speculation or casual observation, but on sophisticated statistical analyses of quantitative measurements and experimental results to identify clusters of people whose combinations of measured characteristics are similar. Thus, to understand the current typological strategy, we must look first at four others, namely the measurement of psychological traits, developmental research, the design of experiments, and research on single cases.

Most psychological research on human individuality has proceeded by first separating, out of the complex of characteristics that makes each person unique, some one particular characteristic and by then putting together some questions or tasks that would indicate the extent to which the individual manifests it. Such sets of questions or tasks are called *mental tests*. The first trait to be singled out in this way was general intelligence, and research on this one characteristic has constituted a sizable proportion of all work done in differential psychology. A wide variety of intelligence tests for various ages and special purposes has come into existence. The next step was to single out various kinds of special ability, such as mechanical aptitude, musical talent, or finger dexterity, and to

devise tests to measure these. Other test makers were soon directing
their efforts to traits related to motivation, rather than ability,
producing instruments designed to measure interests, attitudes,
adjustment, and susceptibility to different varieties of mental disease. The construction, publication, sale, administration, interpretation, and criticism of mental tests by the middle of the twentieth
century was a large and flourishing enterprise. Since about 1950,
criticism of the whole undertaking has been more and more vocal
and insistent. This is not the place to go into such criticisms, but a
point that needs emphasis is that mental testing is only one way—
and probably not, ultimately, the best way—to analyze human
individuality. However, it is now a highly developed technology,
and anyone who wishes to understand how individuals differ needs
to be familiar with it.

The sequence of steps in the procedure is a simple one. First,
one specifies a particular trait in which one is interested, defining it
as clearly as possible. Second, one comes up with some tasks or
questions, performance on which can be scored. Third, one gives
the test to a group of persons and arranges their scores in a way
that will facilitate the comparison of each individual score with the
average for the group. While the three steps are very simple, dealing
with the questions and problems that arise in carrying out the steps
has given rise to much complex discussion. The first stage, as Binet
and all of his successors found out, brings problems of definition.
The best way to deal with these is to start with an admittedly
tentative definition that will be refined through a process of successive approximations as results of testing become available. Little by
little, it becomes clear what a particular test measures and what a
particular trait involves. Sometimes what is at first assumed to be
a single trait turns out to be a combination of two or more that can
be separately tested. In the case of intelligence, for example, research over the years indicated that verbal items and nonverbal
items measure aspects of mental ability that, although related, are
differentiable. And it gradually became clear that such tests are
measuring a quality related much more closely to success in school
than to adaptability in other life situations.

At the second stage, questions arise about the adequacy of
the items chosen to measure the designated trait. The most searching questions have to do with *validity*. Does the degree of success

with these tasks really indicate how high the person should be rated on the trait under consideration? Attempts to answer it have led to distinctions between different kinds of validity, to delineation of many sorts of *criteria* (direct, nontest indicators of traits to be measured), and to the elaboration of statistical formulas to use in analyzing the relationships between tests and criteria. It has been recognized that in some cases a person's responses to a test situation can be viewed as a *sample* of the behavior elicited by similar life situations. In such cases, it is usually not difficult to find out how valid the test is. A child who correctly spells all the words on a spelling test, for example, can be considered a good speller. In the case of other traits, however, performance on the test is not a direct sample, but rather a *sign* pointing to the person's general status with regard to the trait in question. For example, on a frequently used personality test, the response, "False," to the item "I am happy most of the time" is an indicator of paranoid tendencies. Another complication arises from the fact that a test may be valid for one segment of the population without being valid for another. Answers to questions do not necessarily mean the same thing for one ethnic or cultural group as for another. Thus for some traits it may be necessary to use different items to test black children from those used to test white children; for some, different items must be used for boys and girls. There is no way we can be sure that a test will be valid for a new group or situation except to try it out.

Another important set of second-stage questions has to do with how accurate or free from chance error scores are. Such questions are classified under the general heading of *reliability*. It was noted very early in the history of mental testing that a person seldom makes exactly the same score if retested under apparently identical conditions or if given two ostensibly similar forms of the same test. Like validity, reliability has turned out to be a more complex matter than was at first supposed. Research has demonstrated that there are many sources of unreliability and that these vary from test to test, group to group, and situation to situation. When a test is being used to evaluate or compare individuals, one must always take this factor into consideration. Because of inaccuracy inherent in the measurement itself, an IQ of 120 cannot be considered higher than an IQ of 117, for example. It is not possible to expunge all unreliability from psychological measurements, but statistical techniques for analyzing how serious it is and procedures for reducing it to a minimum have been worked out.

At the third stage, involving the preparation of norms with which individual scores can be compared, some major questions have had to do with the suitability of different techniques: "Should percentiles or standard scores be used for ability tests? Are age level or grade level scores better for school achievement tests? What statistical pitfalls are involved in the Mental Age and IQ?" More important than these questions, however, are questions about the representativeness of the norm group. Has it been selected in such a way that it is really legitimate to judge an individual by where he or she stands in it? If an intelligence test is designed for children in the public schools, the norm group should include children in the age range for which the test is intended, from all socioeconomic levels and geographic areas, and from both sexes, in the proportions in which the subgroups occur in the school population. One common error of interpretation, however, is to confuse norm questions with validity questions. Just to include the right proportion of Mexican-American (Chicano) children in a norm group, for example, does not make a test *valid* for Chicanos. But an unrepresentative norm group can make persons who take even a valid test appear to rate too high or too low on the basis of the scores they have made.

The processing of mental test scores to further our understanding of individual differences has taken several forms. The first and most fundamental is simply to arrange them in order of magnitude and produce a *frequency distribution* (how frequently each score occurs) such as the following:

Test Scores	Number of Persons
95–99	1
90–94	8
85–89	19
80–84	42
75–79	53
70–74	41
65–69	20
60–64	6
55–59	1

From such an arrangement, one can see at a glance how many persons received scores at each level and how great the total variation in the group was. It became apparent very early in the history of mental testing that there was a great deal of variation on each trait tested. The hypothetical distribution given is fairly typical. If we look, for example, at reading skill in ninth-graders, we may find that some persons in the group read no better than the average fourth-grader, while others are reading as well as the average college sophomore. Individual differences of this magnitude are clearly relevant to educational policy making and have not yet been sufficiently taken into account. It is often assumed that with better teaching all ninth-graders would be achieving at the ninth-grade level. A half century of research on individual differences has turned up no support for such an assumption.

One conspicuous characteristic of frequency distributions obtained from many sorts of measurement and many different groups greatly impressed early researchers. These distributions regularly seemed to take a particular shape. A graphic representation turned out to be a curve high in the middle, falling off rapidly at both ends. This bell-shaped curve fit fairly closely the mathematical formula for the "normal" curve, already familiar from studies of probability when large numbers of chance events are plotted. Early investigators saw in this phenomenon a basic law of nature, concluding that human characteristics are distributed in the population in accordance with the normal curve. But such sweeping generalizations have been toned down considerably with the passage of time, as more data have come in showing that not all traits follow this pattern and that any test distribution can be made to deviate from it simply by making the items harder or easier for the group tested. Because it is very convenient to use normal-curve mathematics in analyzing scores, test constructors try to select items that will produce a normal distribution. In a general way, it is probably true that most human characteristics seem to be distributed in such a way that there will be large numbers of near-average people, somewhat smaller numbers of people clearly above and clearly below average, and much smaller numbers of extreme deviants in either positive or negative directions. Lincoln's comment does seem to be relevant—that "God must have loved the common people because he made so many of them." But there is no way to prove by present testing techniques that this is nature's plan.

Beyond this elementary inquiry into the nature and extent of human variability on psychological traits, there is a second kind of more searching investigation that has constituted the major thrust of research over the years, namely the study of relationships between traits. The analysis of correlations has been so central a feature of research on individual differences that the whole field is often called *correlational psychology*. By finding out how one set of scores is related to another set of scores made by the same group of people, we are able to make inferences about what the measured differences between individuals mean. This is especially valuable where complex concepts are under consideration. As noted earlier, it is fairly obvious what individual differences in reading skill mean; at least some implications are obvious. But what of intelligence, manual dexterity, or social introversion? What do differences here mean to individuals and to society as a whole? Questions such as these have stimulated the computation of innumerable correlation coefficients.

Correlational research can be roughly divided into two varieties. In research of the first sort, test scores are correlated with nontest variables—college aptitude scores with grade-point averages, mechanical ability scores with supervisor's ratings, personality test scores with recidivism rates in mental hospitals. As stated before, this is a principal technique for validating tests, but its usefulness goes beyond this. Various combinations of tests can be appropriately weighted and used to predict scores on nontest variables, a technique called *multiple regression*. Individuals can be sorted into groups or types using weighted combinations of test scores using the *discriminant function*. For a great many practical purposes, where individual differences must be dealt with in schools, offices, and factories, there are specialized techniques for relating test scores to variables in the world outside the testing room. The other main variety of correlational research, in which different sets of test scores are related to one another, has a more theoretical orientation. By giving a large group of people a great many tests and correlating everything with everything else, it was hoped that we could discover the *basic* ways in which individuals differ from one another and find out how traits are organized. The technique for analyzing large numbers of correlations for their underlying meaning is called *factor analysis*. In an early investigation of this kind, less unwieldy than later ones became, Thurstone (1938) administered fifty-six psychological tests to 240 college students. Correlating every set of test scores with every other set resulted in 1,540 correlation coefficients (56 × 55 ÷ 2). The object of the factor analysis he then performed was to locate a much smaller group of variables whose relationships would account for all of the correlations between tests. In place of the fifty-six tests, he came out with seven "primary mental abilities." It looks as though there would be great economy here—if seven variables can replace fifty-six. Psychologists hoped that by constructing tests for just these seven primary abilities they could simplify our whole system of description of individual differences.

Unfortunately, as time passed and more and more psychologists came out with more and more reports, any ultimate simplification turned out to be illusory. In place of the seven primary abilities Thurstone had found in the 1930s, Guilford in the 1960s had accumulated evidence for 120 or more. Furthermore, correlations between scores on factors themselves can be factor analyzed, producing what are called *second-* and *third-order factors*. What has come out of several decades of factor analytic research is a realization of just how complex human differences really are. But, while it has not simplified anything, factor analysis has become an indispensable research technique to use in dealing with complex relationships. Computer technology has made it feasible, in many problems where it would have been impossible, to carry out the involved mathematical work "by hand."

Multiple regression and factor analysis are now considered to be examples of a broader classification of quantitative research methods called *multivariate techniques*. Three assumptions underlie this general approach (Baltes and Nesselroade, 1973, p. 220): "(1) Any dependent variable (or consequent) is potentially a function of multiple determinants; (2) any determinant or antecedent has potentially multiple consequences; and (3) the study of multiple antecedent-consequent relationships provides a useful model for the organization of complex systems." It is apparent then that multivariate methods are much better suited to the study of the complexity of individuality than are one-trait-at-a-time methods. The individual is an organized complex system.

Over the years, another way of finding out about individuality has taken shape, the study of the same persons over long periods of time. Although research of this sort began as early as the 1920s, it is only in this final third of the twentieth century that it has become an identifiable specialty within the broad field of developmental psychology. Developmental psychology, like most of the rest of psychological science, throughout most of its history has not been much concerned with individual differences, except for the work on intelligence testing discussed earlier. One group of researchers was interested in collecting detailed, accurate observational data about typical behavior of children of different ages. Another group consisted of experimentalists who preferred to use children rather than adults in their laboratory investigations of learning, motivation, or social behavior. Still another group focused on general developmental processes that bridge the gap between infancy and maturity. In many of the specific research studies carried out under all of these orientations, comparisons of age groups provided an obvious framework, and results were often presented as growth curves representing the general course of development with respect to the variable under consideration. But the points that made up these curves were group averages, not delineations of individuals.

Some psychologists became dissatisfied with such curves, based on what came to be called *cross-sectional* research. They became aware that curves for mental growth in individual children often did not resemble the curve for group averages at successive ages. They became convinced that to study development one must study the actual process in individuals and extract general principles from individual growth curves, not from successive group averages. The result of this concern was the initiation in the 1920s and 1930s of several comprehensive plans for studying the same individuals over a long period of years. Terman's study (1925) of gifted children, beginning in 1922, was the first major longitudinal investigation. Other ambitious projects were initiated at the Institute of Human Development at the University of California in Berkeley and at the Fels Research Institute in Antioch, Ohio. These plans involved observations of the same individuals over many years, beginning at birth or even before. In several other places, large-scale longitudinal research spanning many years has also been undertaken.

It is not easy to plan and carry out longitudinal research, and conclusions drawn from it have certain inevitable limitations. One limitation arises from the initial selection of persons to be studied. They must be willing to cooperate in scientific research and willing to commit themselves to it over a long period of time. If a study is to start with newborn infants, it is the families, especially the mothers, who must make this commitment. In our highly mobile American society, many families are immediately ruled out because they know that they are not likely to be available for any length of time within range of the research station. Because they can look farther ahead in their lives, people who participate in longitudinal studies tend to be above average in intelligence, income, education, and other indices of status. They cannot be considered representative of the population as a whole. Even in this sort of sample, considerable attrition occurs with the passage of time, leading to another difficulty in interpreting findings. One can never be altogether sure that some vital characteristic affecting one's conclusions has not changed between the first and last round of data collection. It is necessary that the investigator be aware of these limitations and take them into account. There are ways of checking possible biases they may have introduced. Such biases affect some sorts of generalizations much more than others.

Another set of special problems facing the longitudinal researcher has to do with what to measure, observe, and rate. From a practical standpoint, it does not seem worthwhile to go to all the trouble of selecting a sample of the population willing to be studied over a long period of years and then limit one's concern to a single trait, such as intelligence. It is more sensible to combine the efforts of several psychologists with somewhat different interests and to agree on a plan for collecting a variety of kinds of data on each occasion. Because it was the first trait to be measured and studied intensively and because it is related to many other things in which developmental psychologists are interested, general intelligence has been repeatedly tested in most or all of the longitudinal studies, so that much is now known about how it develops in individuals. Because universal human skills such as grasping, crawling, walking, and talking have been studied in many groups of young children in many places, there is a usable body of knowledge about individual differences in the rate and manner of their acquisition. Much less is known about many other kinds of competence on which civilized society depends; for example, the talents that produce great art and music, the sensitivities of wine tasters and persons who can detect counterfeit bills by their "feel," and even athletic abilities. How are people sorted out so that in the course of a twenty-year period adequate proportions of craftsmen, mechanics, physicians, cooks, and policemen are ready to take on these social roles? It is desirable that longitudinal research include some techniques that will add to our knowledge of special abilities and interests. Of equal importance is the development of personality. How do some people become more aggressive, more altruistic, more generous, more self-assured than others? Longitudinal investigations usually try to obtain information about personality development, using interviews, observations, and ratings, as well as personality tests and inventories. It is the choice of specific techniques for assessing all of these aspects of individuality that creates special difficulties in research that is to go on over a long period. Psychology is a rapidly changing subject; new and presumably better assessment techniques are constantly being proposed. But to a considerable extent longitudinal researchers must stay with the techniques called for in the original plan, knowing that over the period of ten, twenty, or thirty years superior techniques have come on the scene. All that they can do about this is to put their best energies into the formulation of the original plans and then accent the fact that there are limitations as well as advantages in the longitudinal approach.

After data have been collected from the same persons at successive periods of their lives, the problem of how to analyze the data becomes the central consideration. For quantitative data, such as test scores, ratings, and records of the number of instances of particular behavior observed under standard conditions, various methods of analysis are now available (Wohlwill, 1970; Nunnally, 1973; Bentler, 1973). Correlational techniques referred to in the preceding section can be varied in different ways to highlight developmental considerations rather than present status. For example, scores on a personality test for dominance taken at age ten can be related to a number of other characteristics evaluated at age sixteen, such as leadership, popularity, and frequency of dating. Factor analysis based on such correlations over time produces factors representing patterns of development rather than patterns of current organization of traits.

Longitudinal research provides, in addition to quantitative data, a rich array of qualitative and descriptive material. The task of analyzing this in any rigorous way has proved to be a challenging problem with, as yet, no generally acceptable solution. The concept often applied to such material is *developmental stage*. Piaget and his associates have contributed most to this line of research, charting qualitatively different developmental stages in the way children think as they grow from infancy to maturity. Because, like most psychologists, Piaget has been interested in universal patterns rather than individuality, this developmental research has not as yet contributed much to the field of individual differences. What these efforts have contributed to our thinking about individuality is a delineation of an organismic theory sharply contrasting with the prevailing mechanistic formulations (Overton and Reese, 1973). Mechanistic models assume that human beings are essentially reactive organisms, like a machine "inherently at rest and active only as a result of external forces" (Overton and Reese, 1973, p. 69). Thinking in this way, it is natural to analyze the person's equipment into parts of measurable size, such as abilities and personality traits, and to account for behavior as the sum of the effects of forces from outside the person on the sum of these parts. From the organismic point of view, this makes no sense. The person is a living system, "an organized entity whose parts gain their meaning and function from the whole" (p. 70). Such living systems are spontaneously active, and their activity is influenced but not initiated or determined by external forces. The categories of *form* and *structure* rather than amount become central, and it is the transformation of structures that constitutes development. The structural aspect of individuality will be considered in some detail in later chapters.

Psychologists have usually preferred experimental techniques to other kinds of scientific observation, including the correlational methods we have been considering. The advantage of an experiment is that the researcher controls the situations in which observations are made, administers some stimulus or treatment, and measures the response to this change in the situation. It must be recognized, however, that this approach has taught us more about general psychological processes than about individual differences. Investigators usually base their conclusions on the average of the measurements for a group of subjects and make no attempt to analyze why different subjects react differently. Some aspects of individual differences have been explored in laboratory and field experiments, however, and attempts are increasingly being made to design experiments that will throw light on individual differences as well as general trends. This is especially true for problems of *causation*. Correlational research can only demonstrate that certain variables go together. It cannot lead to any conclusion about which is cause and which effect. What the experimenter does is to set up two (or more) groups of subjects, comparable in all respects. The variable hypothesized to have some causative influence is administered to the experimental group, not to the control group. Differences between the groups serve as evidence for the causative effect hypothesized. Much of the effort to explain the sources of intelligence differences has taken this form. R. Harrell (1947), for example, was able to demonstrate the effect of a vitamin-enriched diet on the intelligence of orphanage children. Gray and Klaus (1970), with a somewhat more complex design, showed that enriching children's preschool environment also raises tested IQ.

Simple and obvious as the experimental procedure looks, it is riddled with complications. Much effort has gone into the development of techniques to ensure that experimental and control groups do not differ at the outset in any characteristic relevant to the purpose of the experiment. Ways of guarding against the influence of biases, preferences, and attitudes on the part of both researchers and subjects have been extensively explored. It is often necessary to combine two or more experimental treatments, and multivariate techniques have been worked out to accomplish this without undermining the conclusions. We need not go into detail at this point about these or many other complicating factors; we simply mention that there are ways of dealing with them. Experimental techniques have been used for a variety of purposes in addition to the elucidation of causal factors. Groups can be selected on the basis of their performance in one experiment, then compared in another, as was done in Witkin's work on field dependence and independence, to be discussed in a later chapter. Experiments can generate new theoretical constructs that can then be tried out in both experimental and correlational research. Considerable use has been made of natural experiments, such as the adoption of children into homes of a different kind from those from which they came or such as the rearing of identical twins in different homes.

One difficulty with all of the research strategies considered so far is that they require that people be studied in groups. What one can say about an individual on the basis of such research is either which group he or she belongs in or how he or she compares in some respect to other members of the group. Any quality really unique to the individual cannot be detected by such methods. Gordon Allport (1937, 1960) repeatedly pointed out this deficiency. He picked up and popularized a distinction proposed by German scholars between *nomothetic* research, which seeks to uncover principles and processes characteristic of all human beings, and *idiographic* research, which seeks to delineate unique individual systems. The distinction gave rise to much controversy in psychology, especially in the psychology of personality. Argument revolved around the question as to whether it is possible to be scientific about single cases.

Allport attempted to adapt the case-study methods so prevalent in clinics and social services to scientific purposes (Allport, 1942). Many years later, Allport (1965) applied the techniques he had recommended to a series of letters written over a twelve-year period by an elderly woman, proposing three ways of analyzing the material. In the first, *existential* approach, he traced the outlines of Jenny's world view, her orientation to the outer world, her fellow human beings, and herself. In the second, *depth* approach, he used Freudian and Jungian concepts to analyze motivational patterns, defense mechanisms, and ego structures. In the third, *structural-dynamic* approach, he employed computerized content analysis to uncover clusters of habits and attitudes controlling behavior. Allport did not recommend any one of the three approaches to the exclusion of the others, although he appeared to be least interested in the depth analyses. What he did recommend is a *systematic* eclecticism (italics Allport's), the use of organizing principles from various sources to make sense of the individual case.

During the 1960s and 1970s, there have been several new approaches to the scientific study of single individuals. Several have been brought together in the book edited by Davidson and Costello (1969), mainly those applicable in psychiatry and clinical psychology. Others are emerging in developmental psychology. Three varieties of technique appear especially promising. The first grows out of experiments on behavior modification. By following a sequential plan, each individual can serve as his or her own control. A baseline period in which the incidence of the behavior to be modified is counted is followed by a reinforcement period, then, a period in which reinforcement is discontinued, and then another reinforcement period. If the number goes up significantly during reinforcement and drops during nonreinforcement, the effect of the treatment has been demonstrated, at least for one individual. To draw more general conclusions, more individuals must be put through the same sequence. The advantage of this experimental procedure over more traditional ones is that for each individual subject a specially tailored plan can be used as to what specific behaviors will be counted and what sort of reinforcement will be given. A second ingenious plan for doing scientific work on individual cases is the Q-sort technique. Block (1961) picked up this idea, proposed by Stephenson (1953), and shaped it into a flexible technique for combining a large amount of information from many sources about an individual in a way that did not require group norms. What is done first is to place, on separate cards, descriptive phrases or statements drawn from case studies, interviews, or observations. Each individual description, produced by the person being assessed or by judges familiar with the data, involves assigning each of the items to a category, according to how relevant or appropriate a descriptor it is for the person under consideration. Categories range from "least characteristic" to "most characteristic." The number of items to be placed in each category is fixed in such a way as to constitute a roughly normal within-person distribution. For example, 100 descriptive items might be assigned to nine categories according to the following system: 5, 8, 12, 16, 18, 16, 12, 8, 5. Characteristics not very relevant for the particular person tend to pile up near the center of the distribution. Salient features, both positive and negative, appear at the extremes. By assigning a number to each category, the unique distribution for an individual can be quantified and analyzed by a variety of statistical procedures. A third variety of single-case techniques grows out of Kelly's personal construct theory (1955), to be considered in considerable detail in a later chapter. Each person first produces his or her own list of elements to be compared—persons in various role relationships, occupations, places, or anything else on which individuals have opinions and make judgments. These elements are then considered three at a time, and the individual is asked to explain how two of them are alike and how the third differs from these two. The procedure reveals the bipolar constructs the person employs in dealing with people, places, or things. A grid can then be constructed with elements along one dimension, constructs along the other. A variety of statistical procedures is now available for extracting meaning from these individual grids. Even this brief discussion should have served to indicate that a psychologist who wishes to do scientific idiographic research now has some procedures to employ in the undertaking. There are others less extensively tried than these, and more will undoubtedly appear as time passes.

Some of the most interesting work on personality and individuality is now being carried out through the use of combinations of the techniques we have been examining. One can create new typologies, for example, on the basis of similar responses in experimental situations or similar Q-sort combinations rather than theoretical systems. One can use test scores to equate experimental and control groups and as dependent variables in experiments. One can derive Q-sort items from data obtained at different stages of development, as Block (1971) did in analyzing directions of development from early adolescence to middle adulthood. Block constructed a developmental typology by factor analyzing correlations between individual Q-sorts.

The following chapters contain many examples of ways in which combined research strategies have been used in the study of individuality. What we seek is an understanding of qualitative as well as quantitative manifestations, the characteristics that constitute variations on universal human themes, those that are common to distinctive types of persons and those unique to single individuals. We are still a long way from the goal, but research tools are now at hand to use in its pursuit, and ingenious psychologists are sure to come up with others.

❧ 3 ❧

Origins of Individuals: Heredity and Prenatal Development

For centuries, people have realized that each person's mental and emotional makeup, like his or her physical features, was to some extent determined by heredity. When families get together, the ways in which children resemble their father and mother, as well as their grandparents, uncles, and aunts, are always being pointed out. Sir Francis Galton, almost a century ago, documented the fact that men and women of genius usually come from families that have produced other eminent persons. Literature and history furnish examples of families cursed by a strain of hereditary madness. Hemophilia appeared and reappeared in members of Europe's royal families. It would be possible to go on and on multiplying examples of folk knowledge about heredity. However, it was not until 1865, when Gregor Mendel reported to an obscure scientific society the results of his experiments

37

on plant hybrids, that scientific research on heredity really began, and it was not until 1900 that Mendel's ideas, rediscovered, were developed into the science of genetics.

During this early period, when simple physical characteristics in plants and lower animals were being explored, psychologists were not involved in the experimental program. Their first serious scientific work on heredity utilized correlational rather than experimental strategies. In the early 1900s, while DeVries and others were continuing Mendel's work, Binet and Simon were attempting to measure intelligence. Their first scale was published in 1908. Most psychologists assumed at the outset that this scale and the others that followed it were revealing differences in pure "native" mental ability, so that for the first time they seemed to be in a position to measure each individual's hereditary endowment. This opened up all sorts of exciting research possibilities. But this assumption about what scores on intelligence tests meant did not go unquestioned for long. Some psychologists—and their number constantly increased—pointed out that by the time a child reached the age when testing by one of these instruments could be carried out, he or she had been subjected to a great many sorts of environmental influence and that at least some of the differences the tests were showing could be accounted for by differences in how favorable for mental growth these environments were. Thus began the perennial controversy over nature versus nurture, which has set the pattern for correlational research during most of the twentieth century.

How did psychologists go about obtaining evidence on this question? They started with the kind of observations people had always found most natural, looking at family resemblances. Keeping in mind what Mendelians had shown about genes and what had been noted in a descriptive way long before Mendel, they reasoned that, if individual differences rest on heredity, then the closer the degree of relationship, the more similar individuals should be, in mental ability as in such physical characteristics as height and facial contours. Using large numbers of cases, one would expect parent-child or sibling correlations to be higher on the average than grandparent-child correlations, uncle-nephew correlations, or cousin-cousin correlations; one would also expect all of these correlations between related persons to be higher than those obtained for unrelated persons paired at random. This is just what was found. Parent-child and sibling correlations for intelligence consistently run about .50, about the same as for height. Lesser degrees of relationship produce lower correlations for mental ability as for physical characteristics.

Furthermore, hypotheses about differences in family correlations that would reflect differences in how similar environments were did not receive much support from research findings. It was hypothesized, for example, that correlations should run higher for same-sex siblings than for brother-sister pairs, because they share more experiences as they grow up. Another such hypothesis was that correlations should run higher between siblings than between parents and children, although the average degree of genetic similarity is the same in the two cases, because children share the same home environment, whereas the parents' formative years have been spent in different ones. Some researchers looked for higher mother-child correlations than father-child correlations, because mothers have more influence on very young children than fathers do. A thorough search for evidence with regard to all of these hypotheses was made by Conrad and Jones (1940). They administered the Army Alpha examination to 997 individuals in 269 family groups, constituting one of the most adequate population samples anyone up to that time had obtained. None of the environmental hypotheses was supported. All correlations between parent and child, regardless of sex combination, between brother and brother, sister and sister, or brother and sister, turned out to be .49. Heredity alone could account for this much similarity. Whether it actually does or not cannot be demonstrated using correlational evidence only. Correlations cannot prove anything about *causes* of relationships.

In other studies designed to show whether environmental influences might have something to do with family resemblances in mental ability, correlations between adopted children and their adoptive parents were compared with correlations between these same children and their true parents. Some estimation was involved here, because most foster parents and many of the true parents of children placed for adoption do not take intelligence tests. Correlations between child's intelligence and parent's education, which

tend to run lower but consistently positive, have been used in most
of these comparisons. What these studies have generally found is
that child's intelligence is related more closely to the education of
true parents than of foster parents (Honzik, 1957), pointing again
to the influence of heredity. Looking at the averages for groups
rather than at correlations (which show the relative positions of
individuals within each group) has shown clearly, however, that
improved environments do lead to higher scores on intelligence
tests. The averages for children reared in good adoptive homes
consistently turn out to be considerably higher than the averages
for children reared in poor homes or in institutions (Skodak and
Skeels, 1949; Goldfarb, 1943). A recent study (Scarr and Weinberg, 1976) shows that the conclusion holds for black as well as
white children.

We shall not consider family correlations in any more detail,
because they are no longer considered a source of very useful evidence on the nature-nurture issue. Increasingly research has been
concentrating on twins. There are two kinds, *identical* or *monozygotic* (MZ) and *fraternal* or *dizygotic* (DZ). Monozygotic twins
are produced by the separation of a single fertilized egg into two
parts at the time of the first cell division. The two individuals carry
exactly the same assortment of genes. Dizygotic twins are produced
from two fertilized eggs and are thus no more alike genetically than
ordinary siblings are. When correlations for intelligence based on
monozygotic twin pairs are compared with correlations based on
dizygotic twin pairs, the former are always considerably higher. In
different studies, the MZ correlations have ranged from .79 to .98,
as compared with DZ correlations ranging from .44 to .74 (Jensen,
1972, p. 300).

There is no longer any argument about the statement that
heredity plays a part in the development of abilities and personality
traits. The questions being asked now are "How large a part does
it play? Can we by some sort of statistical manipulation tease out
the relative contributions of heredity and environment for different
traits and in different situations?" The index being used is called a
heritability coefficient, based on separating out the variance in a
distribution of scores that can reasonably be attributed to different
sources. A heritability coefficient (h^2), whatever the particular

formula used in its computation, represents the ratio of hereditary variance to total variance in the distribution. The more recent formulas try to take into consideration assortative mating, the tendency men and women show to marry persons somewhat similar to them in intelligence. Heritability coefficients are specific to particular populations and societies. For intelligence, in England and the United States, they tend to be about .80. This has been interpreted to mean that four fifths of the variation in mental ability we encounter in our society can be attributed to heredity and only one fifth can be attributed to environment (Jensen, 1972; Vandenberg, 1971). For special abilities and personality traits, obtained h^2 values are typically lower. Of special interest is some evidence that the lags and spurts in intellectual development that make growth curves for the early months of life very irregular seem to depend to a considerable extent on heredity. Wilson (1972), comparing curves for the first two years on scales of infant development for MZ and DZ twins, found the sequential pattern of scores to be more similar for the MZ than for the DZ pairs.

Another large "batch" of research studies uses the strategy of comparing correlations for MZ twin pairs growing up in the same home with those for MZ pairs separated in childhood and reared in different homes. Environmental influence on mental development is indicated by the fact that correlations are consistently lower for separated MZ pairs than for the others (Jensen, 1972). These figures certainly do not show, however, that environment is *all*-important. The twin correlations are still far higher than those for ordinary sibling pairs or for unrelated children, even when the twins have been separated very early. Only in the case of marked environmental differences does one twin turn out to be enough higher than another to make a significant difference in what that twin is able to do with his or her life.

We shall not devote more time to the great mass of research material dealing with the relative contributions of nature and nurture, because they do not actually contribute much to our understanding of *individuals*. Heritability coefficients for traits such as intelligence and aberrations such as schizophrenia are mainly used for social purposes. Such coefficients are part of the evidence policy makers may wish to use when trying to solve social problems of inequality in income, education, and political power or to make good decisions about how to deal with abnormalities and pathologies. Even for such purposes, they are not as useful as many people think they are.

It is commonly assumed that defects caused by heredity are permanent and irremediable, whereas defects based on environmental handicaps can be readily corrected. This is just not true. What can be done about a problem is often independent of what caused it. Diabetes is a hereditary disease, yet millions of diabetics are leading perfectly normal lives because of insulin therapy. Mental retardation caused by severe malnutrition in prenatal life is just as much of a handicap and as impossible to overcome completely as mental retardation resulting from heredity. Policy makers have somewhat different options in dealing with conditions that are mainly caused by heredity and those mainly caused by environment, but many of the courses of action they consider fit either situation.

Whatever the heritability coefficients may be in the population, what an individual is like always depends on both kinds of determiners, and there is no way of calculating heritability for individuals. People sometimes go wrong when they interpret heritability as though it were applicable to individuals, assuming that hereditary and environmental influences are additive and can be considered separately. For example, we sometimes see attempts to break down the IQ of a boy (let us say he is named Edward), estimating that his genetic endowment is about 96 points and that the contribution coming from a good home and community has added another 20, giving him a total IQ of 116. Suzanne's IQ of 76 is split into a hereditary component of 96, like Edward's, reduced 20 points by the influence of an exceptionally poor home and neighborhood, causing her to test 76. Or we sometimes see statements that four fifths of Tommy's high IQ of 150 is based on heredity, one fifth on environment. These interpretations of individual scores are altogether wrong and lead to the failures and false starts that have been so prevalent as we have attempted to understand, appreciate, and foster the growth of unique individuals. For this reason, we shall pay more attention in this chapter to research designed to help people understand heredity and early development as an organized *process* rather than a compound of two ingredients. The story begins for any one individual just before his conception, the first of many occasions on which, out of a large number of possibilities, one particular assortment is selected.

The more we have discovered about the way genetic processes work, the clearer it has become that each individual represents a unique selection from an almost infinite number of possible individuals. Large as the earth's population has become—3.8 billion at present writing—the number of possible human genotypes is infinitely larger than this number, of the order of 70 *trillion* (Gottesman, 1974). This is because of the enormous number of genes in the human chromosomes and the much larger number of ways in which they can be combined in sexual reproduction. One person's set of forty-six chromosomes is made of three to five million genes. Any gene serving a particular purpose in development may exist in several different varieties or *alleles*. Unless a person is an MZ twin, he or she starts out in life with a genotype different from that of anyone else who has ever lived on earth or will ever exist in the future.

When the sperm cell and the egg cell unite to initiate a new life, each contains only half of the genetic material in the forty-six chromosomes of the parent from whom it comes. A chromosome is a threadlike particle, visible under a high-power microscope, made up of the many genes that are the basic hereditary units. Except for germ cells during the process of meiosis, the breakup that precedes fertilization, each cell of the body contains two parallel sets of twenty-three chromosomes each, one from the mother, the other from the father. These are replicated each time the cell divides, as it must innumerable times during a person's life. What happens during meiosis, prior to the fertilization of egg by sperm, is that the chromosomes of each parent split up in chance ways, so that each daughter cell contains twenty-three chromosomes. At fertilization, the two sets combine to form a new whole, the basic hereditary blueprint from which the new individual will be made.

In our search for the origins of individuality, the details of how the process of meiosis occurs need not concern us. They are enormously complicated. What is important to understand is that one string of genes in a chromosome is paralleled by another string of genes. Genes are always paired. One gene of each pair has reached the new individual from its mother, the other from its father. At each gene location, the father and the mother have two paired genes received from their own parents, only one of which is passed along to the new individual. Which of the two it will be is unpredictable. What we call *chance* determines the allocation. It is this that makes family resemblances so diverse and surprising. A little boy may happen to receive most of the genes determining facial appearance with which his mother endows him from the set she was given by her father. Relatives will then repeatedly comment about how much the boy resembles his maternal grandfather, especially if the genes from his mother happen to be dominant over those from his father so far as these characteristics are concerned.

Mendel's discovery of dominance and recessiveness was one of the landmark scientific accomplishments of his time, but it has turned out to be less significant in the development of human beings than in that of the pea plants Mendel studied. As an example of what Mendel discovered, we can take one sort of hereditary difference in peas, the production of round or wrinkled seeds. When he crossed pure strains of these two varieties, he found that all of the resulting seeds were round. But if he then allowed plants raised from these seeds to fertilize each other, in the next generation almost exactly three fourths of the seeds were round, one fourth wrinkled. Mendel's brilliant explanation, repeated over and over for other hereditary characteristics of pea plants, was that hereditary determiners come in pairs and one member of each pair is dominant over the other. An individual plant that inherits a gene for round seeds from either parent will produce round seeds, regardless of whether the other gene codes are for round or wrinkled seeds. It will be impossible to tell by looking at the seed itself whether its genes are alike or different with respect to this characteristic. But plants with unlike genes will enable half of their progeny to produce wrinkled seeds. That is what it means to say that the "wrinkled" gene is recessive.

One further discovery contributed an important building block to the impressive structure of what has come to be called *classical* genetics. While in every cell chromosomes are paired, one chromosome pair is different from the others. In males, it consists of a large chromosome called X and a much smaller one called Y. In females, it consists of two X's. There are in the X chromosome genes that are not matched by corresponding genes in Y. It is because of this noncorrespondence that the so-called sex-linked characteristics are transmitted as they are. For example, conditions such as color blindness or hemophilia are carried by recessive genes on the X chromosome. A girl who receives such genes from her father's X chromosome will manifest the trait only if she happens to receive genes of the same sort from her mother. This sometimes happens even when the mother has been free from the trait herself, but it happens much more frequently to boys than to girls. A boy receives a Y chromosome from his father and thus can have no dominant genes to cover up the effects of recessive X genes he receives from his mother. Sex-linked traits are likely to skip a generation—to show up in the grandson of a man who is affected but not in the daughter-mother who is the link between them.

The elegant simplicity of the Mendelian model had a great appeal for scientists and stimulated an enormous amount of experimental research. In much of it, the fruit fly *Drosophila* was used as a subject. The small size of these flies made it possible to keep thousands of them in the laboratory for breeding purposes. The fact that a fly reaches reproductive maturity in two weeks made it possible to rear many successive generations in a short space of time. The fruit fly has only four chromosomes, so that the number of genes, while very large, is still much smaller than the number on the forty-six human chromosomes. Hypotheses and principles derived from experiments on *Drosophila* could be tested out on other animals and checked against data from human populations, especially the observations of monozygotic and dizygotic twins, to determine how applicable they were to other species.

As time passed, it became increasingly apparent that the processes of heredity were too complex to be explained by the original Mendelian model. Perhaps the most important source of complications is that only a small fraction of the characteristics in which human beings differ is under the control of a single gene pair. Most of them cannot be fitted to this model of what is called *segregative* inheritance. Some important characteristics do fit it—

the blood groups, for example, and certain particular varieties of extreme mental retardation. Phenylketonuria is the condition that is best understood. This genetic defect reduces the activity of an enzyme in the liver that at a certain stage of development is needed to convert phenylalanine to tyrosine. This failure interrupts a chain of chemical processes that must occur in sequence if development is to be normal. Understanding this process has made it possible to prevent retardation by providing extra quantities of the necessary chemical at the proper time. Furthermore, it stimulated research on other varieties of genetic defect that might be corrected if understood. Most of the characteristics in which psychologists are most interested, however, such as intelligence and temperamental qualities, follow a pattern of *polygenic* inheritance. Underlying such traits is a combination of genes exerting influence simultaneously and at successive stages of development. The picture is also complicated by numerous exceptions to the dominance principle. Dominance turns out to be not an all-or-none matter; different degrees of blending of the effects of paired genes can occur. Even the number of chromosomes is not always the same for members of the same species. Some human beings have more or less than the normal forty-six, and either deficiencies or excesses affect development in ways only partially understood at present. Whenever we attempt to apply what is known about heredity to our own lives and the lives of others, we must keep in mind that our knowledge is still very incomplete.

Some implications for our thinking about individuality are, however, quite clear. Uniqueness arises from the fact that a limited, although large number of simple determiners can be combined in an inconceivably large number of ways. There is a large element of chance in these combinations. The strain of unpredictability in nature to which Peirce pointed a century ago has been documented in great detail in genetics. What an individual will be like is partially but not completely predictable. Because children receive their genes from their parents, we can say with some assurance that they are likely to resemble their parents in some ways. What we cannot predict for individual cases is the exact nature of the resemblances, the ways in which the baby will be like its mother, its father, its grandmother, its ancestors many generations back.

Insights into the nature of things have been greatly extended in recent decades by pushing research in genetics beyond the abstract concept of the gene to the actual chemical molecules and the processes in which they are involved. The same phenomenon of diversity arising from combinations of a limited number of components also shows up here. The numbers involved in these analyses are so large as to stagger the imagination. A human body consists of billions of cells, each cell made up of an inconceivably large number of molecules, and the molecules themselves are highly complex entities. Molecules of protein are chains of amino acids ranging in length from a few dozen units to several hundred. But all of these huge molecules are constructed from only twenty building blocks. There are twenty amino acids, but they can be combined in an inconceivably large number of ways.

What the molecular biologists have accomplished is to show, at least in principle, how the process of genetic transmission works to produce in the proper sequence all of the diverse protein molecules of which the organism consists. They worked with organisms very much simpler than any that had been used in genetic research before, using bacteria, especially the common variety, *Escherichia coli,* normally present in the human intestine. It is an organism that multiplies very rapidly, simply by separating into two parts every twenty minutes. Thus the scientist can observe three generations in the space of an hour. Because its reproduction is by simple fission, not by sexual combination, all of the genetic material is contained on one long fiber, rather than on paired chromosomes as in higher species. However, small as it is, one of these bacteria is made up of several thousand different varieties of molecules. The task the molecular geneticists took on was to explain how this whole assortment could be duplicated in twenty minutes, directed somehow by the molecules on the genetic chromosome.

The chromosome fiber consists of a chemical substance called *deoxyribonucleic acid,* better known as DNA. When its structure was puzzled out, it turned out to be a double helix (two strands, running in opposite directions, wound around one another) linked together by hydrogen bonds between paired subunits. The breakthrough discovery was that each of the subunits in the chain, called *nucleotides,* was one of four organic compounds, adenine, guanine, thymine, or cytosine. In the parallel strands of the double helix, adenine (A) is always linked with thymine (T), guanine (G) with cytosine (C). It is the *sequence* of A-T and G-C combinations that controls the synthesis of proteins in the cells. A particular sequence of three nucleotide combinations in the DNA molecule leads to the production of one of the twenty amino acids in the protein molecule. Since there are only four ways in which two things of one kind can be combined with two things of another (A-T, T-A, G-C, C-G), there are sixty-four possible triplets (4 × 4 × 4). There are thus sixty-four sets of instructions governing twenty processes; the genetic code provides more than one way in which some of the twenty amino acids can be produced.

This is what is meant by the statement, so often made, that what chromosomes carry is *information*. Just as it is the sequence of letters in a word and the sequence of words in a sentence that carry meaning, so it is the sequence of chemical structures, into which only certain other structures will fit, that "programs" the orderly development of the molecules that make up an organism. Computer technology showed how such sequential programs work, and scientists familiar with the diversity of structure in organic molecules were able to translate the concept of program into chemical terms.

Jacob (1973, pp. 264–265) comments on the analogy in these terms: "It [DNA] is a long polymer formed by the alignment of four subunits, the four organic bases, repeated by millions and permuted along the chain, like the letters of the alphabet in a test. It is the order of these four subunits that directs the order of the twenty subunits in proteins. Everything then leads one to regard the sequence contained in genetic material as a series of instructions specifying molecular structures and hence the properties of the cell; to consider the plan of an organism as a message transmitted from generation to generation; to see the combinative system of four chemical radicals as a system of numeration to the base 4. In short, everything urges one to compare the logic of heredity to that of a computer." Once the structure of DNA was understood, it was possible to understand how it can duplicate itself again and again in the nucleus of the germ cells. The two strands split apart, beginning at one end, and each nucleotide combines with a free nucleotide of the only sort it can combine with. An A unit in one strand picks up a free T unit. The T unit in the other strand picks up an A.

In order for the DNA instructions to result in the actual building of protein molecules, it is necessary that another substance very much like DNA serve as an intermediary. This substance is RNA, ribonucleic acid, different from DNA only in the substitution of another nucleotide, uracil, for thymine. The production of RNA begins, like the duplication of DNA, with the separation of the two strands of the double helix. Guanine units again pick up units of cytosine, but adenine units pick up units of uracil. It is the RNA strands that link up with amino acids to form proteins. (Actually, the intermediate process is more complex than this. Three varieties of RNA participate in sequence—messenger RNA, ribosomal RNA, and transfer RNA—but these details of the process need not concern us here.) The materials available to be picked up are present in the living cell, which is now known to be a far more complex structure than it was at first supposed to be. The chromosomes are in the nucleus or central portion. The peripheral portion or cytoplasm contains small particles called *ribosomes,* which attach themselves to units on the strand of messenger RNA to form the particular protein the code calls for. Other substances making up the cytoplasm and manufactured in it facilitate the process.

Somehow by means of this sort of process, a single cell is transformed into a complex, highly structured human being. We know far less about how this occurs than we know about what goes on in the single cells of bacteria used by molecular geneticists in their research. In order for all of these different structures to be developed, different genes must come into play in different sorts of cells at different times. One discovery in molecular biology has been of special importance in showing how, in principle, this can occur. Jacob and Monod in the early 1960s discovered that there are three kinds of genes (Jacob and Monod, 1961). Only one variety, the *structural* gene, actually participates in protein building. Another variety, the *operator* gene, has the function of switching the structural genes on and off. Genes of a third variety, *regulator* genes, control the operator genes by repressing or derepressing them. Influences from the cell's environment that affect the cytoplasm determine whether the regulator genes will act as repressers or de-repressers at any given time. A feedback mechanism is involved. When the concentration of the enzyme being produced by the protein-synthesizing process reaches a certain level, it switches off, in a manner analogous to the working of a thermostat in a system of temperature regulation. There is still a great gap between what is known about this process and a complete account of the growth that occurs during prenatal life, but a beginning has been made in bridging it.

On a less fundamental level, we can describe the changes that occur as *differentiation* of three kinds, differentiation in time, often called *histogenesis*, or the genesis of cells; differentiation in space, often called *regionalization*, the genesis of more and more different regions of somewhat independent development; and differentiation in shape or form, often called *morphogenesis*. Out of a single germ cell, millions of new cells, differing from one another in shape, substance, and function, must be created. Waddington (1966) poses the problem very clearly: "The student of embryos is faced with the need to understand how a part of the egg turns into [the] liver, another part into the brain, a third part into the forearm, and so on" (p. 44). About all that can be said at present to link this process with the better-understood genetic processes is that different genes come into action and carry out their functions at different stages, then subside and give way to other genes. Differentiation is a process in time. There are pathways of change, and, once a region of the developing organism has initiated such a pathway, it tends to follow it until that particular line of development is complete. What is involved is a sequence of protein syntheses controlled by genes.

Besides the temporal order specified in the sequence of genes, another factor becomes important in prenatal development and retains its importance as long as the life of the organism lasts—the impact of environment. For any single cell, other cells around it constitute an environment. As the number of cells increases, the environment for cells occupying different positions in the cluster becomes differentiated, affecting both the shapes of cells and the chemical processes occurring in them. Thus the indissoluble fusion of hereditary and environmental influences begins in the earliest stages of life. The mother's nutritional deficiencies may produce permanent handicaps. Optimal development cannot occur if the raw materials to be synthesized are not present in sufficient amounts in the prenatal environment.

At all stages of prenatal development, a process of *auto-regulation* is apparent. The developing individual is a self-stimulating system in which feedback from what has just occurred governs what will occur next. It is only recently in the history of human thought that we have come to realize how essential such regulative processes are. Like the thermostat that switches on the current when the temperature drops below a specified level and switches it off again when a specified higher level is reached, the process called *homeostasis* maintains constant temperatures and chemical compositions in living organisms. The autoregulation in a rapidly growing organism is even more remarkable. It requires a mechanism for keeping the process of *formation* of an organ in its proper channel through a complex interplay of on and off signals. Autoregulation operates from the first instant of life. As the organism becomes more complex and differentiated, two special kinds of structure designed especially for this function come into being, the nervous system and the hormonal system. These systems, more than any others, underlie the behavior we observe in individuals.

Turning more specifically to questions related to the origins of behavioral individuality, we find some of the most profound thoughts about it in the later writings of Zing-Yang Kuo, explaining, after a lifetime of scientific study of development in various species, both in natural environments and in the laboratory, what he had found out.

> Ontogenesis of behavior is a process of modification transformation, or reorganization of the existing pattern of behavior gradients in response to the impact of new environmental stimulation; and in consequence a new spatial and/or temporal pattern of behavior gradients is formed, permanently or temporarily . . . which sometimes adds to the inventory of existing patterns of behavior gradients previously accumulated during the animal's developmental history.

At the beginning of life, the individual possesses
an enormous range of behavioral potentialities limited
only by species differences in anatomical structures and
functional capabilities. As ontogenesis proceeds, new behavior patterns are actualized out of the potential patterns and added to the existing *repertoire,* at the same
time [that] ontogenetic processes set a limit to the actualization of another pattern" [Kuo, 1970, pp. 188–191].

One important fact to keep in mind about a developing
organism is that it is spontaneously active. Activity is not initiated
by stimulation from outside; it occurs long before there is any
nervous system to transmit such stimulation. It is the orderliness
with which this activity unfolds that we must understand. Kuo
(1967) has furnished one of the best accounts of the process. Two
concepts are of crucial importance in his theory. The first is the
concept of *behavioral gradient.* An action always involves the total
organism. There are no isolated reflexes or simple habitual movements of only one part of the body. But while all parts of the organism are active—limbs, inner organs, nervous system—some parts
are more active than others. Thus we find a gradient or pattern of
energies, changing from moment to moment. To quote Kuo again:
"Thus the concept of behavior gradients includes not only the
degree of difference in intensity and extensity of the various parts
of the body involved in an overt movement but variations in the
internal organs. These intrinsic (internal) and extrinsic (external)
variations and their feedbacks are formed into complex, interwoven,
but definite and orderly patterns: *the patterns of behavioral gradients.* These patterns are in a process of continuous change, for the
different parts and organs vary constantly in intensity and extensity.
The goal of the science of behavior, then, must be to discover the
ordering and laws of such changing patterns or gradients" (Kuo,
1967, p. 94).

Kuo's other vitally important concept is the concept of
behavior potentials. As has been emphasized repeatedly in this
book, any organism, but especially the human being, has an enormous number of possibilities for the development of behavior patterns and their combinations into what we label *abilities* and

personality traits. In a single life, only a fraction of these will ever be actualized. The limits to such possibilities, for a species and for an individual, are set by morphological structure and functional capabilities. In Kuo's vivid words, "Common sense suffices to point out that a horse can be trained to dance, to walk in slow pace, or to run, but no horse can be made to say the Lord's Prayer" (Kuo, 1967, p. 128). Much of Kuo's research, formal and informal, was designed to demonstrate that potentialities far exceed normal actualities. He believed that one major purpose of the "epigeneticist" (the term he preferred for the behavior scientist) was to discover such behavioral potentialities, so that new patterns of behavior would be available at any time when we see that it would be desirable for animals or people to act differently from the way they normally do. For example, he trained some Chow dogs to fight cats and others to play amicably with them—and some to be friendly to cats in the house and fight them to the death outside in the yard. He demonstrated that whether mynah birds fly high or hover near the house depends on how they are brought up. Kuo's 1967 book contains delightful descriptions of many sorts of unusual behavior in animals and birds of the many species with which he worked.

He identified five factors that are always involved in the development of particular patterns of behavior gradients out of the many behavioral potentials the organism possesses: (1) morphological factors, (2) biophysical and biochemical factors, (3) stimulation, (4) developmental history, and (5) environmental context. To ignore any of these factors (as psychologists have repeatedly done) is to come up with distorted and inadequate pictures of behavioral development.

Another broad, comprehensive account of what the developmental process, prenatal and postnatal, involves is that formulated by Schneirla and his students and coworkers (Aronson and others, 1970). They see the process as a fusion of maturation and experience. Experience is defined as the total developmental history of all stimulation to which the organism has been exposed at all stages, including the trace effects in the nervous system and elsewhere of this stimulation. Maturation includes growth in size and amount of tissue and the differentiation of tissues, including the trace effects of earlier differentiations. One cannot separate these things. At any point in time, the organism *is* its total history from conception to the present instant. As explained before, this is why analyses into hereditary and environmental components do not help us understand individuals. *What will be* arises from *what is,* and *what is* is a resultant of the whole history of what has happened when the processes coded in the chromosomes occurred under particular circumstances. This is the irreducible fact about development, and all the arguments ever uttered about nature and nurture cannot change it.

The basic processes of embryological development occur in the same manner and the same order for everyone. But each newborn child is in many ways unique. Because there is no one else who started with exactly the same sequence of nucleotides in the DNA molecules of which his or her chromosomes are constituted, the individual's blood composition, fingerprints, inner organs, skin, and behavior are not exactly like anyone else's. All organisms are spontaneously active, but some are more active than others, and they are active at different times and in different ways. Such activity puts its unique brand of individuality on the organism. Human beings after nine months of prenatal development are all born with eyes, ears, and brains. But the relative size, shape, and growth potential of every part of the integrated whole varies from person to person. Human beings all require that the same chemical substances be present in the food that nourishes them, before and after birth, but, as Williams (1956) showed, the amounts of each that individuals need and can utilize varies markedly from one person to another.

In spite of the limits that have been imposed on behavioral potentialities by prenatal development, the individual at birth can still be said to be *overendowed.* He or she will develop far more brain cells than will be needed for the thinking that will actually be done in a lifetime. He or she has the equipment that would make it possible to learn millions of facts and skills. He or she can make all sorts of movements, can utter a tremendous variety of sounds. The selection of possibilities to be actualized, begun during prenatal life, continues after birth. Both the particular assortment of possibilities and the process of selection are unique in each individual case. The individual will never be duplicated.

≋ 4 ≋

The First Two Years
of Life

Newborn babies differ from one another as much as older children and adults do in size, shape, and maturity level. The idea that most of them are "normal" and a few "premature" has become more and more obsolete. Even in infants born at exactly forty weeks gestation time (and variations in gestation time, from thirty-seven to forty-two weeks, are not at all uncommon) the range of differences on a scale designed to indicate how far the individual's development has progressed is the equivalent of three to four weeks of growth (Dubowitz, Dubowitz, and Goldberg, 1970). When two babies come home from the hospital, little Dan may look and act like a baby several weeks old, whereas little Peter next door seems too frail and immature to be considered a real person.

The differences, however, are far more complex than these overall statements suggest. Maturity is not a general characteristic applying equally to all parts of the person. Different organ systems have their own growth schedules and are affected by different circumstances. Length or height, for example, is determined to a large extent by the genes an individual starts with, but conditions in the uterus also have some effect on the length a baby is at birth. Prenatal growth characteristically slows down somewhat during the last six weeks of pregnancy, and if it happens that a child genetically programmed to be tall must spend these weeks in the womb of an undersized mother, the slowdown may be greater than usual. What happens in such cases is that this child during the first few months of postnatal life goes through a period of "catch-up" growth, so that he is considerably bigger for his age at, say, six months than he was at birth (Tanner, 1974). Another child may show just the opposite effect. This means that, although detailed charts showing average measurements for infants of different ages are available, it is not possible to predict accurately for individuals in the earliest stage of life. Growth rates themselves differ from person to person.

Tanner (1974) has summarized many other sorts of differences that have been measured in newborn infants. How far along the development of the bones is can be assessed from x rays of knee and ankle. Differences here are partly a matter of heredity, partly a matter of nutrition. On the average, the bones of girls are more mature at birth than those of boys, and the bones of black infants are more mature than those of white infants, but there are sizable differences between individuals of the same sex or race. The maturity of the nervous system can be assessed by observing posture, mobility, muscle reflexes, and responses to stimuli—light, heat, cold, and so on. Differences are apparent here also. Babies differ in their "brain waves" or electroencephalograms (EEGs), measured in response to flashes of light. Again, girls are a little ahead of boys on the average and blacks a little ahead of whites in their development, but it is variation among individuals of the same sex or race that is most striking. Other neurological measures, such as the conduction velocity in nerve fibers, also vary from individual to individual.

Aside from their consequences in how infants are handled and responded to, the physical differences do not have any important psychological concomitants, at least none that are known at present writing. But during the 1960s and 1970s there has been a great deal of research on psychological characteristics themselves.

Ingenious technological methods, some of considerable complexity, have been devised to monitor infant activity and facilitate inferences about what infants perceive. Observers have been trained to make accurate assessments of variables such as amount of movement, acceleration and deceleration in heart rate in response to changing external circumstances, vocalization, and discrimination between persons. While, as usual, many investigators have not been interested in individual differences, a few have. The answers to long-standing questions about development are important to psychologists seeking to understand individuality, questions such as "How do large environmental differences such as those that go with race or social class affect the process of development? What are the effects of different philosophies and techniques of child rearing? What are the relative contributions of intrinsic and extrinsic factors (maturation and learning) in development?"

One major result of this research concentration on the earliest weeks of life has been a growing respect for the competence, adaptability, and behavior potentialities of the newborn. As Horowitz (1974, p. 1) puts it, "It soon became apparent that not only was it possible to make reliable observations of very young infants but that the infant organism was more competent, more complex, and more fascinating than had been thought possible."

Let us look first at measurements of individual differences in infancy planned and carried out in the psychometric tradition. Escalona (1968), one of the first to attempt longitudinal research of this sort, classifies the dimensions of infant behavior along which individual differences have been measured under eight headings. The first is *activity level,* defined as the amount and vigor of body motion typically shown by a given infant in a wide variety of situations. The second is *perceptual sensitivity,* the degree to which the infant is reactive to sensory stimulation in general and to specific stimulation in the various sensory modalities. The third is *motility,* defined as neuromuscular activities that lead to displacement in space. (Some infants are high in activity level, as defined, but not in the kind of movement that changes the placement and position of the body.) The fourth is *bodily self-stimulation,* meaning thumb sucking, rocking, stroking, rubbing, and many other things the infant does to parts of its own body. The fifth is *spontaneous activity,* another more specialized category than general activity having to do with behavior in situations where the infant is "awake and alert, not subject to somatic discomfort, and not exposed to specific and focused stimulation from without" (Escalona, 1968, p. 36). Escalona considers this an especially important category for research on individual differences, as it has to do with the kinds of "behavior schemas" the person has developed. The sixth dimension is *somatic need states and need gratification*—primarily, how the infant deals with hunger and fatigue. The seventh is *object-related behavior,* the "totality of behavioral events in which the infant responds to the perception of objects or things in the environment" (Escalona, 1968, p. 44). The eighth and last is *social behavior,* the way the infant responds to persons.

While this classification covers all of the behavior in regard to which infants during the first year of life have been observed to differ, investigators since the time of Escalona's work have tended to concentrate on more specific variables. There has been a great deal of interest in how long the baby pays attention to a stimulus once he or she has noticed it. A group at the Kansas Infant Research Laboratory (Horowitz, 1974) worked out a sensitive way of measuring this. The infant in the experimental room lies or sits (depending on age) in a standard position, and two observers behind a screen on which pictures are projected watch its eyes through peepholes, recording the length of time the object shown is fixated. The important variable, however, is not the fixation time on the first trial, but how rapidly habituation occurs in subsequent trials and how rapidly recovery from this habituation takes place when a new stimulus is presented with the old one. Infants as young as five or six weeks showed that they recognized as familiar a checkerboard appearing on the screen, with other stimuli interspersed between presentations, by quickly turning their eyes away when the checkerboard appeared. Their attention to this object could be aroused again, however, if music or the sound of the mother's voice accompanied it when it appeared on the screen. For our purposes, the most interesting aspect of this interesting set of experiments is the fact that distinct patterns of individual differences became apparent. Self (1974) found that the babies could be categorized as *rapid habituators, short lookers,* or *slow habituators.* The rapid habituators came down from more than one hundred seconds of looking time to about ten seconds in four presentations. The short lookers gazed at the stimulus only a few seconds even on the first trial and did not change much on subsequent trials. The slow habituators showed only a moderate amount of looking time on the first trial, actually increased this on the third, and looked about as long on the fourth as they had on the first. The addition of music affected the three types of infant differently. The short lookers showed the most change, gazing more than sixty seconds at the stimulus on the first music trial but coming down as the situation was repeated. The rapid habituators took another long look on the first music trial, but not as long as the first trial, and again they habituated rapidly. The slow habituators maintained about the same level, music or no music. We do not know, of course, what significance belonging to one or another of these types has for later development, but the fact that not much more than a month after birth babies differ in the way they respond to pictures and remember which they have seen before is an intriguing one. The three types suggest the very early appearance of cognitive styles, which we shall be considering at some length later.

Other investigators have used acceleration and deceleration in heart rate as an indicator of attention (Hirschman and Katin, 1974). In the earliest days of life, babies tend to respond to stimulation with acceleration; from then on until nine to eleven months the typical response is deceleration. Then there is another shift, and acceleration again becomes the typical response to novelty. Hirschman and Katkin speculate that this may represent a shift from an "orienting" to a "defensive" kind of arousal and back again. Kagan (1972), looking at this U-shaped developmental curve of cardiac response, suggests that the acceleration beginning at nine to twelve months coincides with a shift from passive assimilation of experience to active inquiry. Individual differences would seem to be important, but so far have not been studied.

The idea that personality tendencies may originate very early in life also comes out of research done by Ricciuti and Poresky (1972). In these experiments, babies in a standard laboratory situation found themselves confronted with four successive stimuli, chosen to elicit behavior expressing arousal, approach, withdrawal, and affective responses (laughing, crying, and so on). There were eight infants in each of four age groups; three-month-olds, six-month-olds, nine-month-olds, and twelve-month-olds. On each occasion, first a doll was presented, then a teddy bear, then—suddenly—a jack-in-the-box, and finally a buzzer loud enough to be disagreeable. There were individual differences in the emotional responses—how pleased they were with the teddy bear, how startled or frightened they were at the jack-in-the-box, how much crying they did when the buzzer sounded. Furthermore, the individual differences were greater the older the age group. Again we do not as yet know what such differences lead to, but the experiment corroborates common observation that some babies show more pleasure in cuddly toys than others do and that some are more susceptible than others to startle and fright.

With regard to all of the eight main varieties of infant behavior on Escalona's list, evidence has accumulated that children begin to manifest the behavior at a very young age and that individual differences exist. So far, only a few longitudinal studies have attempted to find out how such differences are related to later characteristics. First let us look at longitudinal research on intelligence. For a long time, the study of individual differences during the first two years of life was cast into this mold that had seemed so suitable in the study of school-age children. Binet, as we have said, hit on the idea of a scale of mental development in which successive levels were expressed as ages, each level representing the average age at which children could answer a particular set of questions and carry out a particular set of tasks. It was a beautifully simple system, and when the intelligence quotient, the ratio of mental age to chronological age, was added to it, it seemed to provide a means of predicting the level at which any child would be functioning during later childhood and as an adult. (This was, of course, an oversimplification, as later discussions will show.) It was natural to suppose that this system of measurement could be extended down the age scale, using months rather than years to indicate mental age during the period when very rapid changes in ability are occurring. Just as a ten-year-old can succeed at tasks at which a six-year-old fails, so anyone can see that a ten-month-old baby can do things that are beyond the capability of a six-month-old. The psychologists saw their job as one of arranging in a scale various indicators of how far along in their development various infants were. A number of such infant scales have been published over the years and have proved their usefulness in assessing the current developmental status of individual children. They differ from intelligence tests for older children, however, in having little or no value in predicting developmental status at later periods. The correlation between IQ during the first year of life (or DQ, developmental quotient, as it is now commonly called) and IQ at the time of entering school is practically zero. DQs during the second year are a little more predictive, but not much.

What this means in practical terms is that a baby who seems unusually bright and is able at an earlier age than others to discriminate colors, grasp toys, crawl, walk, and say recognizable words may or may not do better in school in later years than his or her less precocious sibling or neighbor. One simply cannot predict how bright a child is going to be by giving an infant test (Lewis and McGurk, 1972; Pease, Wolins, and Stockdale, 1973). An exception to this generalization should be noted for some kinds of severe mental retardation, which are apparent in early infancy. These are the cases, however, in which an intelligence test is superfluous, as the defect shows up in any ordinary observation.

This lack of relationship between intelligence ratings in infancy and ratings at later periods has given rise to much discussion. Out of it has come a realization that what we call *general intelligence* does not exist at the beginning of life but results from the merging of more or less independent developmental processes. McCall, Hogarty, and Hurlburt (1972) have used infant scales to analyze some of these processes. They have shown that it is possible to select subsets of items at one point on the age scale that are related to another subset of items at the next point on the age scale and that one can predict fairly successfully from what individual children do on the first subset how well they will do on the second. These related subsets of items, however, may be made up of things that look like quite different abilities. For example, a set of items designed for the first six months, involving manipulative exploration that produces perceptual contingencies, such as shaking a rattle, can be used to predict how successful individuals will be during the second six months at imitating fine motor and verbal behavior. This imitative subset of items for the six- to twelve-month period is in turn predictive of success during the twelve- to eighteen-month period with items having to do with verbal labeling and comprehension. This set in turn is predictive of verbal fluency and comprehension at the next six-month period. What is most important about this line of investigation is that it points the way toward an understanding of cognitive development through the exploration of somewhat autonomous developmental systems. Piaget and his associates have been doing research of this sort for many years, but it has not been assimilated into the efforts of mental testers to measure individual differences.

Crano (1977), after analyzing the data from the Berkeley Growth Study in a new way, suggested a different explanation of the kinds of correlations obtained between mental ability measures at four age levels during the first three years and scores for particular kinds of behavior, such as activity, speed, positive response to people, and the like, measured at later periods. What infant intelligence scales may be measuring is the basic psychobiological integrity of the organism. The higher this is, the better the child should be able to master the successive challenges life brings. Differential scores on early tests thus may indicate differences in this general soundness, rather than in intellectual level.

Let us now turn to a large-scale research attempt to follow a different sort of infant differences through subsequent periods of childhood. Thomas and others (1963) undertook in 1956 to assess temperamental characteristics of infants at three-month intervals during the first year, then at six-month intervals up to the age of twenty-seven months. Less frequent follow-ups were planned for the later childhood years. They started with 136 infants from upper-middle-class New York families. They made ratings based on specific behavioral information obtained from the parents. The aspects of temperament rated were: (1) activity level; (2) rhythmicity; (3) approach-withdrawal; (4) adaptability; (5) intensity of reaction; (6) threshold of responsiveness; (7) quality of mood; (8) distractability; and (9) attention span and persistence. (It will be noted that there is some overlap here with Escalona's list of observable infant characteristics, given in the previous section, but the two research programs were not related in any way, and their objectives were somewhat different.) The 1963 book reported what they had found for the first twenty-seven months. For each of the variables, there did turn out to be significant correlations between ratings for different age levels. Active babies tended to become active two-year-olds. Those who were persistent at nine months were still persistent at twenty-seven months. Because of the way the ratings came out, however, it is not altogether clear what conclusions can be drawn. On all the variables, rated on a seven-point scale, most children received the same moderate rating. There were few extreme ratings, either positive or negative. It was the tendency of these extreme ratings to persist from age to age that produced the correlations. What one can say with some assurance is that children who are unusually high or low on one of these rated traits are likely to continue to be somewhat deviant.

This shows up more clearly in a second major report on the project (Thomas, Chess, and Birch, 1968). This covered a nine-year period. The researchers succeeded in locating 96 percent of the 136 children who had been rated as infants. They found that out of this group forty-two had at some time during their first nine years developed behavior problems. They compared the ratings of these forty-two children with the ratings of the others and used factor analysis to identify clusters of early characteristics that differentiated the behavior problem children from the rest. The cluster that revealed the greatest difference was one that brought together negative mood, high intensity, withdrawal, and slow adaptability. The behavior problem group also included a higher proportion of children who had been rated either unusually high or unusually low on activity level. What is most valuable about this report and most closely related to present foci of research is the discussion of the ways in which children's characteristics elicit differential treatment from parents. The children in the study were classified into five major groups: (1) difficult children; (2) easy children; (3) children slow to warm up; (4) children high in persistence; and (5) children high or low in activity. Each of these types needs a different sort of treatment from parents and teachers. There are no child-rearing procedures suitable for everybody.

The longitudinal studies that have covered the longest span

of years, from infancy to adulthood, were those at the University of California at Berkeley (Schaefer and Bayley, 1963; Bayley and Schaefer, 1964), the Fels Research Institute (Kagan and Moss, 1962), and the Menninger Foundation (Escalona and Heider, 1959). So far as clear evidence of cognitive or temperamental characteristics continuing from infancy to maturity is concerned, the yield is very small. As in the case of predicting later IQ from infant intelligence scores, predicting later personality traits from infant personality traits does not appear possible. But it is through the thoughtful examination of all of the evidence from these studies that more productive ways to think about developing individuality have arisen.

There seem to be, here as with the intelligence test items considered in the previous section, relationships between any one stage and the *next* one. And one needs to watch the transformation of one characteristic into another characteristic that at first glance may look quite different. Escalona calls attention to this by distinguishing between *isomorphic* and *metamorphic* relationships, correlations between measures of the same trait at different ages and correlations between measures of different traits. The words *phenotype* and *genotype* are sometimes used in discussing this same distinction, but they are less useful, because they suggest that we can somehow find the genotypes or basic hereditary endowments of individuals. The latest and perhaps the best pair of terms was proposed by Kagan (1971), namely *homotypic* and *heterotypic* relationships. If activity level in one-year-olds is predictive of activity level in kindergartners, the relationship is homotypic. If activity level predicts reading difficulties, the relationship is heterotypic.

Escalona (1968) has also emphasized another important shift in our thinking about these developmental relationships. When we attempt to account for the differences between persons on the basis of environmental differences, we must remember that between the organismic and environmental variables to be correlated with some developmental outcome it is always necessary to insert an intermediate variable, the *experience pattern* of the person. We must find out how the child experiences his own tendencies and the influences from the world around him if we are to understand

why the stages of his life are related in the ways that they are.*
These insights about how to go about studying the development of
individuality grew out of the Menninger Clinic research. The basic
materials are observational data on 128 normal infants: eight boys
and eight girls at each monthly age level from four weeks through
thirty-two weeks (Escalona and others, 1953). After getting a large
amount of information about each child, the investigators were
able to assess each one along the dimensions described earlier in the
chapter, namely activity level, perceptual sensitivity, motility, bodily
self-stimulation, spontaneous activity, somatic need states and gratification, object-related behavior, and social behavior. Marked individual differences were apparent in all of these dimensions. In one
of the follow-up studies, Escalona and Heider (1959) went back to
the infant data for a sample of the children who were enrolled in
preschool several years later. Looking first only at the data from the
infant files, they formulated predictions about what the child's behavior in school would be like. They then checked these against
actual observations of school behavior and counted their "hits" and
"misses." About two thirds of their 882 predictions turned out to be
correct. Clearly, there had been some continuity in individual personality development. But the study was unsatisfying in many ways.
The principal flaw is that there is no way of being certain how
much success in predictions of this sort would be anticipated through
chance alone. There also was no way to get at the nature of the
developmental processes linking infancy to early childhood in different individuals. Why had some quiet, passive infants developed into
lively, resourceful preschoolers? Why had some unusually active
infants become shy and unhappy? Escalona became convinced that,
complex as the problem is, psychologists must look at the interactions between *all* of a child's characteristics, the opportunities provided by the environment, and the way in which the mother and
other caretakers dealt with the baby. (As mentioned earlier, Thomas,
Chess, and Birch, 1968, came to a very similar conclusion.)

---

* The traditional use of the pronoun *he* has not yet been superseded
by a convenient, generally accepted pronoun that means either *he* or *she*.
In using *he,* the author acknowledges the inherent inequity of the traditional
preference of the masculine pronoun.

Rather than to carry out further follow-up studies, Escalona (1968) went back to the original data and attempted to conceptualize these interactions. Thirty-two of the records were selected for this analysis, the two at each age level who had been rated highest for activity level and the two who had been rated lowest. The active were then compared with the inactive on all of the other variables, looking for differences in treatment and in experience pattern that were related to activity. The theoretical system she formulated was based on concepts first elaborated by Kurt Lewin (1935, 1936), in which personality is described in terms of regions and the boundaries between them. The result was a characterization for each child of his or her stable pattern of experience (SPE), based on (1) the frequency of strong bodily arousal; (2) prominence of internal somatic sensations, especially hunger and fatigue; (3) balance between behavior activations responsive to internal and somatic causes and those responsive to external stimulation; (4) importance of distance receptors (sight and sound); (5) importance of near receptors (touch and passive motion); (6) most prominent modality (vision, sound, touch, or passive motion); (7) least prominent modality; (8) frequency of optimal states of animation. Escalona described each child in terms of these factors and related this whole *adaptational syndrome* to her evaluation of developmental outcome. (This was not in any sense the ultimate outcome, but simply an assessment based on several criteria of how satisfactory the infant's development seemed to be at the time of the observations.) Good general developmental status was related to several aspects of the SPE. It occurred when strong bodily arousal was at least moderately frequent, when responsiveness was greater to external than to internal stimulation, when distance receptors were frequently activated, and when states of optimal animation were frequent. Probably the most important finding was that, while the specific behavioral assessments on which the SPE ratings were made did not correlate individually with developmental status, the SPE *patterns* did. It was the right combinations of factors rather than the right factors themselves that mattered. In concrete terms, Grace, who was subject to strong stimulation from both without and within and who received a great deal of care and attention from her active, sociable mother and the other members of her family, was accelerated in her overall development. But so was Robert, who was not very reactive to inner stimulation but much more reactive to external stimulation and who was enthusiastically although rather unskillfully handled by his inexperienced mother. Different combinations of personal characteristics and treatment seemed to work well in different cases.

In another study by Kagan (1971), the subjects were 180 infants who came to the laboratory to be observed in detail at four months, eight months, thirteen months, and twenty-seven months of age. Kagan did not attempt to assess all aspects of development but selected certain ones that his previous research had led him to think were especially important. He focused especially on *attention,* what the baby attended to and for how long, but he also noted and coded the frequency of smiling and vocalization, the time spent crying or fretting, and what the child did in a period of free play in a room with toys. Some additional, testlike procedures were introduced at twenty-seven months. Cardiac deceleration was monitored during all experiments in which the infant was in a fixed position. The theoretical construct on which Kagan based his experiments was the development of *schemas* or programs for the processing of information from the environment. Kagan defines *schema* as "a representation of an event that preserves the temporal and spatial arrangement of its distinctive elements without necessarily being isomorphic with the event" (1971, p. 6). According to this way of thinking, one of the main things the individual must do during the first year or two of life is to construct a supply of schemas to use in sorting out and classifying the stimulating energies with which he or she is constantly bombarded. The concept *schema* is more inclusive than *image, symbol,* or *word.* It may represent an action, a response to social situations, an interpretation of a natural scene. Its function is to make it possible for the individual to organize and assimilate information.

The results, as in other longitudinal studies of infants, were complex. For one thing, different indices used to measure attention picked up different aspects of the total test situation. "Vocalization most often indexed excitement, fixation indexed time to assimilation, deceleration indexed surprise, and smiling indexed a successful assimilation of an initially discrepant event" (Kagan, 1971, p. 174).

Vocalization and fixation time were not correlated; children high on one of these measures were not necessarily high on the other. Evidently, different children assimilate new experience to existing schemas in different ways. As far as stability from age to age is concerned, there was *no* relationship between individual differences at four months on any of the variables and individual differences at the later ages. From eight to thirteen months and from thirteen to twenty-seven months, the correlations were high enough to be statistically significant, but there was little or no relationship between eight months and twenty-seven months. Results suggested that changes in the dependence of behavior on stable internal structures occur at about the end of the first year. Research based on infant intelligence tests has suggested the same sort of shift. From thirteen months to twenty-seven months, vocalization, deceleration of heart rate, fixation, and smiling all correlated significantly, but, as most of the coefficients were less than .50, it was clear that individual shifts were occurring. This finding, too, corroborates what has generally been found with infant intelligence scales. Like the children with whom Thomas, Chess, and Birch (1968) worked, most of Kagan's subjects had average rather than extreme scores, so that the correlations represented a tendency for extreme children to remain extreme rather than for all of them to maintain the same positions in the distribution. In summary, research on infants, especially in longitudinal studies over at least a short period, has shown that there are individual differences in very young infants, as there are individual differences in older children and adults, but the nature of the links between the early and later periods still eludes us. We do have hints and hypotheses to go on. These are now suggesting more sophisticated designs for research on the development of individuals.

One research approach growing out of the emphasis on the *interaction* of inner and outer sources of stimulation in development is looking at the behavior that babies with different characteristics *elicit* from the adults who care for them, especially mothers. For years, psychologists have studied and talked about the mother's effect on the child, but it is only recently that the problem has been turned around, considering the baby's behavior as stimulus and the mother's as response. Once we begin to look at the situation in this way, it is easy to see that all of the individual differences in infants we have been reporting would naturally lead to differences in the way their mothers treated them and thus to differences in the situation to which the babies must respond.

Lorenz (1956) pointed to the possible significance of such differences when he described the physical characteristics of babies people consider to be "cute." "The head must have a large neurocranium . . . it must have an eye which is below the middle of the whole profile. Beneath the eye, there must be a fat cheek. The extremities must be short and broad. The consistency of the body ought to be that of a half-inflated football, elastic . . . and finally the whole thing must be small and must be a miniature of something" (Lorenz, 1956, p. 222). Common observation shows that a "cute" baby gets more attention from family and friends than a baby who is not "cute." Schaffer and Emerson (1964) called attention to the fact that some babies are "cuddlers" and others "noncuddlers" and that the two types receive different treatment.

But it was not until the late 1960s and early 1970s that this interactive emphasis in research really caught on (Lewis and Rosenbloom, 1974). Individual differences in size and shape and, even more, the differences in crying, smiling, and vocalizing, enter into a complex pattern of mother-infant interaction that serves to channel the development of individual children in different directions. Lewis and Lee-Painter (1974) observed fifty-five mother-infant pairs during 120 minutes of interaction. All infants were within one week of three months of age. Of the group twenty-eight were female and twenty-seven male, and they represented the full range of social classes in the population. Observers went to the homes and unobtrusively recorded what infants and mothers were doing at ten-second intervals during 120 minutes of waking time. This provided 720 ten-second units of mother-infant interaction for each pair. There were many ways in which such data could be analyzed. It was clear, first of all, that there were large individual differences in the time babies spent vocalizing, smiling, crying, and playing and in the time mothers spent holding or rocking the babies. The average baby vocalized during 162 periods, or 23 percent of the time, but the range for different infants was from 4 percent to 62 percent. On the mother's side, the average time spent holding the child was 42 percent, but the range was from 3 percent to 90 percent. Ranges of similar magnitude were obtained for the other variables.

The most interesting results reported had to do with the interactions themselves. Figure 1 is an example. It shows a striking difference between two mother-infant pairs in what happens after the baby vocalizes. The middle row of boxes represents what the mother did during the ten-second period in which the baby was babbling. The numbers beside the arrows indicate the number of ten-second periods in which the behavior occurred. It is evident in the first place that Infant A did a lot more vocalizing than Infant B did. It is also evident that when A vocalized the mother usually talked back. With the exception of one period in which her response was to touch the baby, her response, when she made one, was always a vocalization of her own. Infant B experienced much more variety, with the mother responding sometimes in one way, sometimes in another.

These differences in the nature of one's experience of the world, grafted on to the initial differences in behavior tendencies, lie behind the complex differences we observe in children and adults. Some day we shall know more than we do now about what leads to what. It may be that Infant A will develop more language facility than B because of the vocalization-vocalization relationship. Possibly some of this selecting out of language to be practiced had already occurred during the first three months and that this is why A vocalized more than B did in the experimental situation. It may be that Infant B will develop a greater variety of responses and expectations about responses from other people than A does. Either of these results would be desirable. What findings like this keep reminding us is that we must give up the assumption that there is only one direction in which normal growth can occur. Research of this kind is beginning to produce concrete evidence of the process through which multiple possibilities are transformed into a limited number of actualities. It would be meaningless for us to say that what Infant A's mother does is better for development than what B's mother does until we trace the later growth of the two infants.

In another series of experiments (Korner, 1974), infants were observed and filmed almost immediately after birth in an at-

Figure 1. Differences in Mother-Infant Interaction Patterns.

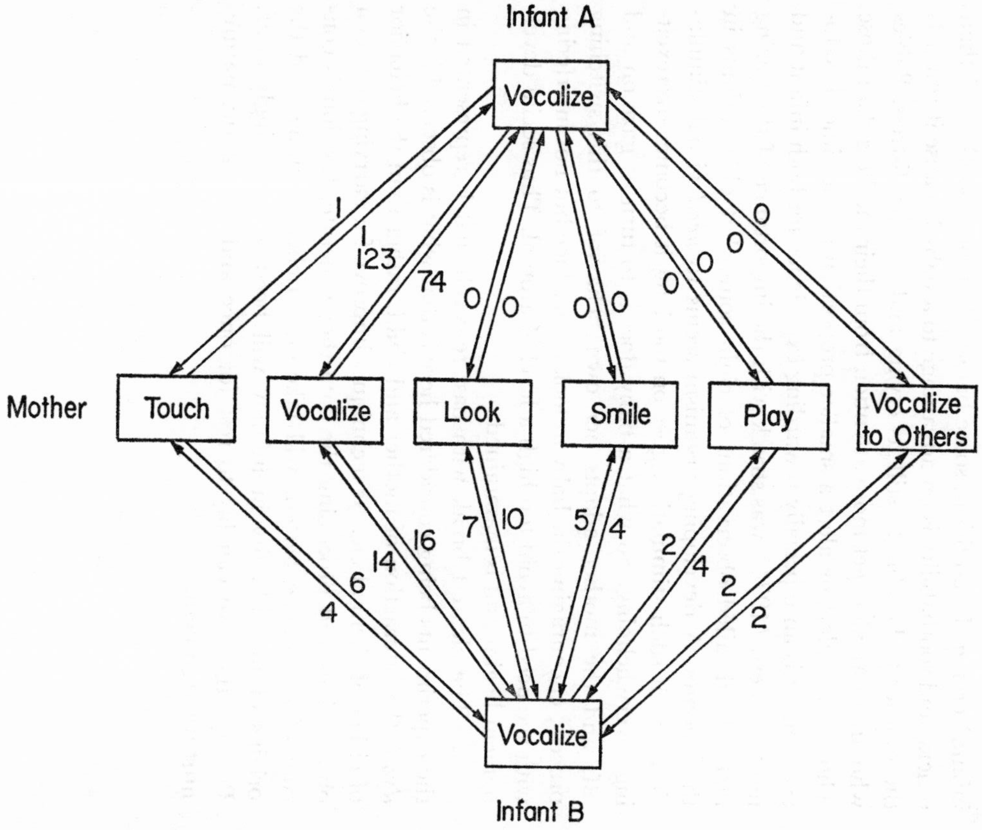

Source: Lewis and Lee-Painter (in Lewis and Rosenbloom, 1974, p. 40).

tempt to detect what aspects of their behavior led to differences in their mothers' behavior toward them. The amount of crying the baby does seems to be the most important variable. Four fifths of the interactions between infant and mother were initiated by the infants' crying. In addition, some babies are more "soothable" than others, and soothability is an advantage to a baby because it rewards the mother to be able to still its crying and ease its distress. Babies who are more alert get more attention from their mothers than those who are less alert or alert a smaller proportion of the time. Eye-to-eye contact is an especially rewarding experience for both infant and mother. Stern (1974) was struck with the importance of this gazing factor in detailed observations of eight somewhat older infants in their homes. A developing organism seems to *need* visual stimulation, but if such stimulation goes on too long it becomes overexciting, overwhelming. So what a baby does is to turn its gaze on and off, and the mother adapts her own behavior to this switching process, encouraging the baby to look at her face but not interfering with the need to avoid too high a level of arousal. Thus social development begins and is maintained.

The clearest break with past research that is represented in the experiments being considered here is that what is observed is the *dyad,* the interaction of mother and child, rather than the behavior of either of them alone. As techniques improve for carrying out such observations and processing the data they generate, Escalona's concept of *experience pattern* will take on a richer meaning, and the origins of individuality in infancy will become increasingly clear. Perhaps then we can lay to rest for once and for all the nature-nurture argument.

❧❧ 5 ❧❧

Intelligence as an Aspect of Individuality

The psychologists who first became interested in individual differences a century or so ago soon exhausted the possibilities of what could be found out by measuring lengths, weights, and reaction times. What began to look far more important were the differences in the ways different people think. Out of the complex matrix of processes we have been considering— genes that start and stop biochemical reactions through which inert material is transformed into living organs; infant behavior, which influences the behavior of adults, which in turn influences the behavior of the infant; deliberate training procedures and chance happenings—there arises a Shakespeare or a Hitler or an Archie Bunker. Forty years after 100 babies go home from the hospital where they were born, their number may include an outstanding physician, a famous novelist, several accountants, carpenters, plumbers, and electricians, a jet pilot, a librarian, a town planner. Among those holding down ordinary jobs, some will be considered excellent workers, some just average, some marginal or unsatisfactory. We are so accustomed to this sorting-out process that we seldom pause to marvel at it. How do these differences originate? The complex society humankind has evolved depends on this diversity in the competencies of different persons if it is to function well.

Early psychologists approached the problem by studying differences in general intelligence in school children. It was convenient to deal with this limited range of differences rather than with the confusing complexity of adult society. For a long time, teachers had been evaluating the competence of individual children by observing how successfully and how easily they mastered the school tasks set for them. It was natural to assume that some special quality or ability accounted for these differences in school performance and that this ability also accounted for differences in adult success. Somewhere along the line, this ability was given the label *intelligence,* and a flourishing line of psychological research began. From our vantage point, looking at possibilities and choices, we can see that the research done by Binet and his followers represented only one road among several that might have been taken. Instead of quantifying *levels* of intelligence, psychologists might instead have analyzed differences in the *direction* of development. Instead of addressing the question, "How *good* is each individual at one sort of mental activity?" they might have asked, "What kinds of competency has each individual acquired and through what developmental processes?" During this final third of the twentieth century, it has become apparent that the focus on levels of intelligence has produced problems as well as resources for human society and that a century of research has given us only a partial understanding of human competence. But in spite of these limitations useful knowledge has been obtained. Let us look at its basic outlines.

It was the French psychologist Alfred Binet who, with Simon, launched the intelligence-testing movement (1908). Descendents of his first intelligence scale are still in common use in schools, clinics, and many other situations. In contrast to his predecessors, Binet recognized that the quality of a child's thinking could not be evaluated by adding up scores on the kinds of simple performances psychological laboratories of the time had been studying—things such as reaction time, sensitivity to visual and auditory stimuli, or memory for nonsense syllables. Instead, one had to devise some means of sampling the thinking that individuals did and then had to find out how good a sample of all their thinking this was. To be fair to children from many backgrounds and social levels, a test must sample performances that there had been opportunity for all to practice. The fact that in most countries of the Western world compulsory education laws were passed during the latter part of the nineteenth century seemed to make it possible to meet this requirement—if one worked with children, not adults. While curricula, of course, vary from place to place, all elementary schools attempt to acquaint children with words and numbers. Binet and his successors avoided the more specialized kinds of school assignments and asked questions designed to produce answers that would vary in quality. On the basis of these answers, they evaluated the child's intelligence.

One of Binet's major contributions to the theory and practice of intelligence testing was to link the measurement system to the naturally occurring improvement with age in children's thinking. It is obvious to any observer that a three-year-old can understand ideas that are meaningless to a two-year-old and that a five-year-old can solve problems he or she was not able to cope with at four. By trying out various questions and tasks on groups of children of different ages, Binet was able to produce a *scale* similar to the system we use to label the sizes of clothes. Just as children vary in physical growth rates, so that one three-year-old may wear a four-year-old jacket and another be better fitted with one labeled for a two-year-old, so a range of mental ages was demonstrated for children of a given chronological age. It soon occurred to psychologists building on the Binet foundation that by dividing the mental age by the chronological age they could obtain an index of how advanced or retarded in his or her *rate* of mental development a child was. (The quotient was multiplied by 100 to get rid of decimals.) Thus the four-year-old who performed like a five-year-old was said to have an intelligence quotient of 125 ($5/4 \times 100$). As time passed, all sorts of technical difficulties with intelligence quotients became apparent and mental testers shifted to more statistically sophisticated ways of scaling, but unfortunately the name *IQ* stuck, became a part of our common language and engendered a great many kinds of errors and misapprehensions.

Whether it is labeled *IQ* or not, what a derived score on any intelligence test shows is how an individual compares with his or her "peers" on the characteristic the test measures. Tests are designed in such a way that when administered to a reasonably large sample of the population in which they are to be used, the scores will produce a bell-shaped, normal distribution. As explained in Chapter Two, this is a mathematical distribution the characteristics of which are well understood. The mean or arithmetic average of a normal distribution falls at the middle of the scale. The standard deviation constitutes a unit in terms of which statements can be made as to how far below or above average individual scores are. Because the proportion of cases falling within each segment of a normal distribution is known, one can readily interpret a score if one knows the system. The test maker decides arbitrarily what number to equate to the middle of the scale and to specified distances from it in standard deviation units. Because when the IQ was actually a quotient the middle or average score was 100, it is customary in intelligence testing to use 100 as the central point. In the widely used Wechsler scales, the standard deviation has been given an arbitrary value of 15. Thus an IQ of 115 on one of the Wechsler scales signifies that the person tested scored at about the eighty-third percentile or that 83 percent of the comparison group received lower scores than this person did. An IQ of 145 places the person in the top 1 percent of the distribution. An IQ of 85 indicates that about 83 percent of the comparison group score higher than the person tested, and an IQ of 55 places the testee in the bottom 1 percent of the distribution. Other tests follow the same system but may attach different numerical equivalents to the mean and standard deviation. The problem of producing a scoring system that will indicate how high or low an individual is has been solved to most people's satisfaction. A much more difficult problem is to determine just what it is that a person is high or low in.

What are intelligence tests really measuring? Early test constructors thought that they knew. They began their search for appropriate test items by defining what they intended to measure. But it soon became apparent that they did not agree very well—their definitions did not coincide. (See Tyler, 1969, for a reprint of an early symposium attempting to clarify these definitions and showing how far apart psychologists were.) People still disagree about what intelligence really consists of, and controversies over testing are partially reflections of these disagreements. However, psychologists engaged in test construction have come to realize that they need not agree on an abstract definition in order to obtain dependable evidence about what tests measure. Regardless of authors' preconceptions about intelligence, the tests they devised showed considerable similarity. Scores turned out to be consistently related to some things, unrelated to others. And it is to the correlations expressing these relationships that we must look for an understanding of what tested intelligence is and what individual IQs mean.

The first universal finding is that intelligence test scores correlate with school success, however measured. Such correlations are by no means perfect, seldom running higher than about .6, but, at all educational levels from kindergarten to college, the better students turn out in most cases to be those with higher IQs, and low-IQ students tend to have difficulty. The higher the IQ, the more schooling a person tends to obtain. In former times, when secondary schools and colleges were more selective than they have recently become, the average IQ for high school students was significantly higher than the average for children in elementary school, and the college average still higher. With our present emphasis on making education at all levels available to everyone, these differences in average score have diminished but not disappeared altogether. Different secondary schools and different colleges vary widely in the average IQ of their students. The more selective the institution, the higher the average IQ, even when the basis of selection does not involve testing at all.

It is not accurate, however, to define intelligence as "general learning ability" just because high scorers do better in school than low scorers do. It is only necessary to watch children on the playground, in the swimming pool, at band practice, or in any other situation where they are acquiring the hundreds of special competencies they pick up as they go along to observe learning processes that do not depend at all on IQ. The evidence points to the conclusion that there is no such thing as *general* learning ability. Years ago, Woodrow (1946) ran some definitive experiments to demonstrate this. More recently, Guilford (1967) came up with more detailed evidence. Individuals differ as to what they learn most readily and what they find especially difficult. It is because of the way we have singled out the learning of academic subject matter for special emphasis that we are likely to overemphasize the ability measured by intelligence tests. When we remove our blinders and look at all the things a person does, we cannot fail to be impressed with everybody's learning ability, and we are less likely to disparage someone who has an IQ of 80 or 90.

What intelligence tests and school assignments both seem to require is that the individual deal with symbols and comprehend complex ideas. Because the subject matter in the curriculum with which elementary school pupils must deal becomes increasingly complex from grade to grade, those whose growth in intelligence is rapid are more likely than the others to be ready for it when it is presented and thus more likely to be able to master it. A distinction Thorndike made more than half a century ago is still useful in clarifying what it is about tested intelligence that predicts success in school (Thorndike, 1926). He distinguished between *altitude* (referring to the degree of difficulty of the tasks a person can cope with), *width* (referring to the number of kinds of task of a given difficulty that a person can accomplish), and *speed* (referring to the amount of time it takes a person to produce a correct response to a task he or she knows how to handle). It is altitude differences that relate most clearly to whether or not one succeeds with high school Latin, chemistry, or literature; whether or not one is admitted to a selective college; and whether or not one obtains a Ph.D. Width and speed help in some learning situations, not in others. The really important difference between the person with a Ph.D. in physics and the average high school dropout is not in how many kinds of simple problems they can solve or how rapidly they can solve them but rather in the level of complexity of the ideas they are equipped to comprehend. There is no evidence that, given enough time, anybody can learn anything. Even if that were true, still, as has repeatedly been emphasized in our previous discussions, time is the one commodity that for finite human beings is not available in unlimited amounts, so that inequalities would persist. Of recent years, a new attack has been made on this old problem of the relationship of intelligence to learning. Cognitive psychology, making use of concepts from linguistics (Chomsky, 1965), information theory (Newell and Simon, 1972), and memory (Anderson and Bower, 1973), is making rapid progress in the experimental analysis of symbolic thinking. But as yet most of our conclusions about the meaning of intelligence differences still rest on correlational evidence.

Although we do not need to do so, we base our evaluation of the prestige of various occupations on the symbolic complexity they call for and the amount of education they require. Thus it follows that occupational level also correlates to a moderate extent with IQ. The military testing program in World War II provided perhaps our most comprehensive data demonstrating this relationship, at least for men (Harrell and Harrell, 1945). They arranged the occupations reported by more than 18,000 Air Force officers in descending order, according to their mean scores on the Army General Classification Test. As has been found repeatedly, people in professional and managerial occupations averaged highest, those in unskilled occupations averaged lowest, and the others in between. The scale used in these comparisons has a mean of 100 and standard deviation of 20. The averages for most professions were 120 or higher; the averages for most clerical and skilled occupations were from 100 to 120; the average for various kinds of unskilled workers were below 100. Within each occupational group, particularly those at the bottom of the list, there was much individual variation. The total range of scores for accountants, for example, was from 94 to 157. For farmhands, scores ranged from 24 to 141.

A related finding, which has shown up consistently for a half century or more, is that children of men and women from different occupational levels also show average differences in IQ. In one of the recent studies, Kaufman and Doppelt (1976) analyzed data obtained for the standardization of the revised Wechsler Intelligence Scale for Children (WISC). At all ages, white children from the top occupational group obtained average IQs of 108 to 110, and averages fell off stepwise for the other groups to reach a level of 86 to 94 for children of laborers. As in previous large-scale surveys, black children averaged lower than white, but the same occupational progression held for them.

Generally speaking, the degree of success a person achieves in the occupation he or she enters is not related to IQ. Here the most detailed evidence comes from an evaluation of a large group of physicians (Price and others, 1963). At the time of the follow-up, some years after graduation from medical school, neither the test scores at entrance nor the grades in courses were related to the degree of success individuals had attained. Evidence that Hoyt (1965) has brought together for a number of other occupations points to the same conclusion. It requires a certain level of the ability intelligence tests measure to *enter* one of the more prestigious occupations, but once one gets in how successful one is depends on factors other than intelligence.

Because social class in America is linked to occupational level, it too shows the same relationship to intelligence. Here most studies show the upper class to be very small and to differ little if at all from the middle class. The difference that regularly shows up is between the averages for middle-class and lower-class children. This has led to considerable discussion of a possible "middle-class bias" in the tests themselves. The important question for practical purposes would seem to be "Are children from lower-class backgrounds 'disadvantaged' only on the tests they take, or does the disadvantage hold for the life situations related to test scores? And if it does, is this because low test scores prejudice teachers and others against poor children, or are the children really lacking in ability needed to do well in school?" Most of the research indicates that the relationship between test scores and school criteria is about the same for disadvantaged groups as for others, thus supporting the conclusion that the tests are probably fair (Cleary and others, 1975). The disadvantage, if such it is, affects the development of the trait the tests are designed to measure, not just the test performance. Within each social class group, children with the higher IQs do better and get farther in school than the others and are likely to achieve higher levels of occupational success than their parents did. Those with lower IQs may find places even lower in the occupational prestige scale than their parents occupied. Waller's (1971) study of a representative sample of Minnesota fathers and their sons provides some evidence for the relationship between intelligence and social mobility. If our system of moving persons up or down on the occupational scale on the basis of their aptitude for schoolwork operated perfectly, we would be faced with the "meritocracy" that some social critics have viewed with alarm, finding it incompatible with democracy (Herrnstein, 1973). Of course, it never has worked perfectly, and there is probably no likelihood that it ever will. But to deny its existence and assume that all lower-class children fail to succeed because they were stigmatized on the basis of inappropriate tests is to fly in the face of a great deal of evidence that many lower-class children do very well on both tests and schoolwork and proceed to successful careers.

Intelligence tests made up of very different sorts of items correlate positively with one another, but these correlations are far from perfect. A person whose verbal IQ is, say, 130 is unlikely to score below 100 on a nonverbal test, although the nonverbal IQ may be lower than the verbal. The person with an unusually large vocabulary (one of the best single tests of general intelligence) is likely to score fairly high on other tests involving numerical reasoning, spatial relations, or general information. There seems to be a common factor running through all cognitive tests. Early in this century, Spearman (1927) labeled this factor "g," and while controversy has raged for many decades over the concept, it is still viable (Cooley, 1976).

As time passed, psychologists became more interested in the part of the variance *not* common to different kinds of tests, the "non-g" portion. Could some sense be made of the fact that correlations between verbal and performance tests consistently run about .5? Why do some subtests consistently show higher correlations with one another than other subtests do? Out of one line of research, making use of factor analysis of tables or "matrices" of correlations between pairs of tests after a large battery of them had been taken by the same people, came the concept of "primary mental abilities." First proposed by Thurstone (1938), the concept accounted for the relationships by postulating several separate kinds of mental ability: verbal comprehension (V), numerical reasoning (N), spatial orientation (S), inductive reasoning (I), rote memory (M), perceptual speed (P), and verbal fluency (F). Since Thurstone's time, these same factors have turned up repeatedly, along with evidence that they can be identified in many age and cultural groups. For example, Flores and Evans (1972) showed that factors V, I, N, S, and M are found in the test performances of both Filipino and Canadian children of the same age. A number of published tests have been built on the concept of primary mental abilities.

But, along with confirmation of Thurstone's findings, time also produced several kinds of confusion in the picture of intelligence psychologists were tracing. For one thing, more and more additional factors kept turning up in different test batteries and different samples of the population. For practical purposes in selection and guidance, measuring six or seven abilities had looked feasible; measuring fifty-six of fifty-seven certainly did not. A second source of confusion has been that tests designed to measure independent kinds of ability still correlated positively with one another. Factor analyzing these correlations produced what were called "second-order factors." How were these to be interpreted? Correlations between second-order factors could then be factor analyzed, so producing "third-order" factors still more difficult to interpret. As stated in Chapter Two, factor analysis did not turn out to be a simplifying technique.

Mathematical as it appears, the technique of factor analysis involves subjective opinion at several points. It is the researcher, not the computer, who must decide, for example, what method of rotation is most appropriate for the data and must attach labels and descriptions to the factors to which the mathematical findings point. Again and again, such questions come up as "Is the 'V' I have identified in Tanzania like the 'V' psychologists in the United States have found? Is the factor pattern for boys the same as the pattern for girls?" Continual progress has been made in finding ways to deal with such questions, however, and, while not all doubt has been dispelled, we can now be reasonably confident that the primary mental abilities represent some real components of intelligence.

The status of the extra factors that keep showing up is less certain. The most comprehensive system that has been constructed to deal with them is Guilford's *structure of intellect* theory (1967). According to this system, abilities can be described in terms of three basic aspects or dimensions: the *operations* they require the testee to carry out, the *content* on which the testee must perform these operations, and the *product* the testee must come out with. Some of the most impressive support for the theory comes from the fact that

Guilford and his students, knowing what they were looking for, were able to design new tests that, included in test batteries to be factor analyzed, produced evidence for the factors predicted. The SI theory has not been widely applied as yet in the day-to-day practical situations where tests are used.

Another quite different theory about the components of tested intelligence involves a differentiation between *fluid* and *crystallized* intelligence (Horn, 1968; Cattell, 1971). According to this theory, the global intelligence tests we have evolved over the years consist of two kinds of items. Items of the first kind require a general intellectual power that has not been channeled in any particular direction. Items of the second kind require developed competence in dealing with certain sorts of material and situations. In the first category, we find things such as puzzles, analogies involving geometric figures, and various other tasks for which schooling is mostly irrelevant. In the second category, we find things such as vocabulary, numerical reasoning, and comprehension of verbal instructions. The strongest evidence for the separation of these two components comes from life span developmental research. Fluid ability develops rapidly during childhood and youth and begins to decline with the attainment of full adulthood. Crystallized ability also increases during childhood and youth but is maintained or even increased during a considerable part of the life span. Education affects most strongly the crystallized ability and tests of such ability most accurately predict school success.

Continuing to build on this basic idea, Cattell (1971) has elaborated another theoretical system, a "structure of intellect" based more on developmental findings than Guilford's is. According to Cattell, a mental performance such as solving a mathematical problem, for example, is determined by three aspects of the person's functioning: (1) *powers,* the general and special abilities the person possesses; (2) *agencies,* unified patterns of behavior arising from particular kinds of learning; and (3) *contributions beyond abilities,* such as motives and character traits. As a person grows, more and more of the powers are *invested* in agencies under the influence of whatever motivations are operating. This is a much more sophisticated formulation than the original distinction between fluid and crystallized intelligence. It fits in well with the overall approach to individuality presented in this book, the creation of actual, limited individuals out of almost unlimited possibilities.

Let us look more closely now at what has been learned about intelligence from developmental research in which the same persons have been tested repeatedly over the years. As was explained in the previous chapter, so-called infant tests of intelligence do not correlate with later intellectual development, but from about the age of eighteen months on there is some continuity in the differentiation of individuals with regard to mental ability. The growth curves themselves differ from individual to individual. For example, one child may appear somewhat backward when he or she enters kindergarten, may make rapid gains for a year or two, and then may level off for several years at an IQ of about 120. Another may show repeated ups and downs, scoring above average one year, below average the next. Still a third may score unusually high in nursery school, somewhat lower in kindergarten, and slightly lower each year thereafter, ending up with an IQ of 98 at fifteen. Although the IQ is not so constant over the years as early psychologists expected it to be, successive testings lead to correlations of from .6 to .8 from about the age of six on. Bright children generally remain bright, dull children remain dull. However, with correlation coefficients of this magnitude one can never be sure by looking at a particular child's first-grade score exactly how he or she will compare with his or her fellows at high school age. Although large IQ shifts that would change a child's classification from, say, "very superior" to "average" are rare, lesser shifts in both directions are common.

Longitudinal research has supported the conclusion we have discussed earlier—that rate and level of mental development depend on environmental influences as well as on genetic endowment. The hope early psychologists had of measuring pure native intelligence, uncontaminated by the effects of stimulation, experience, and training, has been completely abandoned. In the previous chapter, we have examined the complex way in which experience affects the development of individuals during the first two years. It continues to be important. Opportunities to look at shapes, colors, and pictures, and to play with objects and manipulate them, listening to adults, talking to them and asking them questions, reading books, watching television, playing with other children—these are only a few of the innumerable strands in the experience out of which intelligence grows.

Throughout life, the amount of formal schooling and informal exercise of mental capacities in dealing with the challenges of the world influences the level one reaches and the length of time one remains at top level. Until about the middle of our century, it was generally assumed that intelligence, like most physical skills, peaked in the teens or twenties and then began to decline, slowly at first, then more precipitously as old age approached. Comparisons of age groups supported this conclusion. World War I psychologists (Yerkes, 1921), analyzing the Army Alpha scores of more than 15,000 officers ranging in age from eighteen to sixty, reported declines in mean scores from 150 for those under twenty to 120 for those over fifty. A very carefully designed study of practically the entire population of a New England village (Jones and Conrad, 1933) documented the same trend, as did the standardization data on the first individual intelligence test for adults (Wechsler, 1941). Reports from England presented similar findings (Foulds and Raven, 1948; Vincent, 1952). More detailed analyses indicated that the amount of decline varied with the nature of the tests. Scores on speeded tests fell off with age more than did scores on tests allowing unlimited time, and scores on performance tests fell off more than did scores on verbal tests. The same trends seemed to hold for groups with different amounts of education, although more highly educated people averaged higher at all age levels than the less highly educated (Miles and Miles, 1932).

Few generalizations in differential psychology were as universally accepted as this one—that adult intelligence inevitably declined. Although as early as 1940 some data were collected suggesting that some of the apparent decline might reflect what we should now call *cohort* differences, the older groups having grown up under less stimulating circumstances than the younger groups, the generalization was not really questioned until a series of reports came in of longitudinal studies of adults. In the first of these to appear, Owens (1953) arranged for the retesting in 1949–1950 of 127 men who thirty years earlier had taken Army Alpha as college freshmen. He found that instead of scoring lower, as expected, the group averaged significantly higher on the second occasion. A suc-

cession of reports on longitudinal investigations in the United States
and Great Britain corroborated Owens' results (Bentz, 1953; Bayley
and Oden, 1955; Nisbet, 1957; Bradway and Thompson, 1962;
Campbell, 1965). In comparing types of tests, it was generally
found that those showing the greatest increase with age were the
ones that in the cross-sectional studies had shown the least decline.

Since the 1950s, gerontology has become an active research
field, and many aspects of age trends in competencies and motivation are being explored. Life span developmental psychology has
become a reality. New techniques are being devised to assess simultaneously several aspects of the problem of age changes in adults.
One of the most prominent figures in this movement is Schaie
(1974), who uses what he calls *cross-sequential* designs, in which
several age groups are tested several times over a period of several
years. This makes it possible to compare different age groups at the
same time and the same group at different times, to find out about
cohort differences, age changes, and the interactions between them.
In the most comprehensive of these investigations (Schaie, Labouvie,
and Buech, 1973), fifty persons from each of several age groups
were chosen from members of a medical insurance plan. They were
given a comprehensive battery of tests in 1956, 1963, and 1970.
General mental ability was maintained or increased up to age fifty,
although factor scores for inductive reasoning, numerical ability,
and flexibility showed slight declines. After age fifty, there was some
tendency for everything to decline, but again this was much more
marked for some tests than others. The results of longitudinal research are never so unambiguous as brief summaries make them
appear. Allowances must be made for volunteer bias and for the loss
of some subjects along the way. One discovery resulting from the attempt to make such allowances was the discovery of a "death-
drop" effect. Subjects scored much lower than they had previously
if they happened to be tested during the six months before they
died. Jarvik and Blum (1971) concluded from their twenty-year
study of discordant twin pairs that a precipitate drop in intelligence
is a predictor that death is near. All of these results fit in with the
theorizing about fluid and crystallized intelligence. Horn (1976,
p. 472), reviewing much of the research from this vantage point,
concludes "that adulthood development of human abilities is not all

on the positive side . . . but that such development is not all on the negative side either."

An account of developmental research on intelligence would not be complete without taking note of some landmark investigations in which persons at the high end and the low end of the distribution have been followed throughout a large portion of their lives to determine how well they "turn out." The most famous of these projects is the study of gifted children that Terman initiated in 1922 with the selection of about 1,000 preschool and elementary school children and 300 high school pupils, all of whom had IQs of 140 or higher. For fifty years, Terman and, after his death, other psychologists have kept in touch with these people and from time to time have made systematic studies of their progress through life (Terman, 1925; Burks, Jensen, and Terman, 1930; Terman and Oden, 1947, 1959; Oden, 1968). Another follow-up is being made in the 1970s. No summary of this rich store of information about highly intelligent persons can begin to do it justice, but some firm conclusions have emerged that should always be kept in mind when the meaning of tested intelligence is being discussed. First, at all periods of their lives, these people have averaged considerably higher than people in general with regard to many of the things civilized society values—productivity and achievement, mental health, and contributions to the general welfare. Not all members of the group have been equally successful, although very few can be called out-and-out failures. Those who turned out to be least successful had come from homes lower in occupational and educational status than those of the most successful group, and along the way they were rated somewhat lower on desirable motivational qualities, such as self-confidence, integration toward goals, absence of inferiority feelings, and even common sense. They had also more frequently chosen careers not in line with their measured interests. Thus it is clear that background and motivational factors do have some influence on how high intelligence is utilized in life situations. Terman called his first reports on the project *Genetic Studies of Genius* (1925). With the passage of time, the "genius" label has been dropped. With all their accomplishments in the arts, science, literature, business, and public affairs, probably very few of these persons will attain the rare level of eminence that posterity will call *genius.* But the evidence clearly shows that high tested intelligence in a school child does warrant a prediction of high achievement. A very large proportion of bright children become outstanding adults.

Paralleling this lifetime study of the gifted, there is another long-continued investigation showing what becomes of persons who score low on intelligence tests. In Nebraska, Baller (1936) sought out for follow-up men and women who had during their school years been assigned to an "opportunity room" because of IQs under 70, along with other evidence of mental retardation. Charles (1953) made another survey of the same group in their forties. Comparing this group with a normal group consisting of persons who had tested in the 100 to 120 IQ range during their school years, Baller and Charles found that the retarded averaged lower on all of the indices of success and achievement. Their employment record was less satisfactory; their percentage of law breaking and institutionalization was higher. But more significant than these differences, which had been anticipated, is the fact that the majority of persons in the group seemed not to have been greatly handicapped by their low IQs. At both follow-up periods, 83 percent had been at least partially self-supporting, and the jobs they held covered a considerable range of skill and salary levels. About 80 percent of the group had married, and most of their children were doing satisfactory work in school. Other follow-up studies of the retarded have corroborated the Baller and Charles conclusion that most persons who score in the 50 to 70 range on intelligence tests manage to live productive lives.

Combining the findings for high scorers and low scorers to see what they tell us about the nature of intelligence differences, we see that while high test scores may be viewed as a considerable asset leading to high achievement of the kinds civilized society prizes, low test scores are not as serious a liability as one might expect. This asymmetric conclusion is reasonable if we define test intelligence as *aptitude for education.* The high attainments rest on education, obtained in school or self-acquired. Simple survival and adaptation to the practical circumstances of life do not. Intelligence tests measure, not learning ability, but *schoolability.* Much of the confusion and controversy about IQ and its meaning would be cleared up if this fact were more generally understood.

Ever since the early years of the twentieth century, when intelligence tests first came into use, they have been the target of sharp, recurrent criticism. An interesting collection of such attacks and replies, beginning with the debate between Terman and Lippman in the early 1920s and ending with Kamin's scathing indictment in 1975, has been brought together by Block and Dworkin (1976) under the title *The IQ Controversy*. Some of this controversy centers on the content of the tests and the possibility that they are biased against persons who have not grown up in middle-class environments. This criticism has been taken seriously enough that intelligence testing has been discontinued in some school systems and that administrative policies with regard to the use of tests in employment situations have been changed. What persons making this criticism often lose sight of is the fact that tests were designed to measure *individual* differences, not group differences, and that such individual differences are as great in the less privileged as in the more privileged groups and seem to have the same significance. A good summary of the evidence on this issue of test fairness can be found in a special report prepared for the Board of Scientific Affairs of the American Psychological Association (Cleary and others, 1975).

A much more serious focus of controversy has to do with whether intelligence itself, the trait tests purport to measure, has a genetic basis. Are the inequalities in our society, which we know to be related to test scores, inherent in the nature of mankind and thus ineradicable? Much has been made of heritability coefficients, which seem to indicate that from 60 to 80 percent of the variance arises from genetic rather than from environmental sources. We have discussed such coefficients in Chapter Three, pointing to pitfalls often ignored in their interpretation. What should be reiterated here is that heritability is a global concept for a particular group under a particular set of environmental circumstances. Furthermore, it applies to differences *within*, not *between* groups. Even if heritability coefficients for both blacks and whites were as high as the highest estimate made heretofore, namely .80, they would still tell us nothing about the extent to which the difference between the racial groups arises from genetic sources. With present techniques, there is no way to settle this question, as a recent report prepared for the

Social Science Research Council (Loehlin, Lindzey, and Spuhler, 1975) makes clear. In psychology, as in life, there really are some unanswerable questions.

After three quarters of a century of work on general intelligence, we still have no way of measuring overall quality in individual human beings. What intelligence tests are most useful for is to serve as tools we can use in our effort to provide all of our people with all of the education they wish to obtain. Serious errors of interpretation have been made in the past, but time has made it possible to eliminate them. Intelligence as measured is not as important an aspect of individuality as some psychologists once assumed it to be, but it is a more important aspect than the strident critics in the 1970s are willing to admit.

❧ 6 ❧

From Abilities
to Competencies

The general concept of *ability* was one of the most enduring by-products of the intelligence-testing movement. Individuals are assumed to differ from one another in the amount of various hypothetical abilities each possesses. It is obvious that different sorts of work require different sorts of skill. Quite early in the movement, research was initiated to define and measure talents more specialized than general intelligence. Psychologists assumed that persons who attained a high level of skill of some special sort, such as baseball playing, composing, or machine repairing, must initially have had a special talent or aptitude for such activity. They set themselves the task of measuring some of these aptitudes. The first step was to identify an ability that appeared to be necessary in some occupation or group of occupations. Mechanical aptitude was investigated early, because so many kinds of work seem to require it. Clerical aptitude was singled out for attention not much later. It was assumed that the aptitude being investigated was possessed to some degree by everyone, so that differences between individuals consisted of the amount of it each person manifested. At the outset, it was also assumed that aptitudes were innate rather than learned, that they were based primarily on genetic endowment. The psychologist's task was to put together some items or procedures that would indicate how much of the aptitude the testee possessed. These procedures might be samples of the sorts of activities the work required, verbal questions often accompanied by pictures of processes and tools, or simply items that for some unknown reason had turned out to correlate with success on the job in exploratory research. Once this preliminary form had been administered to a suitable group, the development of the finished test could proceed in the same way as was customary for intelligence tests. Reliability was determined by correlating test scores with another version of the same test, Trial 1 with Trial 2, Form A with Form B, odd items with even items. Validity was determined by correlating test scores with criterion measurements obtained after the persons tested had entered the occupation or training program. Norms could be set up based on the distribution of scores obtained in a representative group.

Ideally, the researchers knew, the test should be given before the individuals who were tested had any experience in the occupation, and the criterion measurements should be obtained after they had had sufficient time to show how successful they were. Ideally, all persons who took the test being validated should be hired, low scorers as well as high scorers, so that the correlation between test and criterion would represent the full ability range. Ideally, criteria should be objective measures of how well individuals were doing on the job, rather than ratings, which are at least partly determined by the raters' biases. It is obvious that these ideal conditions for the development of aptitude tests could seldom be found, so that test makers had to resort to various compromises and estimates. Industries financing testing programs were usually not willing to wait six months and train a considerable number of obviously unqualified workers in order to validate a new test that might or might not be useful later in selection. Criterion measurements that looked objective, such as the amount of soap each salesperson sold or the number of lock assemblies each factory worker produced, turned out to be affected by the nature of the salesperson's territory or the conditions in the part of the factory where the worker was situated.

During the heyday of aptitude testing, in the 1930s, it was assumed that all of the difficulties would be surmounted and that all of the human aptitudes and talents required for diverse kinds of work would eventually be measured. Business executives and industrialists would be able to select the best persons for each job. Boys and girls, men and women, would be able to choose the jobs and educational programs in which they were most likely to succeed. Employee selection and vocational guidance would become truly scientific. Needless to say, the goal was not reached, and, as years have passed, hopes that it would be reached faded. The best summary of what was and was not accomplished by the aptitude-testing movement can be found in a book by Ghiselli (1966). Ghiselli collected and organized validity coefficients that had been published during the half century in which aptitude tests had been in use. As one examines page after page of tables and graphs in Ghiselli's book, the most favorable conclusion one can draw is that an astute personnel manager can probably improve hiring practices to some extent but not much by using tests. For one thing, most of the correlations are low, with only a small fraction as high as .40; some are actually negative. Trainability criteria are more predictable than proficiency criteria, and there is little relationship between the two. Knowing which workers would be most easily trained for the work does not tell you which would reach the highest proficiency levels with experience. Tests of intelligence and special intellectual abilities tend to correlate most highly with trainability, as one might expect, knowing the relationship of such tests to school success. Validity coefficients vary enormously from one situation to another. For example, the tests of perceptual speed and accuracy commonly used to select clerical workers have produced correlations with clerical criteria ranging all the way from $-.30$ to $+.49$. The average is about .19. With such results, one can hardly talk about clerical aptitude as though it were real and measurable.

Quite early in the development of aptitude tests, it became necessary to give up the assumption that the abilities being tapped were mainly innate. As has been explained in connection with intelligence, how well a person performs depends both on genes and on experience, and there is no way of separating the two. Two men applying for a special training program in airplane mechanics may both state that they have had no experience with airplanes. But Walt, whose father is a do-it-yourself enthusiast, may have used tools and judged sizes and shapes from his earliest childhood, whereas John, an athlete, son of a businessman, may never have paid much attention to how anything is put together. If Walt scores higher than John on a mechanical aptitude test, it tells us nothing about innate fitness for this kind of work, and, furthermore, gives us no assurance that John will not catch up with Walt or even outdistance him if John seriously undertakes to learn the trade.

Still another difficulty with aptitude testing is that many kinds of special ability that are highly important in the world of work have so far not turned out to be measurable at all. We talk about "born salesmen" or "born teachers," but attempts to analyze what abilities such persons possess to a high degree have repeatedly been unsuccessful. Tests of the simpler aspects of musical talent, such as discrimination of pitch and rhythm, have not turned out to predict how well students do in music school. Tests of artistic talent have been of little or no use in selecting art students. Apparently we have not been able to measure what matters most. It is easy to conclude that in these and many other areas motivation is all-important, so that no amount of basic talent can compensate for a lack of willingness to make an all-out persistent effort. But this conclusion only redirects the question, challenging psychologists to account for these large individual differences in motivation.

Research on aptitude testing has not been all wasted effort. It has left us with a considerable number of well-designed tests available for trial in situations where it is necessary to select the most promising applicants for jobs or training programs. What we know now is that a trial in the particular situation is necessary. As a result of the civil rights movement of the 1960s and 1970s, there are now government policies and regulations requiring such evidence of validity in the particular situation. It is now illegal as well as unethical to select workers on the basis of tests without such evidence.

Aptitude testing, disappointing in the contribution it has made to worker selection, has been even more disappointing in its contribution to vocational guidance. The technique here has been to give a number of tests to the individual and then to construct a profile or psychograph to show at a glance his or her pattern of strengths and weaknessses. Those who initiated this method expected that eventually standard profiles for all the major types of occupation would be available and that, by comparing a person's profile with these profiles, one would be able to identify a kind of work for which that person was well suited. During the optimistic 1930s, investigators produced what they looked on as prototypic evidence that different occupations were characterized by their own occupational ability profiles (Dvorak, 1935). What proved discouraging, however, was that success in the occupation did not seem related to whether or not one possessed the proper profile and that a wide variety of profiles existed within any one occupation. As in the case of intelligence tests, long-range success in an occupation is not predicted by aptitude test scores. Thorndike and Hagen (1959) followed up, in 1955 and 1956, on approximately 17,000 men who had taken the Air Force battery of tests in 1943. Although they turned up some evidence that the average profile of scores differed for different occupational groups, none of the criteria they used for measuring how successful individuals had been in occupations they had entered was related to any of the tests. Thus scientific vocational guidance has continued to elude counselors. There is very little they can tell their clients *for sure* about the significance of scores on tests they have taken.

There is one research program in this confusion-ridden area of aptitude testing that has resulted in a usable technology for helping people decide what kind of work they want to do. This program has been going on for several decades under the auspices of the United States Employment Service and its predecessor agencies, and has produced the General Aptitude Test Battery (GATB) for use in employment counseling. The first step was to collect, in one battery of eleven paper-and-pencil tests and four apparatus tests, measures of all the miscellaneous aptitudes that occupational research had uncovered. Factor analysis was used both in this initial step and in the next step, identifying and naming the aptitudes. Scores obtained by clients of the service in several geographic areas were used as raw data for these analyses. The final result was a

two-and-a-half-hour battery of tests for nine aptitudes: general intelligence (G), verbal aptitude (V), numerical aptitude (N), spatial aptitude (S), form perception (P), clerical perception (Q),
motor coordination (K), finger dexterity (F), and manual dexterity
(M). Each test was scored in such a way as to give an approximately normal distribution for the general population. The mean
was set at 100 and the standard deviation at 20. For each individual, a profile of nine statistically comparable scores could be
constructed.

So far, there was nothing particularly innovative in the procedure. It was the arrangement for bringing these profiles into
alignment with a large number of occupations that was new. This
step involved, first of all, grouping the occupations themselves into
a limited number of job families on the basis of characteristic occupational patterns of abilities. For each job family, the three aptitudes shown in previous research to be most closely related to success
were singled out. Norms for the job family on these aptitudes were
set at a level that would disqualify the bottom third of the workers
holding these jobs. This means that the person who has taken the
GATB can see at a glance whether he or she falls within the range
of successful workers on each of the job family triads. It is an ingenious system for structuring occupational possibilities, ruling out
some, suggesting others for consideration, transforming the quantitative data into information on which decisions can be based.

For example, a young man does not need to know just
where his score on Q, clerical perception, places him within a group
of clerical workers, and, as we have seen, the validity of such tests is
not high enough to tell him this if he did wish to know. What
he does need to find out is whether a career in a clerical occupation
is a reasonable possibility for him. Does he have an adequate
amount of the abilities that such clerical work requires? Tests can
help answer this question even when their validity is not high. The
advantage of the GATB over other tests of similar aptitudes is that
it samples a wider range of abilities and provides procedures that
make test information maximally useful to the individual.

Another large-scale research program, still within the ability-
testing framework, is worth discussing for the light it sheds on the
complexity of human skills. Over a period of years, Fleishman

(1967) made interlocking studies of more than 200 different tasks (mainly tasks related to aviation skills) and tested thousands of persons. Like his predecessors, he correlated scores and carried out factor analyses to ascertain what the basic variables underlying proficiency on all these tasks were. As had many investigators before him, he found that *psychomotor* abilities tend to be highly specific, in contrast to those we call *mental* abilities, which all correlate positively with one another. In all, he identified eleven different psychomotor factors and nine different physical proficiency factors. The basis for differentiating between these two types of factor is not important for our purposes here. What is important is that if one measured all of these factors, one could still not make even a reasonably accurate prediction about the relative success of individuals in carrying out practical tasks. Fleishman and Parker (1962), for example, found that only two of the factor scores were related to performance at any stage of the process of learning to keep an airplane on target in a simulation situation. More than three quarters of the differences between individuals on the criterion task was unaccounted for, even at the stage of learning where some significant correlations with test scores did occur. And the fact that the motor skills utilized at any one stage of training were irrelevant at earlier and later stages further complicates the picture.

Attempting to clarify the nature of the behavior producing the variability, Fleishman and his associates carried out laboratory experiments in which they systematically changed various aspects of the situation—allowing more or less time, for example, or rotating a stimulus through several different angles. As in the case of learning stages, each variation makes for different correlations and a different factor pattern. The goal of constructing a "behavior taxonomy for describing human tasks" became more and more elusive as evidence accumulated. In Fleishman's own words (1967, p. 8), "Finally, let me say that I am not at all sure about the ultimate utility of this kind of taxonomy. It may well be that the kind of taxonomy most useful to one set of applied problems (for example, training) may be different from the one useful for another problem (for example, system design)."

Perhaps what will turn out to be the most valuable outcome of the search for basic aptitudes is the concept of *task,* which is increasingly used in occupational psychology. What is the worker actually doing? What can he or she do? Systematic research on these questions has been carried on for some time by Sidney Fine and his associates at the U.S. Employment Service and the Upjohn Institute for Employment Research. These research efforts have been directed more toward useful products than toward scholarly publications. The most far-reaching result is a system designed by Fine called *functional job analysis,* which constitutes the framework for the third edition of the *Dictionary of Occupational Titles* and the many kinds of occupational information related to it. At the basis of the system is a classification of what workers do, according to whether they deal with data, people, or things. Within each of the three divisions, subfunctions are arranged in a hierarchy of complexity or demandingness. In the data category, the successive levels are *comparing, analyzing,* and *synthesizing.* Using social work as an example of the way the system works, Fine and Wiley (1971) describe tasks at the comparing level as follows: "Likens/contrasts/checks off information in specified categories on application form against list of specific eligibility criteria to signify whether client is within prescribed limits" (p. 43). The analyzing level is illustrated by "Evaluates/assesses urgency of client's presented problem judging circumstances reported and client's behavior/emotional state in relation to general agency guidelines, in order to decide whether case requires emergency or routine handling" (p. 47). Synthesizing is illustrated as follows: "Conceives, intuits, and expresses an original hypothesis concerning the nature of social-psychological problems of an ethnic or socioeconomic group in our society to explain factors and phenomena previously unrecognized or unaccounted for" (p. 51).

Other systems have been proposed for classifying occupations and specific jobs according to the skills workers need to carry out their required tasks, but none has been as influential as Fine's. Cunningham (1971) reviewed a large number of such efforts and proposed a new label for them, *ergometrics,* derived from the Greek word for energy *"ergon,"* and defined as the measurement of human energy application. Most of these researchers are still attempting to fit their findings into the framework of ability measurement, the inadequacies of which have become increasingly apparent. The goal of the researchers is still a general system of ability measurement in which everybody is evaluated on the same dimensions and in which individuality is represented by a profile of scores.

The replacement of this formulation by an entirely different one, in which *repertoire of competencies* replaces *profile of abilities* as the central concept, is what is being advocated here. A competency is a particular skill, something an individual knows how to do. For a psychologist thinking in these terms, the basic questions are "*Which* competencies are in each individual's repertoire?" and "*How,* out of the innumerable competencies in the total human repertoire, does an individual acquire his or her own unique assortment?" Although at present writing no psychological research on these questions is being reported, scattered voices are being raised, many of them in areas on the fringes of psychology, that support such an approach. The movement of which applied psychologists are most likely to be aware is the increasing use of assessment centers for the evaluation of applicants, particularly applicants seeking high-level positions (Bray and Moses, 1972). The most prominent feature of this movement is the focus on behavior, using simulation techniques, rather than tests, to measure aptitudes.

At the other end of the intellectual and social scale from the persons with whom assessment centers deal are persons classified as mentally retarded. Interesting efforts are being made also to analyze the competencies they need if they are to function adequately in society. During the 1970s, several scales have been published designed to inventory specific behaviors of mentally retarded individuals and to indicate specific kinds of training they need. The most recent of these are the *Social and Prevocational Information Battery* instruments, available in forms for mildly retarded adolescents and adults (Halpern and others, 1975) and for moderately retarded adults (Irvin, Halpern, and Reynolds, 1977). The tests are given individually and include simple yes/no questions on job-search skills, job-related behaviors, banking, budgeting, purchasing, home management, physical health care, hygiene and grooming, and functional signs (such as "Flammable," "Fire Escape," and "Help Wanted"). Some sample questions can give an idea of what the test is like: "If you are going walking where there are poisonous snakes, you should wear tennis shoes" (yes/no); "If you are talking on the telephone about a job, it is all right to chew gum or food since you cannot be seen" (yes/no). Still further removed from academic psychology is the burgeoning business of training individuals to locate rewarding jobs for themselves (Bolles, 1975, 1976). In the agencies that are springing up for this purpose, emphasis is placed on informal techniques for persons to use in inventorying their own competencies.

Educators also are increasingly thinking in terms of competencies rather than abilities. The main thrust here is the requirement that certain specified competencies be demonstrated before a student receives a high school diploma. The public rather than the educational theorists seem to be behind such efforts. Gallup (1975, p. 232) cited results of the seventh annual Gallup Poll of public attitudes toward education, showing that more than 75 percent of the respondents agreed that students should not graduate without knowing how to "read well enough to follow an instruction manual"; "write a letter of application using correct grammar and spelling"; "figure out such a problem as the total square feet in a room"; and how to do several other obviously useful things. In several states, attempts are being made to change the pattern of the school system in this direction. In Oregon, nine areas in which competence must be demonstrated have been specified in the administrative rules that the state board of education uses in evaluating local school districts for accreditation. Local districts are required to set specific standards for each of these kinds of competency and to indicate the means for determining whether individuals have met them. Once these requirements are met, proof of competency will be required for graduation from high school. It is expected that the system will be in full operation not later than 1981 (Fairbanks and Hathaway, 1975; Hathaway, 1976).

It is anticipated that a change of this sort will have considerable effect on the whole system of public education. It is an important movement, but it does not yet go far enough. What is needed is (1) to make it possible for each student to leave school with an *individualized* repertoire of competencies in addition to the minimum set and (2) to develop record-keeping systems that would keep track of the competencies each individual possesses. Remodeling school systems along these lines will be difficult, but should not be impossible. Psychologists have much to contribute to this effort to create a school environment in which each student can acquire a unique repertoire of competencies.

One psychologist (McClelland, 1973) has become an articulate spokesmen for the proposal that we should model both the theory and the technology of ability testing to emphasize competence. His strongest criticism is directed at intelligence tests, on grounds discussed in some detail in the previous chapter, in that they measure aptitude for schoolwork rather than general adaptibility and that neither test scores nor school grades tell us much about how successful individuals will be in life situations. The other sorts of ability tests we have been considering in this chapter are just as vulnerable to criticism. McClelland proposes that we shift to the direct measurement of competence. However, the guidelines he sets up for such testing still involve the comparison of individuals with one another and the assignment of scores. He still assumes that all individuals can be evaluated along a single scale. His question is still "How much?" not "Which?" and he is still talking about general competence rather than individualized repertoires of competencies.

Psychologists concerned with personality rather than abilities are also talking increasingly about general competence (Sundberg, Snowden, and Reynolds, 1978). As early as 1959, White suggested that attaining competence in dealing with the environment is a basic motive force in human beings. At a time when motivational theorists, whether psychoanalytic or behavioristic in orientation, were assuming that the objective of all motivated behavior was to *reduce* drives like hunger, thirst, or sex, this was a somewhat radical idea. Since then, much evidence has accumulated supporting the idea that not only human beings but also animals are motivated to increase as well as to reduce the level of stimulation, to satisfy curiosity, to explore, and to seek new experience. It is now taken for granted that what White calls "effectance motivation" exists.

Some personality theorists are interested in measuring the general personal competence they consider important. Goldfried and D'Zurilla (1969) worked out a three-step procedure for constructing a measuring instrument to be used in a particular situation or with a particular population. Their own work was done with college freshmen. The first step in their procedure is to analyze the environment or situation to discover the problems that a person who functions in it must deal with. The second step is to obtain a collection of solutions or responses to these problems. The third step is to have these alternative responses evaluated by judges and assigned numerical ratings for effectiveness. In their research, they obtained the basic data for the first two steps from the students themselves. The final product, however, was still an instrument on which individuals could be scored and compared with one another (Goldfried and Kent, 1972). As in the case of McClelland's proposals, the question is still "How much?" not "Which?"

It is especially in the clinical application of techniques of behavior modification that assessment procedures are being devised without the limitations that adherence to the established mental testing principles imposes. The informal techniques used in connection with behavior therapy point the way toward an individualized, nonnormative means of characterizing persons. One can record, for example, how long a hyperactive child keeps his glance directed at a book he is reading. As training proceeds, one can see whether such attentive behavior is increasing as a result of the reinforcement contingencies being utilized. There is no need to validate looking at the book as a measure of attentiveness or to compare one child's score with norms for a group. This approach seems applicable to the general problem of assessing competencies in life situations.

As cruder concepts about behavior modification have given way to comprehensive theories of social learning, in which cognitive and affective as well as behavioral changes are recognized, this replacement of trait formulations by direct sampling of competencies has received increasing consideration by theorists, if not by researchers. Mischel (1973) discussed five varieties of "person variables" that can be sampled in this way: (1) construction competencies (what the person knows and can do); (2) encoding strategies and personal constructs; (3) behavior-outcome and stimulus-outcome expectancies in particular situations; (4) subjective stimulus values, motivating and arousing stimuli, incentives and aversions; (5) self-regulatory systems and plans, rules, and self-reactions in performance and organization of complex behavior sequences. The first of these categories, the person's repertoire of competencies, is what we have been concerned with in this chapter;

most of the others will be taken up in later chapters. One of the most valuable outcomes of the social learning movement may be that we cease to think of an individual personality as the sum of a number of trait measurements or a profile of scores and begin to assess directly what the individual can *do*. Although systematic research is scarce, we find it natural to characterize individuals in terms of their competency repertoires. The hypothetical Sue Sanders, for example, is a person whose competencies include professional skill as a hairdresser, business skills required for the management of her shop, expertise in the growing of rhododendrons, skiing, cooking for large groups, practical nursing, and the care and feeding of Abyssinian cats. Each year she adds to her repertoire skills such as cake decorating, Chinese cooking, automobile repairing. It is this unique combination of things she knows about and can do that more than anything else defines her as an individual.

How do these unique repertoires of competencies develop? There has been little or no research directed specifically to this question, although the development of particular kinds of competence, such as language, social relationships, and motor skill, is now receiving some attention (see Connolly and Bruner, 1974). Common observation suggests that occupational skills are acquired through some sort of training, formal or informal, and that, because the sequence of jobs a person holds is subject to a great many chance influences, no two people participate in exactly the same training experiences. Hobbies and leisure activities also generate special competencies, such as sailing, bowling, horseback riding, macramé, clarinet playing, acting, and raising vegetables. A complete list of the things Americans find to do in their spare time would consist of hundreds, if not thousands, of items. As in the case of jobs, probably no two persons experience exactly the same sequence of opportunities to engage in particular recreational activities. Thus each combination is unique.

During the childhood years, one of the most important functions of *play* may be to produce these individual repertoires, although in the hundreds of research studies and the extensive theorizing the problem of play has stimulated, this individualizing function is seldom mentioned. Weisler and McCall (1976, p. 494), reviewing such studies, define play as consisting of "behaviors and behavior sequences that are organism dominated rather than stimulus dominated, behaviors that appear to be intrinsically motivated and apparently performed for 'their own sake' and that are conducted with relative relaxation and positive affect."

Ellis (1973) has discussed some thirteen theories about why play occurs. The three modern theories that appear to be somewhat related consider play to be a kind of *stimulus seeking*, an effort to produce an optimal level of *arousal*, generated by the *competence* or *effectance* motivation postulated by White. Play is rooted in the biology of the species, dependent on both heredity and environment. Because flexibility is advantageous to our species, the germ plasm has come to contain a predisposition to seek novel stimulation and emit new responses, to explore, in investigate, and to manipulate. The result is variability. Each person varies in the way he or she reacts to a situation at different times; different persons vary in the way they react to the same situation. It is clear that the development of individual repertoires of competencies would facilitate such variability and thus would be highly adaptive for the species as a whole. At present, such theorizing is necessarily speculative, but, in our attempt to understand how unique individuality is generated through the selection and organization of human possibilities, the study of play seems a likely place to look.

The attempts to characterize individuals in terms of their competencies showing up in occupational, educational, developmental, and personality psychology are of great potential importance. For one thing, they cut across boundaries. Instead of assessing intelligence and achievement in school children, skills in job applicants, and symptoms in psychiatric patients, we can examine what each person in any of these categories can and cannot do. One can capitalize on the developed competencies and set up situations in which competencies not now present can be acquired, whether these are basic educational competencies, occupational competencies, or interpersonal or intrapersonal competencies. The competency approach thus provides individuals and their helpers with clear guidelines as to what to do next.

Another potential benefit is the generation of the concept of *complementarity* to supplement the concept of competitiveness so prevalent in modern society. Mental testing as it has been practiced for more than half a century is both an expression and a stimulator of this competitiveness. One's worth is measured by how superior or inferior to other people one is. One's psychological health is judged by the location of one's score in a distribution representative of the population. Competencies represent a completely different way of structuring our perceptions of others. The more competencies other people have the better for each of us, and it is essential for the functioning of complex society that individuals develop different repertoires of competencies. The absolute limits of each person's living time make all-around competence for one individual impossible. We need one another.

7

Individuality as Structure: Basic Concepts

Thinking of individuality as a limited, although complex actualization of some of the multitudinous human possibilities requires us to consider structure, configuration, pattern. We can use the general term *possibility-processing structure* to cover all these concepts having to do with the ways in which the person controls the selection of perceptions, activities, and learning situations. Any individual can carry out, simultaneously or successively, only a small fraction of the acts for which his sense organs, nervous system, and muscles equip him. Only a small fraction of the energies constantly bombarding the individual can be responded to. If from moment to moment a person had to be aware of all of these stimulating energies, all of these possible responses, life would be unbearably complicated and confusing. The reason that one can proceed in most situations to act sensibly without having to make hundreds of conscious choices is that one develops organized ways of automatically processing most of the kinds of information encountered. In computer terms, one does what one is "programmed" to do. Much of the programming is the same for all or most of the human race; much is imposed by the structure of particular cultures and subcultures. But in addition there are programs unique to individuals, and these are fundamental to psychological individuality.

We can get some sense of the way in which possibility-processing structures come into existence if we watch a three-year-old in an unfamiliar room containing many objects, materials, and toys. The child wanders around at first, picking up one thing or another, letting it drop, idly piling blocks together, making a few marks on a paper with a crayon. (Even these random, haphazard actions show some structure based on previous experience with similar objects and materials.) Before long, the behavior changes. The child settles down in a corner to build a block tower, sits in front of the piano and pounds the keys, or opens cupboard doors looking for food. The next time the child is brought to the same room, patterned activity is likely to appear immediately. The varied possibilities have taken on a structure for the person.

Psychologists have been slow to recognize that the patterning of activity is the most individual thing about a person. The study of individual differences has been almost exclusively concerned with the amounts of various components that are present, components such as intelligence, extraversion, altruism, aggression, or paranoid thinking. Most of the researchers who have investigated patterned behavior have not been interested in individual differences. Organic chemists could never have distinguished between most of the complex substances that make up the biological world had they continued to do nothing except measure the amounts of carbon, nitrogen, oxygen, and rarer elements in organic substances. Starch and all of the many varieties of sugar contain the same proportions of carbon, hydrogen, and oxygen—two atoms of hydrogen and one of oxygen for each atom of carbon. It was the discovery of the structure of the organic molecule, of the way atoms are linked to the hexagonal benzene ring, that constituted the real breakthrough. Psychologists studying individuality are just beginning to think in analogous terms and to produce the technical tools for research on structure.

It is obvious that we constantly use a structural approach in our day-to-day dealings with people. The baby learns very early to distinguish the mother's face from all of the other faces it sees. As we grow, we all learn to distinguish an astonishing number of individuals with astonishing rapidity without measuring anything, simply by perceiving distinctive physical conformations. We recognize instantly unique individual patterns of speech, movement, facial expression. And the distinctions we make between persons we like and dislike, persons we trust and do not trust, persons we choose and reject as friends, mates, or fellow workers rest mainly on assessments of the psychological shapes of individuals.

Individuality in anatomical and biochemical structures is a fact resting on solid research evidence. Williams (1956) presented a considerable body of information about these aspects of individuality. He showed that the organs of individuals, organs such as the heart or the stomach, differ markedly in size, shape, and placement in the body. More importantly, he demonstrated that there are large differences in the composition of body fluids, such as blood, digestive juices, and the like; in enzyme levels in tissues and body fluids; in pharmacological response to specific drugs; and in quantitative needs for particular nutrients, such as minerals and vitamins. Each person has a unique metabolic pattern, as shown by which parts of the nutrients ingested are utilized and which parts excreted in the urine. The significance of this diversity has never been as apparent in medical practice and in human affairs in general as Williams hoped that it would be. He expected that medicine, psychiatry, psychology, education, and even philosophy would be changed when people realized how different individuals are. The practice of transplant operations has made knowledge about the uniqueness of individual organs and tissues more widespread. We know now that the best way to make sure that a kidney transplant will not be rejected is to obtain the organ from the identical twin of the person who is to receive it. We know that after heart transplants massive doses of drugs that inhibit rejection of foreign tissues must be administered and that they must be individually monitored because of the uniqueness of each person's response to the drugs. We know these things in the particular context of transplant operations, but the knowledge has not permeated our thinking in other areas.

In recent years, psychologists and other social scientists have been devoting more attention to the study of organization and pattern, characterizing the whole approach under the label *structuralism*. It is not really a very satisfactory name for what is being studied. The word *structure* has too many architectural connotations and suggests something physical and static. We tend to contrast structure with process or with function. The organized entities that constitute individuality *are* processes and activities that function to carry out the individual's purposes. Rather than concrete, tangible entities, the psychological "structures" are often inaccessible to conscious awareness. The person cannot tell us what these controlling patterns are; we must infer them from actions.

But whether or not the name for the way of thinking is well chosen, some of the recent discussions of structures and structuralism do serve to clarify what it is that we are trying to understand. One of the most illuminating is that of psychology's most eminent structuralist, Piaget (1970), whose long and productive research career has contributed so much to our understanding of the development of intelligence and logical thinking. According to Piaget (1970, p. 5), "The notion of structure is comprised of three key ideas: the idea of wholeness, the idea of transformation, and the idea of self-regulation." A structure is a system of self-regulating transformations, never observed directly, but inferred from its effects. The idea of *wholeness* has to do with the interdependence of elements; a structure is more than an aggregate in which independent elements are arbitrarily associated but do not affect one another. Thus a family of five is a structure; a group of five persons sitting in a doctor's waiting room is not. The idea of *transformation* has to do with the active, constructive aspect of structures that allows them to persist even as they constantly change. As a person's experience is channeled through them, they produce certain patterns of activity, not others. The primitive structures revealed in the young child's interaction with the objects and people around him are transformed through this interaction but still maintain their identity, as Piaget's research has shown. The idea of *self-regulation* refers to the fact that compensatory activity occurs in response to

influences from outside the structure, activity that serves to maintain its integrity. This is a concept carried over from research on
biological systems through which the processes discussed in Chapter
Three were discovered. Feedback and the organism's response to it
are what is meant by self-regulation. Piaget emphasizes the fact that
structures are active, not passive entities. The word *construct* might
be a better designation than the static word *structure*. *"There is no
structure apart from construction"* (Piaget, 1970, p. 140; italics in
original). Perception "calls for a subject who is more than just the
theater on whose stage various plays independent of him and regulated in advance by physical laws of automatic equilibration are
performed; the subject performs in, sometimes even composes, these
plays" (p. 59).

It may seem strange, in the light of these illuminating
thoughts about psychological structure, that Piaget's research receives so little attention in this book on psychological individuality.
The reason is that Piaget and his coworkers have never been interested in individual differences. What they have attempted to lay
bare are the structures characteristic of all human beings at successive stages of development. There are undoubtedly idiosyncratic
aspects of the structures individual children reveal in their answers
to the investigators' questions, but so far no one has undertaken to
describe them, catalogue them, and explore their correlates.

Another book dealing with the impact of structural ideas on
psychology is that of Mucchielli (1970). His definition of structure
is similar to Piaget's, emphasizing organization and dynamic stability.
But his special contribution to the psychology of individuality is the
emphasis he places on *meaning structures*. The book begins with a
pregnant sentence: "The most rudimentary attempt to understand
someone, the simplest approach, the most immediate—and already
this is the whole of psychology—consists in grasping, always in an
appropriate fashion, what things, persons, events *mean to him*"
(Mucchielli, 1970, p. 1). One effect that an emphasis on meaning
structures has is to eliminate the gaps between cognition and feeling, experience and activity, and Mucchielli proceeds to consider
"affective-postural-behavioral" structures in which cognitive interpretation, emotional attitude, and the disposition to act in a particular way are intertwined. He cites numerous examples from his

clinical practice showing how therapy is facilitated by the search for such structures.

A more recent book consisting of chapters by various persons, *Structure and Transformation,* edited by Riegel and Rosenwald (1975), brings out still other facets of the structural approach. The linguistic theory initiated by Chomsky (1957) is discussed in considerable detail, as are cognitive structures in general. The most stimulating addition to what has previously been said about structuralism, however, is in the chapter by Wozniak (1975), which explores the relationship between dialectics, the dominant theoretical system in the Soviet Union and other Marxist countries, and cognitive developmental theory, as best exemplified in Piaget's work. Wozniak (1975, p. 29) first defines the structuralist method as the "analysis of stability in the midst of change . . . a structural analysis represents an attempt to discover latent organization within the objects and phenomena of study to explain both the momentary stability and the constant change that takes place in those objects and phenomena." What dialectics is concerned with more than the other structural theories is the change aspect of this concept. "Motion is absolute; rest is relative" (Wozniak, 1975, p. 32). How does structural change come about? How are structures transformed? The Marxist position is that the process is always and essentially a struggle of opposites—thesis, antithesis, and synthesis. The significance of this point of view for the psychologist seeking to understand individuality is that it sensitizes one to the contradictions and conflicts within a person's present systems of organization. This is the yeast that transforms them. A lively dialectical movement has come into existence in American psychology, focused on problems of development. Riegel (1975) is one of its most articulate spokesmen.

Similar in many ways to the ideas of the structuralists are those of the general-systems theorists, who, during the last few decades, have been attempting to build a foundation for both biological and social theories (Bertalanffy, 1968). The central concept is that of the *open system,* characterized by continuous interchange with the environment, drawing in material and energy, discarding material and energy, but maintaining its identity throughout the process. The open-system concept became especially valuable in the construction of psychological theories when it was extended to cover information as well as material and energy. Wilden (1975) points out that, whereas the classical physical universe is a universe primarily of matter and energy, the human universe is primarily one of information. Psychological structures such as those Piaget and Mucchielli have delineated can be seen as systems for processing information. During the years since World War II, information-processing technology has grown at a faster rate than any other technology, and computers have not only dealt with quantities of information far greater than human beings have been able to deal with before but have also helped to make organized mental processes intelligible. A very influential book that introduced systems concepts into cognitive psychology was that of Miller, Galanter, and Pribram (1960). The authors set up a model that fit the process of human thinking, one that objective psychologists could accept without fear of getting bogged down in a slough of introspection. Since that time, computer simulations of mental processes have become common. They constitute an important source of hypotheses about psychological structures and processes (Simon, 1976).

General concepts such as structure, open systems, and computer programs enable us to bring together evidence from disparate lines of research in our effort to understand how limited individuals deal with almost unlimited possibilities. As stated before, one does what one is *programmed* to do; it is these individual programs that we must examine. In the next few chapters, we shall be looking at several kinds of psychological entities that can be viewed as programs. They appear under a variety of labels. The word *schema,* used by Bartlett (1932) to designate an organized structure controlling what is remembered, became the core concept in the work of Piaget (1952) on the development of intelligence. Recently, Neisser (1976, p. 54) has made it central to a theory of perception, defining it simply as "that portion of the entire perceptual cycle which is internal to the perceiver, modifiable by experience, and somehow specific to what is being perceived." The term *strategy* has been preferred by some psychologists studying how individuals think (Bruner, 1963), because it carries a more active connotation. One major research thrust has been the work on *personal constructs* (Kelly, 1955). Another is the investigation of *cognitive styles,* especially styles of *categorization* (Gardner and Schoen, 1962; Kagan, Moss, and Sigel, 1963), and *field dependence* (Witkin and others, 1954). Moral codes and *values* can be viewed as structures through which possibilities are screened. The same purpose may be served by *vocational interests.*

Looking at all of these research approaches together and including them all under the general heading of *possibility-processing structures* sensitizes us to the likelihood that not all of them are used by every individual. Psychologists have usually assumed that each variable they investigate is present in every research participant. This assumption may be unfounded. Some basic information-processing structures exist in everyone, but these may vary from person to person. For example, an organized value system may be very important for one person and not important at all for another who employs a strategy of unvarying obedience or of always doing what the people around one are doing. The vocational interest system characteristic of physicians may be the major controlling factor for one person, the creed and moral code of a particular church for another.

What most individuals develop is a repertoire of possibility-controlling structures appropriate for different situations. Some may be simple habits, some strategies, some personal constructs, some values. In a developed technology for assessing individuals, we will not give everybody the same tests.

↘↘ 8 ↙↙

Personal Constructs

"This theory of personality actually started with the combination of two simple notions: first, that man might be better understood if he were viewed in the perspective of the centuries rather than in the flicker of passing moments and, second, that each man contemplates in his own personal way the stream of events upon which he finds himself so swiftly borne" (Kelly, 1955, p. 3). So spoke George Kelly at the outset of a book, *The Psychology of Personal Constructs,* that set forth a comprehensive system of thinking about the organization of human personality. The philosophical point of view on which the theory rests has much in common with the one taken in this book, although it seems to have had different roots. Kelly called it *constructive alternatism.* The basic entity is the *construct.* "Man looks at his world through transparent patterns or templates which he creates and then attempts to fit over the realities of which the world is composed. The fit is not always very good. Yet without such patterns the world appears to be such an undifferentiated homogeneity that man is unable to make any sense out of it. Even a poor fit is more helpful to him than nothing at all" (pp. 8–9). These patterns or templates are what Kelly means by constructs, and there is no limit to the number of possible constructs that might be imposed on reality. What a person does and experiences always involves the system of constructs he or she has created previously; behavior is never a simple response to reality itself. Constructs make it possible for a person to anticipate events and act accordingly. A fundamental tenet of Kelly's theory is that the human being is essentially a *scientist* attempting to predict and control the events of his or her own life.

The framework of the theory consists of a fundamental postulate and eleven corollaries. The postulate is "A person's processes are psychologically channelized by the ways in which he anticipates events" (Kelly, 1955, p. 46). The corollaries delineate some of the characteristics of constructs. They are always bipolar; for example, "sincere-insincere," "people who understand me versus people who do not understand me," or "interesting work versus routine work." In other words, constructs always involve discriminations, combining things that are similar and recognizing what the opposite of the category is. Any one person possesses a limited number of constructs, although for some people the number may be very large. Constructs are organized into a *hierarchy* or many-leveled overall structure. Thus all of these examples of bipolar constructs might be subordinate to a higher-level construct of "good-bad" or "hippie-straight." Each person's construct system is unique, and it is constantly being modified through the choice of constructs that appear to provide greater possibilities for the extension of the system. Any one construct covers only a limited range of events, and a person develops a repertoire of single constructs and construct systems, employing sometimes one, sometimes another. Thus to an observer an individual's behavior may appear inconsistent from one occasion to another. Some constructs are more *permeable* than others and thus more susceptible to change. It is the similarity of construct systems that makes for similarities between persons rather than having experienced similar life events. Finally, in order to play a role in a social process involving another person, one must grasp or "construe" the other person's construct system or at least some portion of it.

The focus of more research than any other part of the theory has been constructs about people in social interaction. This is perhaps because Kelly himself, a clinical psychologist interested in helping people as well as understanding them, invented an ingenious technique for analyzing the construct systems operating in relationships between people. This was the Role Construct Repertory Test, usually abbreviated REP. Its original purpose was to facilitate a clinician's understanding of a client. In carrying out the procedure, the subject first supplies the names of persons fitting designated role titles, such as "mother," "a teacher you liked," "a person of your own sex whom you would enjoy having as a companion on a trip," "the most successful person you know." In the simplest form, using cards each of which has a name written on it, the examiner asks the subject to sort the cards, placing together the names of persons who appear similar in some way, and then to explain how they are similar. The procedure is very flexible, and various ways of eliciting the sortings have been used. Most frequently the subject is asked to consider the names three at a time, picking out two of them as more similar and then explaining what is similar about them and how the third person differs.

The REP is not a standardized measuring instrument, and many sorts of variation have been tried. By including a card for the person being tested, information about the person's self-concept can be obtained. If the procedure is being used clinically, including a card for the therapist may reveal something about how the client views the treatment situation. The procedure can be modified to allow group administration, with participants writing in their own answers on prepared answer sheets. Special lists of role titles can be prepared for special purposes, such as finding out how the person views fellow workers, other members of a therapy group, or members of his family. In his book (1955), Kelly suggested a number of ways in which a clinician could obtain and use information to develop and check clinical hypotheses.

It was the development of this procedure into a research technique that most strongly influenced later psychologists. For research purposes, a *grid* is constructed, with role titles along one axis and the constructs revealed by the individual's sortings along the other. What this adds to the original sorting procedure is the opportunity for the subject to apply his or her constructs to all of the persons on the list, not just to the three first compared. Figure 2 shows how this is done. Each *X* indicates a judgment that the posi-

Figure 2. Sample Grid Used in Research on Personal Constructs.

Elements \ Constructs	1. kind–cruel	2. tightening–gentle	3. carefree–conscientious	4. understands me–unsympathetic	5. confident–anxious	6. simple–intellectual
1. self					○	×
2. mother	⊗			×		⊗
3. father	⊗		×		×	×
4. brother		×	×	×		
5. sister	○		×		×	×
6. spouse	×			⊗	⊗	⊗
7. ex-flame		×		○		○
8. best friend	×	○	×	⊗	⊗	
9. ex-friend		×				×
10. rejecting person		⊗			×	
11. pitied person	×					×
12. threatening person		⊗		×		
13. attractive person	×		×	×	×	
14. accepted teacher	×		×		×	
15. rejected teacher		×				×
16. boss		×	×		×	×
17. successful person	×	×	⊗	×	×	
18. happy person	×		⊗	×	×	×
19. ethical person	×		○	×		
20. neighbor	×			×		×

Source: Bannister and Mair (1968, p. 56).

tive pole of the construct applies to the person designated by the column. Grid data have made possible a variety of statistical procedures to be used in analyzing single cases, thus opening up new prospects for research on individuality. The grid technique can also be applied in the analysis of constructs about many other things besides role relationships. Recent research projects in England, for example, have identified constructs that prisoners hold about people, activities, and conditions in the prison situation (Lewis, 1973); looked at sex differences in constructs used in judging female physiques (Stewart, Tutton, and Steele, 1973); and analyzed ways in which people evaluate their environments (Honikman, 1976). Cluster analysis and factor analysis can be applied to grids of single individuals. The degree of similarity between construct systems of different individuals can be assessed. A research group under the direction of Patrick Slater in England has developed a number of computer programs facilitating many kinds of grid analysis.*

Research on personal constructs has proceeded in several different directions. The first is the elaboration of the theoretical concepts and techniques developed by Kelly. Bannister and Mair (1968) discussed what had been done along these lines during the first decade after the publication of Kelly's book. Figure 2 is a simple example they give of the extension of the REP test into the more informative grid. The individual whose constructs were being examined was first asked to think about the three persons designated by the circles in Columns 2, 3, and 5, his mother, his father, and his sister. He indicated, by placing X's in Circles 2 and 3, that his mother and father were similar and, by leaving Circle 5 empty, that his sister was different. He explained the basis for the distinction as the fact that both his mother and his father were kind and that his sister was cruel. He was then asked to place X's in the other squares of the first row to indicate what other persons on the list he considered to be kind, leaving blank the squares under the names of persons he thought of as more cruel than kind. The process was repeated for each successive row of the grid, first deriving a construct from the

* These have not appeared in published form, but information about them is available from Dr. Patrick Slater, Department of Psychiatry, St. George's Hospital Medical School, Clare House, Blackshaw Road, London SW17, England.

three circled entries, then applying it to the other people on the list. With no more than twenty role titles, there could be more than two thousand sets of three to be compared, but to make all possible comparisons would be tedious for the individual and unproductive for the researcher. The process is usually terminated after from twenty to thirty trials. This number of judgments is enough to elicit all of the constructs the individual is likely to apply to the domain of experience being investigated.

In extracting meaning from data such as those shown in Figure 2, one technique commonly applied is to analyze the relationships between constructs (rows) or between persons (columns). How do the constructs fit together in this person's total structure? The simplest way of finding out which persons or constructs are linked together is to count the number of identical entries in each pair of rows or columns. The more of these there are in two rows, the more similar two constructs are; the more of them there are in two columns, the more similar two persons are for this individual. Looking at Figure 2, we see that for Rows 3 and 5, eighteen out of twenty entries are marked in the same way. This means that the "carefree-conscientious" distinction is very nearly equivalent for this individual to the "confident-anxious" distinction. It is not surprising that "carefree" and "confident" should be synonymous, but the identification of "conscientious" with "anxious" at the other pole of the construct is perhaps not what one would have expected—or what another individual would reveal in his or her sortings and judgments. Rows 1 and 2 have very little in common. In fact, what they reveal is a negative correlation between constructs. Persons classified as "kind" are not "threatening"; persons classified as "cruel" are not "gentle." Where about half of the row entries are identical, as in the case of Rows 1 and 6, it means that the constructs are independent of one another, related neither positively nor negatively. Persons considered to be "kind" may be either "simple" or "intellectual"; persons classified as "simple" may be either "kind" or "cruel."

These are simple and obvious ways of analyzing grid data, procedures any clinician or teacher can employ as an aid to understanding a client or a student. Research investigations usually involve more sophisticated correlational techniques followed by cluster or factor analysis, techniques Slater's computer programs now make feasible. Instead of simply placing X's in squares to which a construct applies, the subject can *rank* the persons or other elements the columns designate or can *rate* each of them with regard to a construct. Individuals can be asked to supply their own elements or column headings for the grid, or, at the other extreme, the investigator can supply both the elements and the constructs to be judged. The fact that the grid technique allows so many variations is what makes it so useful in research on individuality.

For a time after Kelly's book came out, psychologists seemed not to recognize that what was being proposed was something genuinely new, not just another kind of personality test. A series of attempts began to use REP grids to measure a trait defined as *cognitive complexity*. Bieri (1961) and Crockett (1965) provided useful summaries of what this line of investigation accomplished. One can obtain a measure of complexity-simplicity from an individual's grid by noting either the total amount of similarity between rows or the total number of different and independent constructs used. Crockett also made use of another nongrid type of score based on the number of constructs the subject used in written descriptions of people. However obtained, these scores could be handled in the standard psychometric ways. It was found that scores for cognitive complexity showed satisfactory reliability and that the trait, while unrelated to ordinary measures of academic intelligence, did have something to do with what we call *social* intelligence. For example, complex individuals were better at predicting the responses of other persons to situations described in a test, and they were less likely to overestimate the similarity between themselves and others. But all of the correlations with these and other criteria turned out to be low, and complications became apparent. The degree of complexity a subject manifested was different for different role categories. For example, a person might use a very simple set of constructs in judging disliked persons and a very complex set in judging liked persons (Crockett, 1965). Bannister and Mair (1968) found that thought-disordered schizophrenic patients received scores that classified them as complex, since their constructs showed a low degree of linkage to one another. This finding suggested that some complexity scores were indications of confusion.

Since about 1965, the attempt to score personal construct protocols for complexity—or, indeed, for any other personality trait—has been largely abandoned. But, although it failed in its initial purpose, it pointed the way to another kind of analysis of individual differences that promises to be more profitable. Landfield (1977) has carried out a series of studies in which he evaluates not just how many constructs an individual employs but how he or she organizes or integrates them. As Kelly pointed out, constructs are organized into higher-order constructs, with the whole system often built on several levels. By techniques designed to assess the number of levels an individual's constructs cover as well as how many different constructs the system contains, Landfield was able to get rid of some of the confusion and ambiguity previous research on cognitive complexity had generated. Using some ingenious criteria obtained from a group in which each member talked to each other member for six to eight minutes, Landfield and his associates demonstrated that persons high on both differentiation and integration, as evaluated from the number of constructs and the number of levels in the hierarchy, were likely to be described as healthy, mature people, whereas those high in differentiation but low in integration were likely to be described as confused and maladjusted. Other differences showed up for other combinations of differentiation and integration.

With the realization that research on personal constructs need not be forced into molds designed for mental testing, rapid progress in many directions has occurred. We cannot report all of the ingenious designs and suggestive findings. But we can dip into the pool here and there to pull out samples. In clinical psychology and psychiatry, there are many to choose from. Bannister's work on schizophrenic thought disorder has already been mentioned. In one of these experiments, Bannister and Salmon (1966) compared schizophrenics and normals, using two types of grid. The first required subjects to rank photographs of people with regard to adjectives such as *kind, mean,* and *selfish.* The second required them to rank objects, such as drawing pins, loaves of bread, and washing machines, on constructs appropriate to such objects; for example, "long-short," "curved-straight," and "heavy-light." The relationships between constructs were analyzed for each person on each

type of grid. While everybody produced higher correlations for
things than for people, schizophrenic thought disorder showed up
much more markedly on the people grid than on the object grid.
Thus the locus of the thought disorder was clarified.

Another psychiatric study, this one of a single case, an arson-
ist, is of particular interest (Fransella and Adams, 1966). The objective was to find out what the fires meant to the individual who
started them. The patient was presented with six different grids
designed to reveal different aspects of the mental structure underlying the fire setting. The elements of the first were adjectives descriptive of emotions—words such as *disturbing, tearful, revengeful,
peaceful,* and *guilty.* The constructs that he was requested to use in
ranking these elements were aspects of the fire-setting situation, such
as "moment of putting match to fire," "the blaze of the fire," "smell
of wood burning," and "sexual arousal." For each construct, the
elements were ranked according to how well they described his
feelings. What the investigator did with the rankings was to correlate each construct row with every other construct row and then
select two unrelated constructs to serve as axes against which the
rest of the relationships could be plotted. It turned out that almost
all of the feelings expressed by the patient's rank ordering were
related more or less closely to the moment between putting the
match to the structure and seeing the flames leap up. It was the experience of lighting the fire that evoked emotion, rather than the
fire itself. The other five specially designed grids brought out other
features of the patient's mental organization—the facts that he saw
himself as an upright, decisive character; that the feeling experienced when setting a fire was related to his positive feelings about
himself; that he did not see himself as hostile to his wife or others
but rather as a just punisher of wrongdoers; and that hospitaliza-
tion had failed to produce any major change in his construct system.
Because of the high negative correlation between the sort of person
he admired and thought he was and the sort of person he described
as "likely to commit arson," the investigators concluded that he might
commit the crime again under tempting circumstances without in-
tending to and without feeling guilty or remorseful about what he
had done. This case has been presented in some detail because of
the significance of experiments on single cases for a psychology

of individuality. One of the most influential and long-lasting effects of the personal construct movement may be this methodological gain. The utility of such techniques shows up with particular clarity in cases such as the one described. No study of the characteristics of arsonists as a group would have revealed this person's underlying structure. And, without an understanding of such structures, legal and psychiatric treatment of such persons will continue to be ineffective.

The volume edited by Slater (1976) provides several examples of ways in which personal construct ideas are being applied in mental health settings. The techniques can often clarify the nature of particular patients' difficulties. In one case (Rowe, 1976), for example, they revealed that a depressed woman's basic construct of "emotional versus tough" was perpetuating her depressed state of mind. Emotional people, according to her construct system, brood and worry about things, but this worry is what prevents calamities. Thus it is necessary to worry even though it keeps one depressed, because the alternative is to be tough and uncaring. Personal construct grids can be used to facilitate the treatment process. By having both patient and therapist produce grids descriptive of the patient, one is able to find out which aspects of the patient's thinking the therapist understands and which he does not understand. By having both members of a couple fill in grids describing their relationship, the bases of differences between them can be identified. Grid techniques can be employed to monitor changes that occur as therapy proceeds. Grids can be used to delineate the salient features of an individual's self-concept. They can clarify the reasons why some depressed patients attempt suicide whereas others with similar symptoms and in similar circumstances do not.

Salmon (1976) explains in detail how personal constructs can be assessed in children of four years and older, subjects for whom other methods of personality assessment have never been very satisfactory. The flexibility of these methods is a major advantage. One can explain truthfully to even a very young child that the purpose of the questions is to find out how a person sees things and thinks about them. The sorting procedure, used individually, is readily understood. Elements to be sorted can be objects, models, pictures, names of people, and descriptions of situations. There are many ways besides the usual comparison and contrast procedure to elicit constructs from children. One can utilize conversations or interviews or have a child write essays about people. Questions by the investigator serve to clarify the child's meanings. Ranking or rating of elements can be carried out by young children if instructions are adapted to their natural ways of making such judgments. For example, the investigator can first ask, "Which of these people is most good-natured?" and then can remove the card or picture chosen and ask, "Now, of the rest of these people, who is most good-natured?" One proceeds in this way until all items have been ranked.

One way of summing up the significance of personal construct techniques for the mental health field is to say that they are essentially interview aids, ways of enabling men and women, boys and girls, to express things they would not have been able to put into words in response to general interview questioning, regardless of the skill of the interviewer. The implications of this conclusion—that construct grids are first and foremost facilitators of communication—are being pursued by Bonarius (1977). He has developed a variation of the REP procedure designed to be used by any two persons who wish to understand each other better. The Repertory Interaction Test (RIT) takes the form of a game, the rules of which are summarized in a manual that both players read before they begin to play. The participants alternate as question askers and question answerers, progressing from less to more sensitive material. Interpretations are checked with each other as they are made.

Besides psychiatry and clinical psychology, other areas of human concern are being explored using techniques pioneered by Kelly (1955). Architects and community planners are interested in these areas. They see the possibility of finding out how their clients evaluate buildings and aspects of their environment and thus not having to rely on their own criteria, which may or may not match those of the clients. Honikman (1976) used pictures of living rooms as elements to elicit constructs and then factor analyzed the grids to discover what the major groupings of characteristics were. For most of the clients interviewed, the first component was a distinction based on whether rooms were on the one hand, "comfortable, homely, lived in" or, on the other hand, "formal, not homely, uncomfortable." The second component differentiated heavy, crowded-looking rooms from light, spacious ones. By asking appropriate questions, the investigator was able to find out just which features of rooms influenced these judgments.

Another ingenious application of these techniques was an English study designed to show how long-term prisoners think about their worlds (Watson, Gunn, and Gristwood, 1976). The constructs were stressful situations, such as "getting the sack"; "getting caught by the police"; "being laughed at"; and "having nowhere to live." The elements were responses one might make to such situations, such as "punch out" (a graphic English expression); "feel depressed"; and "get drunk." What was discovered here that would not have come to light ordinarily was that the most likely response to stressful situations was not any sort of antisocial behavior but rather unpleasant affective states. Construct structures prisoners produced showed that situations characterized by a lack of material things were likely to lead to thieving and depression, whereas it was the interpersonal frustrations, such as being laughed at, that were likely to lead to violence. These results may not be surprising, and they reflect, of course, what prisoners say rather than what they actually do, but the potential usefulness of understanding the structure of their thinking in order to deal with them intelligently is self-evident.

One more example of the use of techniques based on personal construct theory as facilitators of individual expression of thoughts and feelings comes from anthropology. Simons (1976) adapted the procedure for use in Java to find out what the community midwife thinks about matters related to birth control. In Java, midwives are the central persons in putting birth control programs into practice. They are the ones who are in a position to give out information, to refer women to clinics, and to provide advice and support. Since attitudes about contraception are linked to many other values and attitudes, just asking "Do you believe that birth control is a good thing?" does not give much of a clue as to whether or not it will be practiced. Simons used questions as elements in a grid, questions such as "Do you think a large family means many burdens if the parents are poor?" "Do you think that, however many children a person has, the Lord will provide for them?" "If there were a course about family planning for a week in a clinic, would you come?" and "Do you think it is especially important for parents to have a dutiful son?" One row of the grid was assigned to each midwife, and her answers to the questions were recorded in the squares below them. The grid representing all of the midwives was then factor analyzed to reveal basic structure underlying the answers to the questions. It could then be determined where each midwife was located with regard to this structure. It turned out that there were four principal components or factors. The first had to do with attitudes for or against birth control. The second contrasted submission to the will of God and to nature with the practical attitude that individuals or villages should be rewarded for having fewer children. The third represented the difference between actively promoting birth control yourself and being guided by the opinions of others. The fourth had to do with general orientation toward procreation. It was interesting to find that a midwife's position on this last component was not related to her position on the first, which indicated how favorable she was toward birth control. It is quite possible for a Javanese woman to favor birth control and still see a large family as a blessing. After studying the placement of individual midwives on all of the components, the investigators concluded that the midwife professes and tries to preserve traditional beliefs and values. Her dominant reference group is the community. However, that is not her *only* reference group. She also has modern constructs related to the health center. What she tends to do is to use community constructs in the community, health center constructs at the health center. Midwives differ in the amount of connection the systems have for them, however, so that some are more likely than others to refer village women to birth control clinics. The study shows why progress has been slow in promoting birth control, but it also suggests ways of accelerating it. And it provides another illustration of the way in which analysis of the structure of thinking processes can throw new light on old and intractable problems.

Many more examples of ingenious research could be cited, but enough have perhaps been given to demonstrate the flexibility and versatility of the theory and techniques. What aspects do those most involved in the movement think are most likely to be emphasized in the future? In the *1976 Nebraska Symposium on Personal Construct Psychology* (Landfield, 1977), the question was considered in several thoughtful essays and in the discussion that followed their presentation. The participants were more interested in directions in which the *ideas* are developing than in techniques and applications. One of the major emphases is on interpersonal communication. We have already described the Bonarius procedure for facilitating mutual communication in persons who are not patients or clients, without the participation of a psychologist in the interchange. Communication at a level deeper than ordinary conversation is a fundamental need in our complex modern world. Digging below the surface for constructs underlying expressed attitudes, opinions, demands, and actions might have a beneficial effect on relationships between parents and children, workers and employers, bureaucrats and citizens.

A second major emphasis is on the utility of personal construct theory in dealing with development and change. Woven into the fabric of Kelly's system is the realization that constructs and construct systems are changing constantly, but that the change is not haphazard. A person never suddenly trades in his or her repertoire of constructs for a new one. Different constructs differ in their permeability; some absorb new information much more readily than others do. And some constructs affect the structure of a person's whole construct system much more drastically than others do, when change does occur. Those at higher levels of the hierarchy have more far-reaching effects than those lower down. Several kinds of research already mentioned have to do with change processes. Having a patient fill in grids at different stages of therapy is one example. Longitudinal research on children is another. Schools at all levels from kindergarten to graduate school would seem to constitute resources for the study of developmental change in construct systems.

Another current emphasis is the consideration of affective as well as purely cognitive aspects of the process of construing and of nonverbal as well as verbal indicators of constructs. The distinction between rational thinking and emotion is etched deeply into the construct systems of most individuals in the Western world. One of the special attractions of Kelly's theory is that it transcends this distinction. The index of Kelly's book (1955) has no entry for the word *feeling* and very few references for the word *emotion*. The theoretical system does not need to distinguish these concepts. Constructs arise out of experience as it comes, with cognition and affect inextricably interwoven. However, in the twenty years since Kelly's book appeared, by far the largest part of the research has rested on cognitive constructs, verbally expressed. The desirability of broadening the scope of research to cover the whole panorama of human activity was brought out in the discussion at the Nebraska Symposium.

As we look at the directions in which personal construct theory is developing, it is gratifying to see that it has not solidified into an orthodoxy but instead has tended to merge with other theoretical systems that resemble it. This is partly a consequence of changes that have occurred in psychology as a whole that have led, to a climate much more congenial to the theory than the climate was in Kelly's time. We have discussed some of these changes in Chapter One. Mancuso (1977) and Sarbin (1977) describe this overall transformation of psychology in terms proposed in 1942 by a philosopher, Stephan Pepper, as a replacement of the prevailing *root metaphor* by a different one, human-as-machine giving way to human-as-scientist. Instead of *mechanism,* we have adopted the world hypothesis Pepper called *contextualism;* instead of looking for the *causal sequence,* we examine the historical *event* in all its ramifications. Mancuso's research is tying socialization and moral development into the personal construct framework. Sarbin is bringing construct theory into alignment with his own extensive work on social roles. Another participant, Rosenberg (1977), is linking personal construct thinking to the active research in social psychology on the perception of persons and to his own studies of implicit personality theory. In the chapter by Mair (1977), the profound significance of metaphor in human thinking is highlighted, as well as the implications probed of the metaphors that Kelly himself used, implications we have only begun to see. Through fresh construing, the person opens up a world of possibilities previously invisible and thus creates new reality.

Personal construct theory is deeply involved in the transformation of our views about what psychological science is. On a theoretical level, the transformation is well developed. But how about research procedures, the means by which we arrive at conclusions? If every person is essentially a scientist trying to make sense of the world, as Kelly believed, then the distinction between experimenter and subject that has been almost universal in psychological research is untenable. The results of every experiment reflect to some extent what the subject thought its purpose was as well as what the experimenter intended. The kinds of experimental controls that physical scientists use are not appropriate or adequate as controls for extraneous variables in human (or even animal) research, because these extraneous variables are anticipations and assumptions, not necessarily the same for all subjects. What this fact means, if we take it seriously, is that it is incumbent on us to write some new rules for scientific research in psychology and the other social sciences, construing persons joined in the endeavor as scientific collaborators rather than as observer and observed.

It took Kelly himself some time to appreciate what he was doing to psychology. According to his own somewhat whimsical account (Kelly, 1970, p. 256),

> It seems that, once upon a time, psychologists became enamoured of science. It was quite a passionate affair, but very one-sided. Psychologists were deeply hurt by the harsh turn of events. But instead of abandoning their suit . . . they loudly protested their continuing infatuation, taking advantage of everyone who could be made to stand still and listen. . . .
>
> I used to think this public display of blighted affection was ridiculous. Why didn't psychologists get on with the job of understanding man? If they did their job well, the scientific establishment would soon enough lay claim to all they had achieved. . . .
>
> So I was amused. The overserious involvement with science had culminated in rejection. Yet the psychology I found so amusing is the harlequin among the sciences. In that classic theme, man is reminded that the clown he observes is himself. . . . So it is with psychology, a discipline so entangled in its own consistencies that it moves from pomposity to pathos, and, in doing so, portrays man better than he knows.

From the vantage point we have taken in this book, we see this as an insight the importance of which can hardly be over-emphasized. If the subject matter of psychology is not a finite collection of behaving objects but rather the limitless domain of human possibilities from which generation after generation of individuals draws without depleting the resources, then our science cannot be content with models borrowed from physics and chemistry. We must create new models, new rules for playing the game of scientific inquiry, new guidelines for our research. George Kelly realized this.

≫≫ 9 ≪≪

Values, Attitudes, and Interests

Of all the structures through which human possibilities are selected and actualized in individuals, value systems are the most comprehensive and probably the least understood. The term *values* has been variously defined, and there is still considerable ambiguity about which psychological characteristics belong in the category. Allport (1961, p. 454) defined value as "a belief upon which a man acts by preference." The definition given by Brewster Smith (1963, p. 332) was "conceptions of the desirable that are relevant to selective behavior." Morris (1956) did not attempt a definition but called attention to three ways in which the term is commonly employed: as a tendency to *prefer* one thing to another; as an *anticipation of the outcome* of preferential behavior; and as a concept about what is *desirable,* whether or not it is in fact preferred. These writers agree that a value is a firmly held belief that may govern preferences and choices of a fundamental, nontrivial kind. This brings the concept clearly into our class of possibility-processing structures. The most recent and care-

131

fully thought-out definition of what we are concerned with in this chapter is that of Rokeach (1973, p. 5): "A *value* is an enduring belief that a specific mode of conduct or end state of existence is personally or socially preferable to an opposite or converse mode of conduct or end state of existence. A *value system* is an enduring organization of beliefs concerning preferable modes of conduct or end states of existence along a continuum of relative importance."

Rokeach goes on to distinguish between instrumental and terminal values and to consider how values are related to attitudes, interests, social norms, needs, and personality traits. "To say that a person has a value is to say that he has an enduring prescriptive or proscriptive belief that a specific mode of behavior or end state of existence is preferred to an appositive mode of behavior or end state. This belief transcends attitudes toward objects and toward situations; it is a standard that guides and determines action, attitudes toward objects and situations, ideology, presentations of self to others, evaluations, judgments, justifications, comparisons of self with others, and attempts to influence others. Values serve adjustive, ego-defensive, knowledge, and self-actualizing functions" (Rokeach, 1973, p. 25). One of the things that distinguishes research on values from research on many other aspects of individuality is its interdisciplinary character. For centuries, philosophers have been thinking about values. Anthropologists are very much concerned with values in the cultures they study. Sociologists use value concepts in analyzing societies. And value concepts, somewhat differently defined, underlie the whole science of economics.

Psychologists embarking on empirical investigations make use of ideas from all of these sources. The first step in such an investigation is to assemble a collection of statements or items. At this initial stage, a good deal of subjective judgment about what is relevant inevitably affects the research. There is no universal catalogue of human values and no established criteria for pruning and shortening the list one is working with to make sure that nothing essential is being omitted.

The measurement techniques used in research on values also differ in an important way from those commonly employed in personality study. They are *ipsative* rather than *normative*. In ipsative measures, it is the individual's distinctive pattern of high and low scores that one looks at rather than the position the individual occupies in a distribution for a group. Items in a value-measuring instrument may require the person to indicate which of three things he or she likes best and which least, to rank several life goals in order from most to least important, or to sort statements into categories ranging from most to least acceptable. Such requirements make it impossible for the person to come out with high scores on everything, as one can in taking ability and most personality tests. By preferring one alternative, an individual necessarily relegates others to less preferred positions. With a different set of alternatives, one's response to any particular item might be different. The use of ipsative measures imposes limits on conclusions that can be drawn. When we compare an individual with group norms, or compare, say, groups of students in India and the United States, with regard to any one value, we must remember that comparisons are relative to the whole value pattern in which this value was embedded. For example, Myra may seem to place a lower value on wisdom than her classmates do, because her score for this value is well below the group average. But the true state of affairs may be that Myra places a much higher value than most of them do on social recognition, mature love, and an exciting life. (These are all items from Rokeach's list.) The rank for wisdom is forced down by the higher placement of the other three. A value system must be thought of as a *structure* rather than as a sum of several measured quantities.

The earliest and probably most influential major research on values was that of Allport and Vernon (1931). They set out to measure the six values that the German philosopher Spranger (1928) had differentiated:

1. *Theoretical*—valuing the pursuit of truth by intellectual means.
2. *Economic*—valuing useful, practical activities.
3. *Esthetic*—valuing artistic qualities and beauty.
4. *Social*—valuing helpfulness to people.
5. *Political*—valuing power and influence.
6. *Religious*—valuing mystical experience and spiritual things.

The Allport-Vernon measuring instrument, revised in 1951 and again in 1960 as the Allport-Vernon-Lindzey *Study of Values,* has been used in a large number of research projects in which the relationships of values to other psychological characteristics have been investigated. At the time that the *Seventh Mental Measurement Yearbook* (Buros, 1972) appeared, the total number of such studies had reached 687. Generally speaking, special groups tested have shown the kinds of values one would expect them to. Creative architects and mathematicians assessed at the Institute of Personality Assessment Research scored high on the theoretical and esthetic scales. Business persons, teachers, technical students, seminarians—these and many other groups present different value profiles of characteristic shapes. The Allport-Vernon-Lindzey *Study of Values* (1951) is a simple tool that has turned out to be useful for many purposes. But for psychologists seeking to understand the part values play in the development and expression of individuality, the tool is not really adequate. The main difficulty is with the Spranger typology. Does it cover all of the values by which people live? Is it appropriate for persons with less education than the college groups to which it has typically been administered? Are the scales really measuring basic values or only more superficial interests? Although the Allport-Vernon-Lindzey inventory has been the most popular instrument in research on values, it is not the only one.

A quite different approach was that of Morris (1942, 1956). The sources of the items used in this investigation were the world's major religions and the cultures based on them. Morris (1942) began by distinguishing three basic components or orientations, the Dionysian, the Promethean, and the Buddhistic. "The Dionysian component is made up of the tendencies to release and indulge existing desires. . . . The Promethean component . . . is the sum of active tendencies to manipulate and remake the world. . . . The buddhistic component . . . comprises those tendencies in the self to regulate itself by holding in check its desires" (Morris, 1956, pp. 1–2). Different combinations of these tendencies generate value profiles characteristic of various cultures. In later statements of his ideas, Morris described the basic orientations without using the religious labels, calling them *dependence, dominance,* and *detachment.*

In beginning his research, Morris wrote thoughtful descriptions of seven ways of life that characterized what he considered to be the most important value profiles. He asked college students to react to these and to suggest others. The result was an instrument called Ways to Live, consisting of thirteen descriptions that could be ranked and/or rated by participants. The first of these "ways" illustrates what the instrument was like.

> In this "design for living" [Way 1], the individual actively participates in the social life of his community, not to change it primarily, but to understand, appreciate, and preserve the best that man has attained. Excessive desires should be avoided and moderation sought. One wants the good things of life but in an orderly way. Life is to have clarity, balance, refinement, control. Vulgarity, great enthusiasm, irrational behavior, impatience, indulgence are to be avoided. Friendship is to be esteemed, but not easy intimacy with many people. Life is to have discipline, intelligibility, good manners, predictability. Social changes are to be made slowly and carefully, so that what has been achieved in human culture is not lost. The individual should be active physically and socially, but not in a hectic or radical way. Restraint and intelligence should give order to an active life [Morris, 1956, p. 15].

The thirteen ways can be summarized as follows:

1. Balance, moderation, and order.
2. Independence and self-direction.
3. Sympathetic concern for other people.
4. Pleasure and enjoyment.
5. Companionship and group activity.
6. Action and domination.
7. Dynamic integration of enjoyment, action, and contemplation.
8. Simple, carefree enjoyment.
9. Quiet receptivity.
10. Stern self-control.
11. Contemplation and renunciation.
12. Energetic action, construction, overcoming obstacles.
13. Humility in letting oneself be used by great purposes in the universe.

The research carried on with the Ways to Live scale consisted mainly of comparisons between groups of students in many countries, China (before 1948), India, Japan, Norway, and Canada, and in several colleges in the United States. Factor analysis of the correlations between ratings of the thirteen ways to live reduced the number of basic orientations to five: (1) social restraint and self-control, (2) enjoyment and progress in action, (3) withdrawal and self-sufficiency, (4) receptivity and sympathetic concern, and (5) self-indulgence or sensuous enjoyment. It seemed that the factor analysis brought us back close to the Dionysian, Promethean, and Buddhistic thinking from which the research started. Both resemblances and differences in the national groups were apparent. All of the students rated factors 1 and 2 (in the reduced list) highest, but it appeared that students in the United States valued the first, "social restraint and self-control," less highly than the other national groups did. Students in the United States were also lower than the others on factor 4, "receptivity and sympathetic concern," and higher on factor 5, "self-indulgence," than the others. For the group from China, the factor receiving the highest rating was factor 2, "enjoyment and progress in action." The 1940s were, of course, a time of great events in China's history. Morris analyzed in considerable detail possible reasons for the differences that turned up, social, psychological, and even biological reasons (age, body size, physical type). Prothro (1958) added an Arab group to the ones Morris had tested, finding similar factors and fairly high correlations with the order in which other students had ranked the "ways."

Even though the factor analyses indicated that at least five factors were required to account for the correlations, Morris continued to carry along his initial assumptions that value structure is basically three-dimensional and that dependence, dominance, and detachment were more fundamental than the empirically derived factors. Whether or not one agrees with this conclusion, the evidence that values are linked together in some sort of structure and that they are complex and complexly determined is important to consider. The Ways to Live instrument has not been widely used in subsequent research, perhaps because it was the creation of a philosopher, not a psychologist, and thus was not in the main channel through which psychological information flows, perhaps because it requires from the research participant an investment of time and intelligent consideration that cannot be counted on in groups other than well-motivated college students.

A more recent large-scale research undertaking designed to clarify differences in value structures and their correlates is that of Rokeach (1968, 1973). In the earlier book, Rokeach brought together papers he had written over a period of years during which he had been struggling to organize attitudes, beliefs, and values into some sort of coherent system. The narrowest of the three concepts is *belief;* the broadest is *value.* "An adult probably acquires tens of thousands of beliefs, thousands of attitudes, but only dozens of values. A *value system* is a hierarchical organization—a rank ordering—of ideals or values in terms of importance" (Rokeach, 1968, p. 124). Like the researchers who preceded him, Rokeach derived his list of basic values from various sources, the writings of philosophers, contributions of graduate students, and interviews with thoughtful adults. He found it reasonable to prepare separate lists of *terminal* and *instrumental values.* Terminal values represent end states of existence, such as security, peace, and freedom. Instrumental values represent modes of conduct through which end states are attained. The final lists, distilled from a much larger number of items, consisted of eighteen items of each type. The eighteen terminal values were the following end-states: (1) a comfortable life, (2) an exciting life, (3) a sense of accomplishment, (4) a world at peace, (5) a world of beauty, (6) equality, (7) family security, (8) freedom, (9) happiness, (10) inner harmony, (11) mature love, (12) national security, (13) pleasure, (14) salvation, (15) self-respect, (16) social recognition, (17) true friendship, and (18) wisdom. The eighteen instrumental values were being (1) ambitious, (2) broad-minded, (3) capable, (4) cheerful, (5) clean, (6) courageous, (7) forgiving, (8) helpful, (9) honest, (10) imaginative, (11) independent, (12) intellectual, (13) logical, (14) loving, (15) obedient, (16) polite, (17) responsible, and (18) self-controlled. The terminal values can be characterized as "things to strive for" and the instrumental values as "ways to be."

The structure of one's value system is revaled by one's rank ordering of the items in each of these sets. To facilitate this ranking, each item is printed on a separate, removable, gummed label. The respondent peels off the one considered to be most important and pastes it in Box 1. The next most important goes to Box 2. Thus one proceeds until all eighteen have been ranked. Shifts and revisions are easily accomplished as one goes along, since the labels peel off without difficulty. The reliability coefficients for various groups were reasonably high, but they varied considerably from person to person, with some placing the items in almost identical positions on successive occasions, others showing almost no consistency at all. Rankings of terminal values tended to be more stable than rankings of instrumental values. Why some persons manifest stable value systems and others do not is at present an unanswered question. We shall return to it later.

The special importance of Rokeach's work with this value survey is that it is based on a wider range of subjects than former investigators had studied. It was administered in 1968 to the national sample of American adults, 1,409 persons in all, polled by the National Opinion Research Center (NORC), certainly the most representative group ever questioned about their values. Rokeach was able to compare subgroups in the population, such as blacks and whites, men and women, conservatives and liberals. The instrument has also been used in a large number of other studies that explored relationships of values to attitudes, personality characteristics, and behavior. The simplicity of the technique is a great advantage. Value rankings obtained in this way are only negligibly related to one another. Almost all possible combinations appear in individual rankings. The fact that one assigns first place to "happiness," for example, tells us almost nothing about where other items will be placed. The highest correlation between "happiness" and anything else is $-.23$ with "equality," and this is obviously too low to make any sort of individual prediction possible. Rokeach, like most psychologists who come into possession of a large number of correlation coefficients, carried out a factor analysis of the correlations, low as they were. Seven factors emerged, but together they accounted for only 41 percent of the variance, so that they are not very meaningful as characterizations of the value structures of individuals. As in other value research, there does seem to be a central set of values on which almost all subjects agree. Americans in the

NORC sample ranked the terminal values "a world at peace," "family security," and "freedom" highest, "an exciting life," "pleasure," "social recognition," and "a world of beauty" lowest. As explained before, this finding on an ipsative instrument does not mean that Americans are against pleasure or social recognition. Ranking forces some items to the bottom of the list. Among the instrumental values, "honest," "ambitious," and "responsible" ranked highest, "imaginative," "obedient," and "logical" lowest.

Differences between subgroups were generally in line with expectations. Men showed themselves as more materialistic, achievement oriented, and intellectual; women were more religious and more concerned about peace, love, and happiness. In most cases, however, differences were not large. For example, males, on the average, ranked "ambitious" second on their list of instrumental values, whereas females ranked it fourth. Differences between social classes also made psychological sense. It is interesting to note in this connection that the gap between different educational groups was wider than the gap between rich and poor. The poor and the relatively uneducated ranked "a comfortable life" and "clean" higher than did the well-to-do and well educated. These were the largest differences found, arising perhaps from the likelihood that people higher in the social scale take comfort and cleanliness for granted. The poor and the less well educated also gave a higher rank to religion and to conformist virtues such as politeness and obedience. There were fewer differences between blacks and whites than between social classes, and those there were paralleled the differences between income and educational groups, suggesting that socioeconomic position has more to do with values than race does. One item distinguished sharply between the blacks and the whites. "Equality" ranks second for blacks, eleventh for whites. The difference is even sharper when the racial groups are matched for income and education.

"Equality" turned out to be a pivotal value in other comparisons as well. Supporters of seven different 1968 presidential candidates differed most on this item. Kennedy and Johnson supporters ranked it fourth, Wallace supporters fourteenth. In contrast, supporters of all seven candidates placed "freedom" in third place. This contrast led Rokeach to formulate a general model of political ideology (see Figure 3). "The major variations in political ideology are hypothesized to be fundamentally reducible . . . to opposing value orientations concerning the political desirability or undesirability of freedom and equality in all their ramifications" (Rokeach, 1973, p. 169). Support for the validity of the model was

Figure 3. A Freedom-Equality Model of Political Variations.

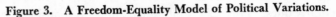

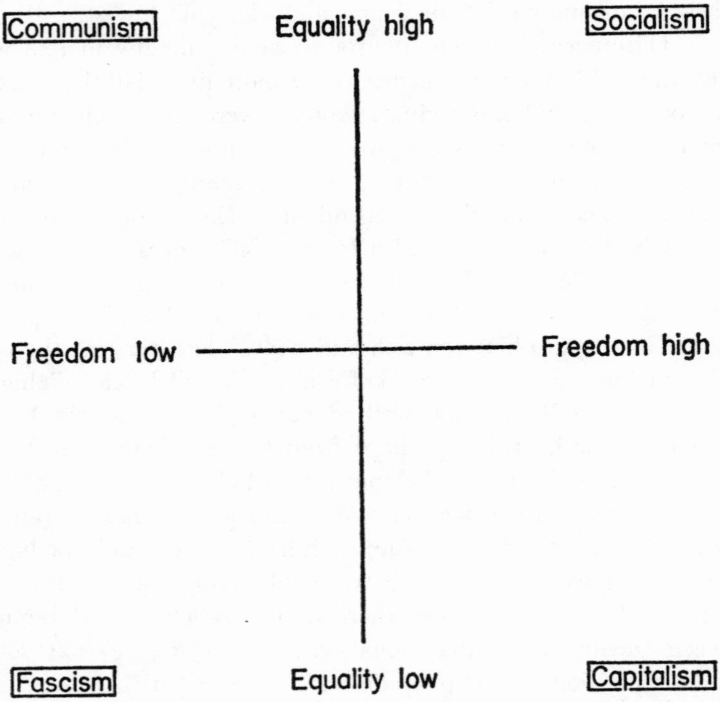

Communism   Equality high   Socialism

Freedom low ——————————+—————————— Freedom high

Fascism   Equality low   Capitalism

Source: Reproduced from M. Rokeach, *The Nature of Human Values* (p. 170). Copyright © 1973 The Free Press, a division of the Macmillan Company.

found in frequency counts judges made of values expressed in the writings of Lenin, Hitler, Goldwater, and several socialists. The socialists ranked "freedom" first, "equality" second. Lenin ranked "equality" first, "freedom" seventeenth. Hitler ranked "freedom" sixteenth, "equality" seventeenth. Goldwater ranked "freedom" first, "equality" sixteenth. Since Americans all rank "freedom" high, differences in this country are mainly differences in how "equality" is valued.

Rokeach reports a number of intriguing little studies that point to a relationship between values and behavior. College students who joined the National Association for the Advancement of Colored People in response to a special invitation ranked "equality" higher than nonjoiners did. Students not participating in civil rights demonstrations ranked "a comfortable life" tenth; participators ranked it eighteenth; participators ranked "equality" fifth; nonparticipators ranked it seventeenth. Regular churchgoers ranked "salvation" much higher than did those who seldom or never attend church. Employees who returned pencils lent them for filling out a questionnaire ranked "honest" higher than did those who kept the pencils. Prison inmates ranked "honest" somewhat lower and "wisdom" much higher than nonoffenders did. Compatible roommates were more similar in their value rankings than noncompatible roommates were, and clients terminating counseling after one interview were less similar to their counselors than those who continued. Value similarity makes for compatibility. In another direction, hippies and nonhippies differ in various ways, with hippie youths valuing the present more than the future, utilitarian social arrangements and inner harmony more than competition and achievement. As has been often demonstrated, values differ for groups representing different occupations. This evidence about how values are linked to behavior is fragmentary but impressive. In general, results are in line with what one would have predicted. "Equality" differentiates political groups; "a world of beauty" separates artists from nonartists. Three of the values on the list stand out by being related to more than half of all the behaviors and attitudes studied: "a comfortable life," "equality," and "salvation." This finding suggests that socioeconomic, political, and religious values are the ones most closely linked to behavior.

In summary, the Rokeach research program has shown that individuals differ in value structure and that the differences manifest themselves in many areas of human life. While one might quibble about some of the detailed results, a strong case has been made for the general conclusion that values are indeed important possibility-processing structures.

Another recent attempt to identify value systems and find out what they are related to is that of Sundberg, Rohila, and Tyler (1970). The instrument used to assess values, the Sundberg-Tyler

(S-T) Values Q-sort, grew out of the theoretical ideas on which
this book is based.* The fundamental principle is that the world
with which a person deals consists of possibilities rather than of
definite things or specific demands and that the individuality and
the variability exemplified in the person's behavior depend on the
way in which possibilities are selected and structured. Values are
possibility-processing structures. The value Q-sorts were only one of
a considerable number of techniques employed in an intensive study
of early adolescents (about fifteen years of age) in several American
locations, in the Netherlands, and in India. As other investigators
had done, Sundberg and his associates surveyed definitions and discussions of values and collected a large number of value statements.
Some were drawn from inventories such as that developed by Allport, Vernon, and Lindzey; from the anthropological research of
Kluckhohn and Strodtbeck (1961); and from the work of Morris
(1956, already discussed). Some were obtained from boys and girls
themselves in response to such questions as "Who are you?" The
investigators also wrote statements themselves, based on their experience and their reading. All in all, more than 500 statements
were assembled for the original pool. This number was then reduced
to a workable size by eliminating statements children did not understand, by combining items with similar content, and by getting rid
of duplication.

A distinction somewhat similar to Rokeach's distinction between terminal and instrumental values was adopted for this
research. Statements were classified either as "personal assumptions"
or as "personal directions." Personal assumptions are the beliefs,
principles, or hypotheses the individual holds about the world. Such
statements as "Most people can be trusted" and "If one wants to be
successful, one must work hard" fall into this category. Personal
directions are the principles or criteria a person employs in acting or
moving toward goals. An example is "I enjoy activities and adventure." The word *direction* was used rather than the word *goal* to
suggest a dynamic sequence of activities rather than a static structure.
It was not always easy to assign a statement to one of the two cate-

* The unpublished manual for the S-T Value Q-Sort may be obtained from Consulting Psychologists Press, 577 College Avenue, Palo Alto,
Calif. 94306.

gories; the distinction, clear enough in the abstract, becomes blurred when applied to concrete statements. But through repeated attempts the researchers produced a set of fifty statements classified as personal assumptions and forty statements classified as personal directions. Each was typed on a separate card to be used in a seven-step Q-sort. Preliminary studies indicated that the reliability of these sorts was adequate for research purposes. As Rokeach had found, individuals vary greatly in the stability of their expressed values.

The largest project in which this instrument was used was a comparative study of adolescents in India and America (Sundberg, Rohila, and Tyler, 1970). In a small American city and an Indian city in which the schools were of comparable size, twenty-four boys and twenty-four girls were selected from a larger group in which several group tests had been given, selected in such a way that the distribution of socioeconomic levels would be approximately the same for the national samples. Seventeen hypotheses about differences in values were formulated, based on analysis of the two cultures. Responses to the items on the Q-sorts were then examined to determine whether or not they supported the hypotheses. The results were complex and often difficult to interpret. Some of the comparisons did support the hypotheses. Indian adolescents did assign higher positions in the Q-sort to values having to do with deference, conformity, and external control, and Americans assigned higher positions to values having to do with sensuous enjoyment and sociability. But expected differences were not found on values having to do with individuality, autonomy, free will, self-expression, service, getting ahead, and democracy. Traditional values we had hypothesized on the basis of religious literature, such things as asceticism and resignation in India and puritanical morality in the United States, did not show up at all in these young people.

Perhaps the most important idea coming out of this and other research with the S-T Values Q-Sort is that there is a large amount of similarity between widely separated groups of high school-age people. This is the same conclusion Morris reached in his work with college students. If we look only at whether the placement of a statement is above or below the middle category of our seven-step Q-sort, we find that 18 percent of the statements were similarly accepted or rejected by persons of both sexes in both countries. An additional 13 percent were similarly placed by Indian and American girls or Indian and American boys. Thus is seems that about 31 percent of these ninety items represent values held in common by the two groups so far apart geographically and culturally. They are items having to do with the desirability of having friends, helping people, traveling, working, expressing oneself, and enjoying one's youth. (The one statement almost everybody rejected was "Old age is better than youth.") While boys and girls show some differences, they are enough alike to produce a correlation of .85 between American boys and girls and .78 between Indian boys and girls. Socioeconomic differences are also few in number. Individuals within the groups do differ from one another in value structure. We need to develop conceptualizations that can be used to describe the ways in which individuals deviate from the common human pattern. Universal values, values characteristic of particular cultures and subcultures, and individual values all enter into preferences and choices. We need to consider them all simultaneously, along with alternative possibility-processing structures that for some persons make values irrelevant.

Down through the years, psychologists have expended far more research energy on attitudes than on values. Rather early in the history of psychometrics, ways to measure attitudes were devised, making it possible for social psychologists to investigate people's attitudes toward such things as religion, black people, war, movies, and conservation. At first most of the research was correlational, relating attitudes to other attitudes and to background and experience. Later the focus of research shifted to attitude change, and experimental procedures of various kinds were employed. The principal difference between attitudes and values is that an attitude is directed toward a particular object or situation, a value toward a much wider range of things. Anti-Semitism is an attitude, but belief in Nordic superiority is a value, as is tolerance for and acceptance of diversity. One value may affect a large number of attitudes, and an individual's value system may govern his or her attitudes toward almost everything. But, although values are broader and more basic structures, attitudes also constitute structures through which possibilities are screened. Smith, Bruner, and White (1956) made an intensive study of ten adult men who held differing attitudes toward

Russia and found evidence that this one attitude was deeply im-
bedded in the subjects' personalities, serving different purposes for
different individuals. Another influential book (Adorno and others,
1950) initiated a torrent of research on the authoritarian personality. The project started as an investigation of anti-Semitism, but
the complex of attitudes, ideology, and defense mechanisms that it
revealed does not fit readily into the categories of either attitudes or
values. Some of the ways individuals acquire for screening and organizing possibilities are not classifiable into the common psychological categories. Because of the increasing difficulty of interpreting
the results from research on attitude-personality relationships, attitude measurement no longer appears to be a promising approach to
the assessment of individuality. One's assortment of attitudes toward
people and things is certainly unique. But the basic values underlying the attitudes would seem to be a more economical and meaningful way of characterizing an individual.

   Vocational interest patterns can also be viewed as structures
through which possibilities are screened. Research on interests, like
research on attitudes, has a long history. As early as 1927, Strong
brought out an inventory made up of work-related items toward
which respondents indicated their likes, dislikes, and preferences.
What gave the Strong Vocational Interest Blank its unique character was that each scoring key—and more and more were constructed as the years passed—was based on only those items for
which tabulations of responses has shown a clear difference between
a group of successful persons in a particular occupation and a comparable group of persons who were not in the occupation. Thus a
score carried a clear meaning for the person receiving it: "Yes, you
are like persons in this occupation," "No, you are not like persons
in this occupation." Evidence accumulated that people felt at home
in occupations fitting their likes, dislikes, and preferences and did
not feel that they belonged in occupations characterized by different
likes, dislikes, and preferences. It is important to remember that the
similarities and dissimilarities have to do with dislike and indifferent
responses as well as likes. In fact, many of the Strong scales are
based predominantly on dislikes. For example, it is difficult if not
impossible to obtain a score showing similarity to professional artists
without indicating by one's "dislike" responses that one rejects a

large number of things artists reject. As Whitehead observed and as possibility theory stresses, the nature of one's rejections is an important factor in shaping the pattern of one's individuality.

Several important general findings have emerged from fifty years of research on the Strong scales. One is that interests are extremely stable components of individuality, changing very little in adults over long periods of time (Campbell, 1971). Another is that interest scores obtained before one enters an occupation are good predictors of whether or not one will continue in it. Strong (1952a, 1952b) demonstrated this in a twenty-year follow-up of physicians and engineers who had filled out the blank as students. Those whose interest pattern did not match the pattern characteristic of the occupation chosen had more frequently than the others shifted away from their first choice toward an occupation better matching their pattern. Campbell (1971, pp. 49–63) summarizes the results of this line of research.

There is not much evidence that interest scores are related to success in college classes or in occupations, except under special circumstances (Campbell, 1971, pp. 63–67). One of these special situations is sales occupations. Strong's (1934) classic study of life insurance salesmen showed that the great majority of men rated successful on the basis of the amount of insurance written over a three-year period had received high scores on the scale for life insurance salesmen, on which a much smaller proportion of unsuccessful men had scored high. However, this study stands almost alone, even in sales research. In general, what is being tapped by the Strong Vocational Interest Blank is a framework for important decisions, a representation of the ways in which the individual has dealt with possibilities in the past as they arose. This is a concept difficult to incorporate into the trait psychology that has dominated the study of individual differences. As successive revisions of the Strong blank have appeared, there has been a tendency to present interests more as traits or dimensions than as structures. More attention is now being given to basic interest scales, which are simply catalogues of things respondents like, without reference to what they reject. Interpretations of scores attempt to express *how much* interest of each variety is present rather than what shape the person's pattern of choices and rejections has taken on. Strong's insight that the importance of interest scores to an individual considering occupational possibilities is that they answer the questions yes, no, or perhaps has become clouded.

Interest patterns, like value patterns, are structures for processing possibilities. There is some overlap between the two concepts, but they are not identical. What may govern one person's choices, occupational or otherwise, is a value structure in which comfort and security rank very high. Another person, even one who chooses the same occupation, may be attuned to what its members like and reject and may give little or no consideration to the values the work serves. Beside values and interests, there are other kinds of structure through which possibilities may be processed, some discussed in earlier and later chapters of this book, some seldom touched on anywhere. A strategy of always doing what the people around you are doing works well for some individuals in some circumstances. Girls who accept traditional sex roles employ a strategy of doing what people expect you to do. A rigid puritanical conscience can govern a person's dealings with many of life's possibilities without the necessity of examining the values the code expresses. A devotion to a special hobby such as body building or dahlia growing can set up a possibility-processing structure.

In trying to understand how value systems and alternative kinds of structure enable the individual to select and develop a unique assortment of possibilities from among those open to the human race, one gets the feeling that psychologists have not yet hit on the most productive way to formulate the problem. By investigating one variable at a time, assuming that it is present in everybody, we constantly attempt to force individuals into molds that do not fit. We must somehow learn to think in terms of alternative structures and repertoires of action tendencies. We shall return to this problem later.

≈≈ 10 ≪≪

Styles of
Conceptualization

While Kelly and his associates were developing ideas arising from the clinic and consulting room and while the value researchers were seeking answers to questions in social psychology, psychologists in other places were exploring aspects of individuality they had encountered in laboratory experiments. The overall designation for research of this sort is *cognitive style*. The term covers a diverse assortment of characteristics having to do with the different ways people perceive and conceptualize the sights and sounds, words and meanings, with which the world confronts them. Research of this sort proceeds in a different way from the research based on mental testing. The first step is to classify people into *types* on the basis of their performance in an experiment. Groups formed in this way are then compared on a variety of other characteristics, including behavior in other experiments, mental test scores, and actions in life situations. The work of Holzman and Klein (1954) on *levelers* and *sharpeners* was one of the first examples. The experiment used to identify the two types was one in which subjects were asked to judge the size of squares presented in random order. As the experiment proceeded from one set of squares to the next, the experimenter gradually changed the assortment in the set by removing the smallest square and adding a slightly larger one. For example, if the first series to be judged consisted of squares with sides of two inches, three inches, four inches, five inches, six inches, and seven inches, the sides of the next series would range from three inches to eight inches, and by the end of the experiment the squares might range from nine inches to fourteen inches. Levelers tend not to notice these gradual shifts, basing their size estimates entirely on relative sizes. Whereas at the beginning of the experiment they may judge a six-inch square to be "large," by the end they may be judging even a ten-inch square to be "small." Sharpeners seem to approach each square as a new experience, noticing its absolute size. Holzman and Klein demonstrated that people of these two types reacted differently to other situations where senses other than vision were involved. They differed in their judgment of the loudness or softness of tones, for example, and the heaviness or lightness of weights.

Many such style differences have turned up, but only a few have been investigated for a long enough time in enough detail to contribute to our general understanding of how individuals differ. As research on such style differences continued, there was a tendency to convert the types into traits that could be measured by standard psychometric techniques. This introduced a new feature. As long as they were expressed as simple classifications of persons who reacted differently to some situation, they did not involve any judgment about how good or how poor the types were. With trait measurement, one end of the distribution became "high" and the other end "low." In this way, some of the advantages of the nonevaluative observation of differences were lost. However, by the late 1970s a movement in the opposite direction had set in. Kogan (1976), reviewing research on cognitive styles in children, distinguishes between three main types of experimental situation. The first consists of those in which perceptions are more or less veridical, so that it makes sense to consider some scores better than others. The second consists of those in which both kinds of response are equally veridical but in which the experimenter considers one to be superior to the other; for example, more advanced developmentally. The third consists of those in which there is no basis for judging one style to be superior to the other. Situations of the third sort are now receiving emphasis. We are coming to realize that we need not quantify all differences and apply standards of "better" or "worse," "higher" or "lower," to everything individuals do differently. Even if we decide to construct a quantitative scale in order to facilitate the analysis of data, we need not assume that high scores are to be preferred to low scores or vice versa. It may well be that a person scoring low on one particular scale will function better in some situations than a person scoring high.

In this chapter, we shall be concerned with the research on how individuals impose structure on stimulus materials. There is an area of overlap between this body of research findings and the personal construct research discussed in a previous chapter and with the work on information processing to be taken up in Chapter Twelve. The basic question is "How do individuals assign to categories the innumerable things with which they must deal and how do they explain their classifications?" Such research has made use of four principal varieties of task. In one, the subject is asked to sort blocks or pictures of geometric forms varying in shape and color. A second kind, used by Gardner (1964), presents the subject with an assortment of small objects or their pictures on cards—such things as kitchen utensils, toys, or tools—which the person sorts into groups, explaining the basis of each grouping. Both category breadth and qualitative differences have been studied using this procedure. The third approach, designed especially to assess category breadth, makes use of a questionnaire (Pettigrew, 1958), in which each item specifies an average value for some category, such as annual rainfall somewhere, width of windows, or length of whales, and requires the subject to select from a set of alternatives the lowest and the highest values to be expected in the category. In the fourth approach, used mainly with children, each item consists of three pictures; the child is asked to select the two that go together. The style is revealed by these pairings. For example, if one set of pictures consists of a dog, a cat, and a doghouse, the child using a *relational* style will classify the dog with the doghouse, but the child using an *inferential-categorical* style will pair the dog with the cat. In summary, some techniques assess breadth of categorization, some assess qualitative differences, and one, the object-sorting procedure, serves both purposes.

The interest in breadth of categorization illustrates the aforementioned penchant of psychologists for defining and measuring quantitative traits. There would seem to be some resemblance between the concept of category breadth and the concept of cognitive complexity that Kelly's followers tried to define, especially if category breadth is assessed by noting the number of groups a person produces in a free sorting situation and if cognitive complexity is assessed by noting how many different constructs show up in the REP test. And breadth of categorization as a variable of interest to psychologists has suffered the same decline that cognitive complexity did. It turned out not to be a simple, consistent aspect of human nature. At the beginning, theoretical hypotheses focusing on *abstraction* and *differentiation* appeared promising. Abstract thinking was considered superior to concrete thinking, and differentiation was a growth variable increasing with maturity. Gardner and Schoen (1962) administered a number of tests having to do with abstraction and differentiation to a group of seventy women and then correlated all of the scores. Almost all of the correlations turned out to be low; many were negative. Attempts to clarify the relationships through factor analysis did not shed much light. Category width, as measured by the Pettigrew questionnaire, for example, did correlate in the expected direction with the number of groups produced in the free sorting situation, but the coefficient was only $-.19$. The number of groups in the object sorting test correlated only .13 with the number of constructs on the REP test. The theoretical hypotheses about relationships between conceptual differentiation, preferred level of abstraction, and abstract thinking ability, as measured by an intelligence test, were not supported. The complexity of this apparently simple breadth variable is what most impressed the investigators.

Research based on comparisons of age groups has also brought confusion rather than clarity (Kogan, 1976, pp. 63–72). During the 1960s and early 1970s, a number of studies of school-age children seemed to indicate that categories broadened with age, and it was suggested that growth entails a shift from an emphasis on perceptual differences to the use of abstraction and synthesis (Saltz, Soller, and Sigel, 1972). But some workers reported the opposite trend (Neimark, 1974), with overgeneralization in the younger groups and increasing differentiation in the older ones. The picture became still more complicated when research was extended downward to younger and younger age groups. Overgeneralization is characteristic of three-year-olds, overly narrow categorization of eighteen-month-olds (Kogan, 1976, p. 70). In an attempt to analyze individual differences in ways three- and four-year-olds go about the task of categorizing, Block and Block (as reported in Kogan, 1976) tried out four kinds of tasks with eighty-one boys and eighty-three girls. One clear finding was that breadth of categorization was linked to inaccuracy in decisions about whether particular instances belong to specified categories. One would expect, then, that as children become more accurate their categories will narrow somewhat, and this is just what comparisons of preschoolers and primary school children have usually shown. Block and Block also found that, as in the case of older subjects, the scores obtained by different procedures correlate to only a slight extent and that there is not much stability of individual scores from year to year.

Several investigators have reported that relationships involving category breadth differ rather markedly between the two sexes. The correlations tend to be higher for girls than for boys. At the other end of the age distribution, Kogan (1973) found that older women (age 62 to 85) used significantly fewer categories than younger women did, whereas older and younger men did not differ very much. More interesting than these unexplained statistical findings is the fact reported by Block and Block that category breadth in boys and girls was related differently to personality characteristics as rated by preschool teachers. Girls inclined toward broad categorizing were likely to have unfavorable traits attributed to them, for example, "tries to stretch limits," "reacts poorly to "stress," and "is unable to delay gratification." In the case of boys, fewer personality descriptions were related in any way to the category breadth variable; the relationships there showed the same direction as those on the girls' list. It appears that preschool teachers do not find broad categorizers very likable, but aside from this conclusion few others can be drawn. Generally speaking, males produce broader, more inclusive categories than females do, and breadth is related to fewer other variables in males than in females. But the whole picture is complex and not well understood. Kogan and Wallach (1964), investigating personality characteristics involved in willingness to take risks, divided their college student subjects into groups according to whether they were above or below average in anxiety and defensiveness. Then they tried them out on a number of tasks thought to involve risk taking. It turned out that breadth, measured by the Pettigrew questionnaire, was related to the use of skill strategies in situations where one could choose to rely on either luck or skill, but *only* in the subgroup low in anxiety and high in defensiveness. The authors explained this result on the basis of differential confidence, concluding that broader categorization represents a need for certainty, but the explanation still leaves some of the findings unexplained. In another project, the same authors (Wallach and Kogan, 1965) studied creativity in grade school children and found that for girls—but not for boys—broader categorizing is related to creativity. One conclusion that can be drawn from all of the puzzling findings is that to try to measure breadth of categorization as a single trait is a mistake. Individuals do differ, but their differences are not expressed very clearly in these scores. Other research strategies are called for.

As confusion about the meaning of category breadth has increased, investigators have been shifting their attention to qualitative differences. Research is designed to differentiate between two or more types of sorting behavior, and then to find out what people belonging to these types do in situations where sorting is not involved. Some variation of the object-sorting procedure or of the "three pictures" test is used to establish the types. Sigel, Jarman, and Hanesian (1967) identified three principal styles in young children, and these have shown up again and again in people of various ages. The first is the *analytic-descriptive* approach, with objects or pictures grouped on the basis of some concrete similarity, either of the wholes or of parts. Examples are "These go together because they have stripes"; "These are big, the others are little"; and "These go together because they have heads." The second main type is the *categorical-inferential approach,* with objects or pictures grouped together because they belong to the same abstract class: "The dog and the cat are both animals" and "These are all tools that you use to make things." The third main type is the *relational-contextual,* with grouping based on the fact that the people or things are involved in some situation together. For example, one may group together a cow, a man, and a pail, explaining that the man milks the cow into the pail. One boy, faced with the task of grouping occupational titles, put together "draftsman" (misinterpreting its meaning), "postman," and "policeman," explaining: "The draftsman drafts you into the Army, the postman brings you the letter, and the policeman makes you go!" Different investigators have used different labels for the three styles, but the distinctions between them are fairly clear.

There have been attempts to arrange these qualitative differences along some sort of scale, with the categorical-inferential style considered to be most "mature" or "abstract" and the relational-contextual most "immature" or "concrete." As research continued, however, such scaling or evaluation of the merits of different styles became less and less convincing. By no means all of those who employ relational-contextual concepts are immature. Age comparisons do not show a clear progression from a lower to a higher level of conceptualization. Experiments in which people are trained to group stimuli according to a style they do not spontaneously use show that such shifts are not difficult to bring about. Grouping style seems to be a matter of preference rather than ability.

One study that was influential in changing the prevailing assumptions about the meaning of categorizing styles was that of Davis (1971). He administered Sigel's Conceptual Style Test to comparable groups of bright children in the fifth, eighth, and eleventh grades and to college freshmen, thirty at each grade level. He found that individuals were not very consistent in the ways they responded on two occasions four to six weeks apart. The reliabilities for the percentages of responses of the three types ranged from .29 for what Davis called *descriptive-global* responses in eighth-graders to .89 for *relational-contextual* responses in fifth-graders. There was no tendency for consistency to increase or decrease with age. It was clear that some items elicited more of one style of response, others more of another style. There was more difference among items than among age groups. The supposedly mature categorical-inferential style did not become more common at successive age levels, and the supposedly immature relational-contextual style did not become less common. For these samples of boys and girls, who were well above average in intelligence, about 30 percent of the responses were relational-contextual and about 45 percent categorical-inferential. Descriptive responses were less frequent at all age levels. Another finding highly significant for a psychology of individuality was that all subjects used more than one approach. The author concluded that cognitive style is not a unitary process and that it is the individual's *pattern* of responses that is distinctive.

An interesting sidelight comes from the Wallach and Kogan research program to which we have referred earlier. It was the boys whom they had classified as high in creativity who were most likely to use both of these styles in sorting. The boys who were high in intelligence but low in creativity did not use what they called the *thematic* (relational-contextual) approach, although in another task, that of writing stories using designated words, they showed that they were able to put ideas together in a relational way. This again indicates that preference rather than ability is involved in styles of categorization.

Sex differences not yet adequately explained play a part in these style preferences as well as in breadth of categorization. Sigel, Jarman, and Hanesian (1967) looked into the relationships between the personal and social characteristics of four- and five-year-olds and the three categorizing styles. The relationships were in opposite directions for the two sexes. In boys, descriptive categorizing went with emotional control, in girls with lack of emotional control. In boys, emotional control was inversely related to relational-contextual categorizing; in girls, the relationship was low and nonsignificant.

As attention has focused increasingly on the very earliest period of life, attempts have been made to find out about something analogous to categorizing behavior in infants. It is of course necessary to provide very simple stimulus objects, such as blocks, balls, and cutouts varying in size, color, and shape. Ricciuti (1965) reported some evidence that infants twelve to twenty-four months in age spontaneously form groups based on similarity in one of these attributes. Bornstein, Kessen, and Weisskopf (1976) observed some grouping on the basis of color even in infants four months old. In considering this finding, Kogan (1976) suggests that categorical perception may not have to be learned but may constitute part of one's biological endowment. There has been no attempt to analyze individual differences in children at this early age, although there has been some speculation about "perceptual" as contrasted with "functional" groupings in the two- to four-year age group (Nelson, 1973).

Developmental research on these problems has been extended in an upward as well as a downward age direction. Kogan (1974) compared college students averaging about twenty-one years of age with members of a gerontological club averaging about seventy-two years of age on object sorting and photograph sorting. There were differences, but it is not clear what they mean. The older persons used a somewhat smaller total number of categories and were somewhat more likely to use relational-contextual categories, such as grouping matches with a pipe. Do these differences represent changes in abilities or preferences, or do they represent differences in cohorts fifty years apart? More evidence is needed to untangle these strands.

One major research thrust has been to analyze the effects of training to use particular styles of categorization. As mentioned earlier, for a time psychologists considered the analytic-descriptive response to the Sigel triads to be a more mature style than the relational-conceptual. Baird and Bee (1969) attempted to increase the proportion of analytic responses given by first- and second-grade children by rewarding them with candy every time they responded in this way. The proportion of analytic responses went up. Then they attempted to produce a shift in the opposite direction, toward relational-conceptual groupings. In this they did not succeed very well. While they interpreted these results to mean that children were set to learn more mature styles, a conclusion that also fit in with their finding that shifts in the analytic direction turned out to be more lasting than those that did occur in the other direction, the findings can be accounted for in another way, namely that the reinforcement procedures were more specific for analytic than for relational responses (D. R. Denney, 1972). As we have said, it is no longer assumed that the styles can be scaled for maturity. The one conclusion that stands out from these studies is that a child can be trained to use a style different from his or her usual one.

Training experiments have been very popular during the 1970s, and they have corroborated this conclusion that children can readily be induced to think in a style they do not spontaneously employ. Sigel and Olmsted (1970) were interested in young, disadvantaged black children, the sort of population for whom programs of compensatory education are designed. They used a variant of the object-sorting task, presenting the child with twelve common objects, such as cup, ball, top, pencil, and bottle opener, and trying out two different procedures for eliciting responses. In the *active* procedure, the examiner would select one of the objects, ask the child to choose all of the others that belonged with it, and then explain the reason for the choices. Seven objects in turn were presented in this way. In the *passive* procedure, the examiner demonstrated several ways in which the objects could be grouped and asked the child to tell what the basis for each grouping was. The research was designed to permit comparison of the two testing procedures and also to compare results obtained when pictures rather than objects themselves were used as stimuli. It turned out that the children produced more responses in the active than the passive condition and produced more responses to objects than to pictures of objects. These results remind us once more that conditions that appear to be the same are not necessarily identical for persons being studied. But the main purpose of the Sigel and Olmsted experiment was to compare the effects of two training procedures. One, classification training, consisted of practice in grouping things different ways. The other, attention training, consisted of directing attention to similar aspects of objects. The results indicated that children used more different styles after training than before and that classification training was more effective than attention training. After this experience, children were able to produce more alternative responses to each question and to use more varied criteria of classification. Presumably such flexibility is an advantage to a child, in school or out.

In another sort of training experiment, D. R. Denney (1972), working with twenty-three second-grade boys, tried out the efficacy of modeling as a way of influencing categorizing behavior.

Simply observing a videotape of a model selecting two of the three objects pictured in each item of a series of triads and explaining why she chose them did affect children's behavior significantly, shifting it toward the styles the model had used and away from the styles they had used spontaneously in a pretest. In another modeling study, N. W. Denney and Acito (1974) demonstrated that children as young as two could learn to group by similarity through observing a model and that the new skill generalized to materials different from those used in the test. Clearly, these (and probably other) cognitive styles are not fixed, unalterable aspects of individuality.

Out of the work with children, a new distinction emerged that for a time dominated research activity on children's cognitive styles, namely the distinction between *reflective* and *impulsive* orientations. In the initial efforts made by Kagan, Moss, and Sigel (1963) to explore differences in response to Sigel's Conceptual Style Test (the picture triad procedure), it was hypothesized that the most important distinction would be between analytical and functional (relational) pairings, exemplified by such answers as "The zebra and the shirt belong together because they both have stripes" and "The man and the watch belong together because the man wears the watch." An interesting feature of this distinction turned up: Children who analyzed took longer to respond than children who used the relational style. This led to the classification of children as reflective or impulsive, and a search for correlates of these styles was initiated (Kagan and others, 1964). A new test, Matching Familiar Figures, was devised. Each item contained a drawing of a familiar object followed by six variants, only one of which was identical to the standard in all respects. On this test, immediate response ordinarily makes for errors. One must take time to examine the variants carefully in order to choose the right one. On the basis of a combination of time and error scores, children could be classified into four types: quick and inaccurate, slow and accurate, quick and accurate, slow and inaccurate. The majority of children fall into either the first or the second category, and can be labeled *impulsive* or *reflective*, although there are sizable minorities in the quick-accurate and the slow-inaccurate classes.

Evidence quickly accumulated that in school-age children

this style difference was reasonably stable for intervals up to two and a half years (Messer, 1976) and was reasonably consistent from one type of situation to another. It appeared that reflective children did better on intelligence tests and schoolwork than impulsive children did (Meichenbaum and Goodman, 1969; Messer, 1970). Like the cognitive styles previously discussed, this one proved to be susceptible to training, although it was easier to make impulsive children more reflective than to make reflective children more impulsive. As so often happens in psychology, however, what started as a simple distinction began to look more and more complicated as research efforts accelerated (Kogan, 1976). When studies were made of preschool children, the correlations that had been reported for school-age children did not seem to hold. Some investigations suggested that errors played a greater role than time in the differences of style. The question as to whether IQ differences lead to differences in reflectiveness or vice versa was seen as important and was not readily answered. Is this an ability distinction or a preference distinction? Could it be ability at one developmental level, preference at another? What part does anxiety play—and anxiety about what?

It seems doubtful now whether this whole body of research findings belongs under the rubric of cognitive style. It was a sideline branching off from the search for differences in the way people categorize, one that led to some intriguing and challenging findings. At this juncture, perhaps what is called for is a rethinking of the problem. Efforts to do this are being undertaken. But for the purposes of this chapter let us return to the main road and put together what the qualitative differences in spontaneous sorting and similarity grouping seem to mean in a psychology of individuality.

Perhaps the most important generalization arising from these experiments, one that may serve as a foundation for theoretical hypotheses somewhat different from those we are accustomed to, is that where experimental arrangements do not preclude it, individuals use more than one style of conceptualization. Davis (1971), in the study discussed earlier, found that less than a third of the children and adults used one style consistently. What characterizes an individual is the pattern of responses, the likelihood that different tasks and situations will be dealt with in one way rather than an-

other. Why, then, should we call these patterns of behavior *styles?*
Would not *strategies* be a better term? A long time ago, Bruner,
Goodnow, and Austin (1956) proposed that we look at differences
in the ways people think as cognitive strategies they have available
and like to use.

Confusion growing out of failure to distinguish between
competencies and preferences has marred much of the research on
cognitive style differences. As more information has been made
available about preschool children and infants, it is clear that the
use of a particular strategy may reflect both competency and preference. For example, most two-year-olds are not yet able to group on
the basis of similarity (N. W. Denney, 1972b), although some tendency to develop this capacity may be present even in the earliest
months of life. Once a child learns to put baby, bottle, and mother
together on a relational basis, this so-called style is available for the
rest of the person's life, even after learning a little later that one can
put bottle with window glass on an analytic basis or, still later, that
one can group bottle with basket and can on a categorical-influen-
tial basis. Kogan (1976, p. 114) concludes, "As research on styles
of conceptualization has progressed, their differential character has
become strikingly apparent. Indeed, it is questionable whether
modes of conceptualizing are ever abandoned in favor of presumably more advanced modes. Instead, for children as young as two
years of age, alternative modes of conceptualizing may exist side by
side in the child's cognitive repertoire."

Kogan goes on to propose that future researchers explore
the conceptual repertoires of young children:

> The time would appear to be ripe for a reorienta-
> tion of research on styles of conceptualization. Let us
> determine not only what the child prefers to do but what
> he is capable of doing. Let us depart from a rigidly uni-
> linear model in which styles more or less mature follow
> one another according to a developmental timetable.
> Instead, let us plumb the repertoires of our subjects,
> recognizing that all of the styles may be present simul-
> taneously. . . . Consistent with a multilinear model of
> development . . . let us explore the balance and pat-
> terning of styles within individuals. There may be more

to the study of cognitive styles than traditional interindividual differences. Indeed, in its original meaning, the cognitive style concept referred to the patterning of cognitive dimensions within persons. . . . This early usage has essentially been ignored in recent work, and the study of styles of conceptualization is poorer for it" [Kogan, 1976, p. 115].

If, as has been emphasized throughout this book, individuality arises from the imperatives of unlimited possibilities and limited time, then the nature of the conceptual screens the individual develops and uses to simplify experience is important to find out about. We have made only a beginning, and most of our efforts have led into blind alleys rather than open channels, but there is no question about the desirability of continuing the undertaking.

⋙ 11 ⋘

Field Dependence and Independence

There have been many exploring expeditions into the rich territory of cognitive style, but only one has been pursued continuously for more than three decades. A large and rapidly increasing body of knowledge about field dependence and independence has accumulated, knowledge that is turning out to have useful applications in schools, clinics, and other life situations. During the period that Witkin and his associates have been working to produce this knowledge, the products have been packaged under different labels, such as *articulated* versus *global,* and *differentiated* versus *undifferentiated.* But the designation Witkin used first, *field dependence* versus *field independence,* now seems to be most applicable.

As explained earlier, most cognitive styles showed up first in the course of psychological laboratory experiments. This one is no exception. Following World War II, Witkin and a number of co-workers were investigating a perceptual problem, the question of how people locate the upright in space. In other words, how do we

162

know which way is up? Common sense suggests that there are at least two kinds of cues. The first kind is visual. As we look around us, we see walls, trees, poles, and other structures perpendicular to the ground, and we align ourselves with them. The second kind of cue is kinesthetic. Gravity exerts a continuous pull on the body, and we adjust ourselves to it. In ordinary life situations, both these kinds of cues are present all the time. What Witkin and his colleagues did was to separate and vary the cues and to measure the deviations from the upright under these different conditions. In one of these experiments, the subject sat in a tilted chair in a tilted room. The instructions were to manipulate the controls in ways that would bring the body into an upright position, regardless of the angles at which room and chair were tilted. In another experiment, the subject was brought into a completely lightproof room where the only thing visible was a luminous frame within which was a luminous rod. Both frame and rod could be tilted in the same or opposite directions. The subject's task was to adjust the rod to a true upright position, whatever the tilt of the frame.

What stood out most clearly in the results of these experiments were the striking individual differences. Some subjects always aligned themselves with the walls of the tilted room or with the tilted frame, even when this meant that they or the rod deviated as much as thirty degrees from the true upright. Others ignored the visual information and reacted accurately to their inner muscular sensations. Further experiments made it clear that this was not just an "eye versus muscle" distinction. Persons who could not free themselves from the visual stimulation, which in this case was irrelevant, were also unable to free themselves from other irrelevancies. This fact showed up most clearly in their performance on the Embedded Figures Test, in which all the stimulation is visual and no kinesthetic component is involved. The subject is first shown a simple figure, such as a triangle or cube. Then he or she is shown a complex figure and asked to locate the simple figure within it. By and large, the same people who had been good at adjusting chair or frame to a true upright position, ignoring slanted surroundings, were also good at pointing out the simple figure, ignoring distracting lines, shapes, and colors. Correlations between scores made in all three test situations were moderately high, and supplementary studies showed that the differences held for senses other than vision and kinesthesis. Field-independent persons, for example, could identify a simple tune embedded in a complex pattern of sounds or, with eyes closed, identify the raised contours of a simple figure embedded in a complex one. What all these tasks seemed to have in common was a strategy of *analyzing* or breaking up a complex stimulus into its components, as contrasted with reacting to the stimulating situation as a whole.

The outcome of these experiments was a new typology classifying people as *field dependent* or *field independent*. This is not, however, what the quantitative results of the experiments require. What they show in any group tested is a continuous distribution of scores, from very low to very high. Individuals tend to react in one way or the other, but most of them score somewhere between the extremes. But the directional tendencies, extreme or not, are consistent. Correlational studies indicate that a person tends to score at approximately the same level in the different perceptual tests and also in tests of thinking and problem solving where analysis and restructuring are required. Individuals also maintain approximately the same relative levels from early childhood to maturity (Witkin, Goodenough, and Karp, 1967).

Like the style differences discussed in previous chapters, these differences identified by Witkin and his coworkers were for a time assimilated to the prevailing psychometric concepts and viewed as traits or dimensions. It is hard for psychologists brought up in this tradition not to attach different degrees of desirability or undesirability to scores at different levels. At the beginning, Witkin avoided this, simply observing that the field-dependent persons in the tilting room-tilting chair situation were meeting the challenge in one way, the field independent in another. But as time passed, the emphasis changed, and *psychological differentiation* came to be viewed as a kind of ability somewhat like intelligence. The more a person had of it, the better. The relatively undifferentiated were seen as handicapped to some extent in comparison with the differentiated. In the 1970s, the pendulum has swung back toward the assumption that there are two equally valuable styles, each with advantages and disadvantages. Psychological differentiation as measured is, of course, a kind of ability; some persons actually are not able, no matter how hard they try, to locate the simple figure in the complex one or to move the rod to an upright position. But it now seems quite possible that on some other test the "global" kinds of thinkers might do better than those who score high on the differentiation tests. We shall look at some of the research suggesting this a little later. The point here is simply that we are beginning to break free of the shackles that ability measurement imposed on us and look at individual differences without imposing value judgments.

Attempts to pin down just what the characteristic is that is measured by the techniques described have proceeded in several directions. There have been experiments on learning and problem solving, correlational studies relating differentiation scores to scores on a wide variety of ability and personality tests, developmental investigations, and clinical observations and case studies. Hypotheses were set up on the basis of initial findings and then constantly revised as new results were reported. Often a finding that psychological differentiation was not related to something it had been expected to relate to proved to be as important a piece in the puzzle as a positive finding was. It was clear almost from the beginning that cognitive style was not a matter of intellect alone; it had to do with feeling and motivation as well.

Persons showing a high degree of field independence were somewhat more likely to be male than female. They scored somewhat higher on intelligence than the more global people did, but a closer look at this relationship made apparent that it was not based on all types of intelligence test material but mainly on items requiring that details be differentiated from context, as in Block Design and Picture Completion tests (Witkin and others, 1962). Field-independent people had clearer, better articulated self-concepts. A supplementary test was developed for research on this relationship. It is a figure-drawing test, scored for "differentiation of body concept" (Faterson and Witkin, 1970). Field-independent persons were more active, more autonomous, more self-motivated. They were better at problem solving when the solution required that some critical element be taken out of its context and the situation mentally restructured (Witkin and others, 1962). On the kinds of problem represented in most school assignments, it apparently makes no difference whether one is field dependent or field independent (Witken and others, 1977a).

Comparisons of field-dependent and field-independent persons in a variety of learning experiments revealed some interesting distinctions (Goodenough, 1976). There is no consistent difference in how much they learn. It is the way in which they learn things that differentiates. When the experiment had to do with the attainment of concepts, a task in which concrete examples of some abstract concept are presented one after another until the subject sees what the concept is, field-dependent persons reacted immediately to the salient cues, whereas field-independent persons analyzed both major and minor features of the examples, searching for cues that might be relevant. In several kinds of learning experiment, field-dependent persons were more likely to adopt what has been called a "spectator" role, looking passively at each stimulus, whereas field-independent persons adopted a "participant" role, forming hypotheses to be retained or discarded as the experiment proceeded. This "active versus passive" distinction runs through much of the research over the years.

Research in another, quite different direction has shown that the field dependent differ from the field independent in the kinds of symptoms they develop if they become neurotic or psychotic and in the kinds of therapy that help them (Witkin, 1965). Lewis (1971) brought together the evidence with regard to these differences and proposed a theoretical framework to account for them. The basic distinction is between guilt and shame. Field-independent people are more susceptible to guilt, as a result of their separation of self from nonself and their tendency to analyze. The field dependent are more susceptible to shame, which is a more diffuse, ambiguous, socially oriented, feeling. Guilt-driven field-independent patients are more likely to develop such defense mechanisms as compulsive behavior and paranoid thinking. Shame-motivated field-dependent patients are more likely to develop defense mechanisms such as repression or denial of whole areas of experience.

Other parts of the picture delineating the two styles were filled in by research on dreaming (Witkin, 1970; Goodenough and others, 1974). The finding that stands out most clearly here is that field-independent persons are more likely to recall and report dreams, especially under conditions that are less than optimal for remembering them. In a laboratory study, subjects were awakened abruptly after a period in which the apparatus indicated that REM (rapid eye movement) sleep had been in progress. (Much previous research has established that it is during such REM periods that dreaming occurs.) Under these circumstances, both kinds of subjects remembered what they had dreamed. But if the awakening process was gradual rather than abrupt, field-independent subjects were much better at reporting their dreams than field-dependent subjects were. They were also better at recalling them the next morning. This finding fits in with the psychiatric evidence that repression plays a more prominent role in the personalities of the field dependent than of the field independent.

While it was being assumed that psychological differentiation is a trait, it was tacitly assumed that the more field independence a person showed the better. In the years since 1970, the advantages of field dependence have come in for a more searching scrutiny (Witkin and Goodenough, 1977). These advantages are of a social kind. The distinction is between an *interpersonal* and an *impersonal* approach to life. It turns out that field-dependent persons are more sensitive to many aspects of social situations than field-independent persons are. They are more likely to change their attitudes and opinions in accordance with the views of people around them, but only in situations marked by some ambiguity. They like to be with people. They even move physically closer to others in communicating with them than do field-independent people. Field-dependent people tend to be better liked than those of the opposite type and tend to demonstrate greater skill in getting along with people.

The new appreciation of the assets of the field dependent has been expressed in learning experiments that could have important implications for the schools. One would expect that field-dependent children would be more susceptible to social reinforcements than children of the other type. This turns out to be true for negative reinforcement (punishment or criticism) but not for positive reinforcements (praise or approval) (Goodenough, 1976). Praise or material rewards affect both types of children equally, but criticism has a more potent effect on the field dependent. Field-dependent persons are better at remembering the faces and names of persons they have actually met but not at memorizing photographs of complete strangers. It seems that they automatically pay more attention to social aspects of situations and thus remember them better than field-independent people do.

This leads to a generalization that is important in the light of our general purpose, to understand how individuals deal with possibilities. Field-dependent and field-independent persons differ in *direction of attention*. Thus they become aware of different possibilities. One sort of research that demonstrates this has to do with choices which persons of the two types make. Witkin and others (1977a) summarize a number of studies of choices. The field dependent are likely to choose courses and majors with a "people" emphasis in the social sciences and humanities, whereas the field independent are more likely to choose impersonal fields, such as the physical sciences. The difference appears in scores on interest inventories and in career choices as well as in course selection. Also, within any one major or occupation people channel themselves into different branches on this basis. For example, clinical psychologists tend to be field dependent, and experimental psychologists tend to be field independent. Psychiatric nurses tend to be field dependent, surgical nurses field independent. Furthermore, when college students change their majors, the shifts are likely to be in keeping with cognitive styles. In a longitudinal study of an entire entering class (Witkin and others, 1977b), the investigators looked not only at initial choices but at shifts that occurred later. They found that the final major or specialty chosen for graduate or professional study was a better fit for the individual's cognitive style than was the initial choice. For example, students who initially enter a mathematics-science program or a related preprofessional program and continue in it to graduation are significantly more field independent than students who shift to another major. It seems that students who begin with choices incompatible with their cognitive styles revise their plans when they sense that they are in the wrong place. There was some evidence that students are more successful in fields suiting their cognitive styles, although for the group as a whole, grade-point average was unrelated to field-dependence scores.

A considerable amount of effort has gone into the exploration of the sources of the differences between field-dependent and field-independent people. One question is "How early in development do the styles appear?" Another is "What aspects of children's environments are related to the differences?" There is now some fairly satisfactory evidence that preschool children four and five years old have already begun to develop in one direction or the other (Kogan, 1976). The picture is complicated by the fact that the direction of growth is toward increasing differentiation. All children become more differentiated as they grow older, but individual differences persist. Another complication is that the developmental picture is different for boys and girls. At most ages where a sex difference shows up, boys are more differentiated, less field dependent than girls. The puzzling fact is that at the preschool level it is the girls who are most differentiated. The direction of the difference reverses between five and six. Furthermore, the cluster of characteristics related to the field dependence-independence distinction emerges in a coherent form about a year earlier for girls than for boys. Is this a matter of the greater all-around maturity of girls at this stage? We do not know.

Like other psychological characteristics, field dependence or independence develops through the interaction of initial tendencies and experience. So far there has been little investigation of a possible genetic basis for the initial tendency, but the idea has not been ruled out. Perhaps the current interest in research on infancy will eventually lead to an understanding of what aspects of behavior during the first few months enter into the complex interactions through which this and other cognitive styles take shape. We already know a good deal about the development of differences in field dependence at later stages of childhood. Early in the Witkin research program (Witkin and others, 1962), there was a careful scrutiny of differences between mothers of the two types of children in personality and styles of child rearing. On the basis of interviews planned with great care, mothers were classified as IID (interaction-inhibiting differentiation) or IFD (interaction-facilitating differentiation). There turned out to be fairly high correlation between the classification of mothers and the scores made by children on the tests of psychological differentiation (point biserial coefficients of .85, .82, and .65 in the three groups studied). It appeared that the research hypotheses which had entered into the design of the interview procedure were sound.

What were these differences that the investigators expected to find and did find? The personality characteristics characterizing the IFD mothers were self-assurance and self-realization. They were more confident than the IID group about their own ability as mothers, less inclined to worry or blame themselves for mistakes. Self-realization was apparent in their varied interests and activities outside the home. Mothers in the IID group were more given to complaints about their husbands and children, were often shy or overly reserved, and showed conformist attitudes in their social relations. The ways in which the two kinds of women interacted with their children differed even more. Mothers fostering differentiation set definite standards, expressed approval easily, and encouraged children to take responsibility, be independent, and explore. Mothers inhibiting differentiation expressed dissatisfaction with children's intellectual development, appearance, and behavior. They stressed obedience and compliance. Some of them were overly severe, some overly indulgent in their attempts to control their children. Either extreme seems to hamper the development of independence.

Since this 1962 report there have been several other studies of the socialization processes involved in the two orientations (Dyk and Witkin, 1965; Dyk, 1969; Witkin, 1969). Although there is still much to be learned about it, in general it can be said that field independence is linked to the encouragement of separation from the mother and to the imparting of standards for internal control of impulses and decisions. Much of the developmental research was carried on while it was still being tacitly assumed that the field-independent end was the "good" end of the distribution. The considerable social advantages of the more global style had not yet come in for much attention. Some of the assumed disadvantages of field dependence have now been shown not to occur. Field-dependent children are not any more likely to be emotionally overdependent than field-independent children are (Witkin and Goodenough,

1977). Field-dependent adults are strongly influenced by other persons to change their opinions only in ambiguous situations where other persons are seen as likely sources of information. The differences between the two styles are more complex and less obvious than they were at first assumed to be.

Another way of finding out about the sources of field-dependent and field-independent orientations has involved cross-cultural comparisons (Witkin and Berry, 1975; Berry, 1976). Research has been carried out on a number of cultural groups in different parts of the world, including Canadian Indians, Eskimos, African tribes from Sierra Leone, Nigeria, and Zambia, West Indians, Mexicans, and Norwegians. Holtzman and others (1975) started with comparable groups of Mexican and American children and retested them over a six-year period. Witkin and others (1974) compared pairs of villages in Holland, Mexico, and Italy, where one village in the pair was high in the emphasis placed on conformity, the other low. Within each group, the same relationships of test scores to each other and to personality variables that had been demonstrated in the United States seemed to hold, with a few minor exceptions. Differences between families in attitudes and child-rearing practices seemed to affect the development of the two contrasted cognitive styles in the same way.

But the average levels of field independence differ considerably from one culture to another. Scrutiny of these differences has led to several generalizations. Hunting societies such as the Eskimos tend to produce field-independent people; agricultural societies such as the Temne in Africa tend to produce field-dependent people. Societies with a "tight" social structure, meaning that they have many different roles and an elaborate structural organization, tend to produce field-dependent people. Societies with a "loose" social structure, meaning that they have few different roles and not much organization, tend to produce field-independent people. Possibly biological factors enter in. Societies of field-independent people eat more proteins, and their ratio of androgens to estrogens is higher than it is in societies of the opposite type. But the most important factor is the prevailing socialization practices, the emphasis on obedience and on the control of aggression versus emphasis on training for self-reliance and independence. Holtzman's (Holtzman and others, 1975) comparison of Mexican and American children illustrates this distinction. Mexican children are less field independent than their American counterparts. The mothers in the two countries differ in many respects. Mexican mothers are more authoritative and exercise stricter control over their children. They value obedience more, independence less. They give the children less responsibility in the home. Although most of the comparisons involved mothers, some differences in the fathers were also reported. The cross-cultural research has supplemented the developmental research in a very important way in showing what kinds of influences affect the development of the two cognitive styles.

One major thrust of the research program on field dependence and independence, especially in recent years, has been to explore ways in which knowledge about the styles can help in solving practical problems. The two fields in which the relevance of the style distinction has been most clearly demonstrated are psychotherapy and education. In psychotherapy, style differences are apparent in the behavior of therapists, the behavior of clients, and the interaction between them (Witkin, Lewis, and Weil, 1968). Field-independent therapists interact more with their clients than do field-dependent therapists. Field-independent clients express more hostility and less diffuse anxiety than do field-dependent clients. When therapists and clients are matched for cognitive style, they rate one another more positively than when they are mismatched. This positive effect of congruent cognitive styles shows up very quickly, even before the first hour ends (Oltman and others, 1975).

Application to classroom learning and teaching are being discussed with increasing frequency (Witkin, 1976; Witkin and others, 1977a). Field-independent and field-dependent teachers differ in several ways. Besides the differences in choice of specialty area, mentioned before, they differ also in teaching strategies. Field-dependent teachers prefer discussions to lecture or discovery methods, in contrast with field-independent teachers. Various other differences in what teachers prefer and how they handle simulated teaching situations have turned up, but so far there has been little observation of actual classroom situations. It is important to note that there is no evidence that either style makes for more all-around competence.

Students and teachers both differ in *how* they find it most natural to learn and teach, not in *how much* they learn and teach.

It is not clear, however, that teachers and students should be matched for cognitive style. In education, as in therapy, teachers and students like one another better and describe each other in more positive terms if they are similar. Similarity makes for mutual attraction. They also communicate more easily than mismatched groups do. But as Witkin and the discussants of his paper (Witkin, 1976) have pointed out, this does not mean that students will learn more from persons who are like them. Much more research on the effects of different combinations in different subject matter areas will be required to find out how the interactions of style affect the learning process.

The place of field dependence-independence in an overall psychology of individuality is somewhat ambiguous. The findings we have been considering do not exactly fit into the framework set up in previous chapters. On the one hand, what is measured is an ability, and an individual's score shows how much he or she has of this ability. Like other abilities, psychological differentiation increases with age, up to about seventeen, when it levels off (Witkin, Goodenough, and Karp, 1967). But in other respects what is measured does not fit the ability model. The trait is bipolar. There are advantages and disadvantages for persons at either end of the distribution: proficiency in analytic problem solving for the field independent, proficiency in social interactions for the field dependent. Furthermore, the differences transcend cognition, as most ability differences do not, extending to preferences, choices, needs, defenses, and many other characteristics that are identifiable but not measurable. Witkin and Goodenough (1976) have been attempting to remodel the theory (or theories) that have dominated their research program at successive states. The proposed new theory orders the concepts that have emerged from different lines of research into a hierarchy, with the broadest concept, differentiation, at the top, and the others arranged in a branching structure below it. The main branch, from which have grown most of the subbranches we have been considering in detail, the authors now propose to call *self-nonself segregation*. The distinction rests on whether a person relies mainly on internal or mainly on external referents in his or her dealings with the world. (Is this the perennial introversion-extra-version classification in a new form?) Two principal subbranches accommodate most of the research findings. One has to do with autonomy in interpersonal relations, the other with restructuring. People we have been referring to as field independent seek auton-omy and engage in restructuring, in contrast with the field depen-dent. Witkin and Goodenough (1976) emphasize once more that neither style is "better" or "higher" than the other. Each is good for different purposes, different situations.

One important new concept introduced by Witkin and Goodenough (1976) is that of *mobility*. It seems possible that indi-viduals who have developed the characteristics of one style might train themselves in some of the skills characteristic of the other. For example, persons good at restructuring but obtuse about social situations can and do sometimes become more sensitive to the feel-ings of others. It may be more difficult for the person with limited restructuring to acquire the field-independent orientation, but even this is not impossible. Witkin and Goodenough are speculating that whichever their basic orientation, some persons may be more "mo-bile" than others. A mobile person who could shift from one style to the other would have some real advantages. Thus the achievement of mobility might constitute an objective for training in the cogni-tive style domain.

Several cognitive styles that we are not considering in detail in this or the previous chapter have been identified. Some have stimulated considerable research, others very little. They have grown out of different theoretical systems. It is not certain that they in any way belong together under the general label of *cognitive style*. But their potential importance in education, child rearing, occupational choice, and other areas of human concern makes them of some in-terest to psychologists. Eventually, the style approach to individual differences could make the present focus on abilities obsolete. We have mentioned the *leveling-sharpening* distinction, having to do with the way in which experience is assimilated to memory. Levelers tend to blur similar memories and not to distinguish between events that are similar but not identical. Sharpeners make sharp, even exaggerated distinctions, thereby heightening contrasts between past and present. The category of *scanning* has to do with the way in which attention is distributed, whether with a broad beam and a wide span of awareness or a narrow beam focused on a particular area. The dimension of *risk taking versus caution* has to do with whether one takes chances or avoids risky situations. The category *tolerance for unrealistic experience* refers to perceptual differences between persons prone to see movement when looking at stationary flashing lights and those who resist such appearances. The dimension of *constricted versus flexible control* refers to differential susceptibilities to distraction and interference. Preliminary research on personality components of all these styles has been carried out, but not enough to warrant general conclusions. Descriptions of these and several other proposed styles can be found in Messick (1976).

What the research on cognitive style has contributed to a psychology of individuality based primarily on ability and personality trait measurement can perhaps be summed up by a camera analogy. Cameras come at all levels of complexity, just as individuals come at all levels of intelligence. An expensive model differs from a cheap model both in versatility and in the quality of the pictures produced. But each camera must be *set* for distance, for light value, and for type of film in order to take a picture. Ability differences correspond to differences in the equipment cameras consist of. Cognitive styles correspond to the settings. Each of us is preset for maximum efficiency in some kinds of circumstances. Each of us registers some but not all of the countless possibilities around us.

≫≫ 12 ≪≪

Information Processing
in Individuals

During the years since World
War II, we have greatly expanded our understanding of how an
individual shapes and reshapes the system that controls his or her
interchange with the world of energies, objects, and people. What
has enabled psychologists to move ahead rapidly in solving problems far older than the science of psychology itself was the theory
and technology of information processing that accompanied the
introduction of electronic computers. One no longer needed to
abjure everything except observable behavior to be considered
scientific. Almost overnight it became respectable to talk about inner
experience, consciousness, imagery, and intentions. The concept of
"input" at least partially dislodged the concept of "stimulus" from
its preeminent position, with the concept of "output" replacing
"response." But the more significant effect of the adoption of the
computer analogy was that it reawakened interest in the study of
the process between input and output and led to research on aspects
of human experience which had been neglected during the period of

behaviorist domination. One effect of this rethinking has been a merging of concepts that psychology and philosophy had been keeping in separate compartments: sensation, perception, attention, concept formation, memory, language, imagery, and problem solving. As information moves through the system, different subsystems are involved in processing it. It appeared more profitable to study these subsystems than to confine one's research activity within the boundaries established in earlier times—boundaries, for example, between percepts and concepts or between concept formation and memory. The general term *cognitive psychology* includes all the psychological processes people use in processing information.

Early psychologists had studied these cognitive processes by introspective techniques. Present-day psychologists rely mainly on a family of techniques aptly labeled *mental chronometry* (Posner and Rogers, 1977). Time-honored experimental procedures in which the subjects press a key in response to a signal, memorize digits or words, or discriminate between briefly exposed shapes or colors are varied in ways that permit the experimenter to time the successive stages of the action. In an experiment on memorizing random sequences of digits, for example, variations can be introduced in the presentation time, the time between presentation and testing, the amount and kind of interpolated activity, and the instructions given to subjects. This has enabled researchers to hypothesize several successive "stores" in which information is deposited while it is being memorized (Loftus and Loftus, 1976). Using experiments on reaction time to study attention, the experimenter varies the complexity and timing of the signals the subject is to attend to, the nature of the response to be made, and many other features of the situation. Using such methods, Posner and Boies (1971) were able to separate out three components of attention that could be studied separately: alertness, selectivity, and processing capacity. Other researchers have investigated the attainment of concepts, the solving of problems, or the learning of skills. Whichever prototype experiment one starts with, the ingenuity of the experimenter shows up in the ways of varying the procedure to reveal the sequential components of a complex process and the ways in which they are linked to one another. Cognitive psychology as a whole has not had much to say about individuality. Like most psychologists, those interested in information processing usually focus on the general nature of the phenomena. But individual differences do turn up, and some theorists are now attempting to analyze and account for them.

We shall base our discussion primarily on the memory research, bringing in findings from other areas where they are appropriate. The models memory researchers are using have a maplike quality, in that they postulate successive places in which different processes occur. Initial input is to a preconscious *sensory store,* where a large amount of information is retained for a very brief time. Most of it decays or disappears within one second and never gets into the rest of the system. The second division is a *short-term store,* in which limited amounts of information can be held for about fifteen seconds to be "worked on." (Some separate this stage into two parts, making a distinction between *short-term* and *intermediate-term* store.) The third division is a *long-term store,* in which practically unlimited quantities of coded or organized information can be retained indefinitely and retrieved as needed. The ideas considered in the last several chapters all have to do with the contents of individuals' long-term stores.

The central problem for research on memory is the same as the general problem that concerns us throughout this book: "How are a limited number of actualities constructed from an almost unlimited number of possibilities?" The process involves both selection and organization. Sperling (1960), in an experiment that has become a classic, first demonstrated that the amount of information initially entering the system is much larger than the amount processed and retained. In this ingenious experiment, subjects were presented for a very brief time, fifty thousandths of a second, with an array of twelve letters arranged in a three-by-four table. When asked immediately to report all the letters they could remember, they could usually name only four or five, but many of them thought that they had initially known more than this and had forgotten them while they were writing the first few. To check on this impression, Sperling tried a procedure in which, at a signal given by a high, medium, or low tone, the subject would report only the top, middle, or bottom row of the table. He reasoned that a person who could report three out of four letters in whichever row was signaled, not knowing in advance which row it would be, must have seen and recognized at least nine of the twelve letters. In subsequent experiments, Sperling found that the more letters he presented initially, the more subjects could report. He also found that delaying the signal tone by even a fraction of a second drastically reduced the number of letters subjects were able to report, indicating that the initial impression lasts only a very short time. Under ordinary circumstances, people are not aware of this initial information, just as under ordinary circumstances they are not aware of all the other possibilities available to them.

The processes occurring in the part of the system labeled *short-term store* exemplify two principles we encounter wherever possibilities are being transformed into actualities: that it is an active, not a passive process and that it combines selection with organization. In a much-quoted article, Miller (1956) showed that the number of items which can be retained in immediate memory is seven, plus or minus two. Intelligence testers, who had been using digit span tests for many years, were already familiar with this limit. Anyone who could repeat nine digits immediately after hearing them, in one trial out of three, scored at the highest level, Superior Adult III, in the Stanford-Binet scale, Form L. What Miller added was the concept of *chunking*. If one combines several digits into a meaningful unit, such as 1492, 248, or 111213, or combines several letters into a word, one can remember seven, plus or minus two, of the composites. It is seven items of some sort that constitute the limit, and the items can be of any size, even sentences, lines of a poem, or long, ordered series of numbers. Thus we see that one kind of activity occurring in the short-term store is *recoding* of information into larger chunks. This is accompanied by a process of *rehearsal*, by means of which information is kept resonating while it is worked on. Rehearsal serves also to transfer some of the information to appropriate locations in the long-term store. Theorists who postulate an *intermediate-term* store think of this as the part of the system where the interaction between short-term and long-term memory occurs (Bower, 1975).

Long-term memory contains a variety of kinds of information. Bower (1975, p. 56) lists five, with the suggestion that there may well be others. These are

1. Our spatial model of the world surrounding us, symbol structures corresponding to images of our house, city, country, and planet, with information about where significant objects are located on this cognitive map.
2. Our knowledge of physical laws, cosmology, the properties of objects and things.
3. Our beliefs about people, about ourselves, about how to behave in various social situations; our values and the social goals that we seek.
4. Our motor skills for driving, bicycling, playing pool, and the like; our problem-solving skills for various domains; and our plans for achieving various things.
5. Our perceptual skills in understanding language or interpreting paintings or music.

Where, in this whole complex system, can differences between individuals be found? Even the most superficial scrutiny suggests several ways in which each individual would be unique. There are two main varieties of individual differences, analogous to the *hardware* and *software* that characterize computers. We might look for differences in the size, shape, and sensitivity of the components and also in the control processes or strategies used at successive stages. Hunt and Lansman (1975) and Hunt (1976) have found evidence for both sorts of differences between individuals. There are differences, for example, in how long the initial coding process takes through which transitory information is admitted to short-term memory. Hunt, Lunneborg, and Lewis (1975), reporting these time differences, noted also that university students in the top quarter of the intelligence distribution averaged about 35 percent faster than students in the bottom quarter. Hunt suggests that even at the preconscious level there may be differences in the attentional processes by means of which some information is systematically picked up, some ignored and allowed to decay. Some of the evidence here comes from experiments in which different information is presented to the two ears. Kahneman, Ben-Ishai, and Lotan (1973) showed that commercial truck drivers who were good at switching attention from one ear to the other had better safety records than those not so adept at switching attention. (The correlation was only .37, but the relationship is interesting.)

The investigation of these subtle attentional control processes that operate even in the early preconscious stage of the sequence may turn out to have some theoretical and practical value, but what goes on at the next stage is probably of greater significance. There is at least scattered evidence for substantial individual differences in the retention, integration, and transformation of information in short-term memory. As would be expected from the fact that digit span tests and other tests of immediate memory have been included in intelligence scales ever since Binet's time, the overall efficiency of short-term memory is related to what we call *intelligence*. What the more precise and sophisticated new techniques add to the established testing techniques is a breakdown of the overall index into separate parts. The main difference between persons with high and low memory span seems to be with regard to the kind of *chunking* used. This is illustrated very clearly in the study Hunt and Love (1972) made of the mnemonist V. P., who over two sittings improved his digit span from eight to twenty-five numbers by chunking groups of digits into units and then remembering the units. This is an active process, and most people find it difficult to learn, according to Hunt's report. It is also highly idiosyncratic. Probably no two persons, even when they are equally successful memorizers, construct exactly the same chunks. Speed of information processing may be a factor in efficient chunking in experiments or tests, since time limits are usually imposed for the task. The results which Hunt and his coworkers have obtained, however, indicate that the correlations between verbal intelligence and the speed measures obtained from memory experiments are quite low, so it seems unlikely that speed is the most important factor involved.

Another approach to the analysis of individual differences in short-term memory is to look at the ways in which persons classified as mentally retarded handle the task of memorizing new material. In a research program carried out by Brown and associates (Brown and others, 1973; Brown, Campione, and Murphy, 1974), mental retardates were compared with normals in paired-associates experiments on memory. The task is a simple one. Stimuli are presented to the subject in pairs. Later, when the first stimulus of the

pair is presented, the subject is supposed to remember what the
second one was. The comparison showed that what the retardates
did not do was to *rehearse* mentally between trials. The major differences between retardates and normals seemed to be in strategy
rather than equipment, in software rather than hardware.

The importance of strategies for memorizing, especially rehearsal strategies, has been brought out in a number of developmental studies comparing children of different ages. A symposium
published in *Human Development* in 1971 considered research on this
problem in some detail. Belmont and Butterfield (1971) asked nine-
year-olds, thirteen-year-olds, adults, and retarded children to memorize lists of serially presented letters, comparing experimental conditions in which the subject controlled the timing of the presentations
with conditions of forced rehearsal. The results showed the development of rehearsal strategies from age to age. These were such things
as pausing for rehearsal after the third and sixth letters and not rehearsing final letters because they were easy to remember anyway.
Under the forced rehearsal conditions, all the groups became more
alike. Individual differences were not analyzed in these experiments,
but they must have been substantial. For example, only 50 percent of
the adults used the "nonrehearsal of final letters" strategy. Haith
(1971) commented on another interesting difference between the
strategies of five-year-olds and those of adults. Using the briefly presented geometrical forms as stimuli, it was found that adults remembered more when four were presented at once than when only two
were presented at once. Not so for five-year-olds. Their average was
never more than 1.6 forms remembered, regardless of the number they
had been shown. Check experiments indicated that the adults must
have used encoding and rehearsal strategies which the five-year-
olds had not yet hit on. Sometimes different strategies are in conflict. Hagen (1971) summarized several studies of rehearsing and
labeling, another technique often useful in memorizing. Results suggested that the attempt to label stimuli as they are presented inter-
fered with the active rehearsal which facilitates recall, especially
from the age of ten on. Hagen concluded that what we call *short-
term memory* may involve two stages: the very short-term process
that is facilitated by labeling the stimuli to be remembered, the first
to be mastered by very young children, and the somewhat later em-

ployment of more active strategies to facilitate remembering things for a longer time. As children grow, they are learning at two levels, acquiring new skills, not necessarily conscious or intentional, and at the same time are coming to realize that they are *actors* who can determine how they will use the skills they have acquired. There is evidence that useful strategies can be taught to young and retarded children but that they do not necessarily employ them outside the experimental situation.

Meacham (1972) reviewed American and Soviet developmental research on memory suggesting that what we have been calling *memory* is really an epiphenomenon, a blanket term covering various cognitive activities, such as organizing, labeling, rehearsing, and elaborating visually and verbally. Soviet psychologists have been interested in the relationship between voluntary and involuntary aspects of memory. Subjects *choose* to engage in the most appropriate cognitive activities, and this choice is related to (1) instructions, (2) material, (3) knowledge of available activities, (4) compatibility and competition in mnemonic activities, and (5) sociohistorical milieu.

Developmental research at the other end of the age range has also contributed to our understanding of where differences between persons are most likely to occur in this complex sequence of occurrences we are calling *information processing*. Denney and Denney (1973) based their conclusions on comparisons of groups of older and younger adults. The mean age of the older group was eighty-two, the mean of the younger group thirty-eight. The experimental task was a variety of the Twenty Questions game. Older subjects asked fewer constraint-seeking questions and more redundant questions than younger subjects did, so that they required thirty-two questions, on the average, to solve the problem which younger subjects solved with eighteen. The conclusion was that age brings a decline in the ability to direct intellectual processes in accordance with hypotheses derived from perception of relationships. Here, as in the work with children, it is activities, strategies, and control processes, rather than capacities or speeds, that constitute the major differences between people. Waugh and others (1973) came to a similar conclusion in analyzing comparisons between adults of different ages on a two-choice reaction time experiment.

The difficulty older groups have with the task lies in the initiation of the response of choosing rather than in the rapidity of the response itself, once it gets started.

The last word on the question of where individual differences lie has not been said. Although most of the research evidence supports a conclusion that the most significant differentiators are strategies or control processes rather than the size, shape, or sensitivity of mental components, there is some evidence that does not point in this direction. Huttenlocher and Burke (1976) reported differences in digit span between four-year-olds, seven-year-olds, nine-year-olds, and eleven-year-olds that could not be accounted for on the basis of rehearsal or self-imposed strategies. Similarly, Lyons (1975), using adult subjects, found that individual differences in digit span found under normal conditions of presentation persisted under drastically changed conditions, such as speeding up the rate of presentation so greatly as to make rehearsal and other usual strategies unusable. High subjects remained high, low subjects low, under all conditions, suggesting that some sort of general ability may be involved. This is, of course, what intelligence testers have been assuming. Perhaps the soundest conclusion which can be drawn at present is that both quantitative differences in capacity for memorizing and qualitative differences in the strategies used are present.

Problems having to do with the part that intentions play in information processing are being extensively and intensively investigated by Posner and his associates (Posner and Snyder, 1974). Their general focus is on *attention,* and the experimental technique most frequently used is the measurement of reaction time. Accurate measurements are made of separate parts of the subject's performance. One task used is the Stroop color word test. The subject looks at a card on which color words have been printed in ink of various colors. For example, he may see the word *red* printed in blue ink or the word *yellow* printed in green. The conflict between tendencies to respond to the sense of the word and the sight of the color itself allows the experimenter to analyze the facilitating and interfering effects that occur under various conditions. Posner and his coworkers have found that attention involves two components in addition to general alertness, one automatic and unconscious, the other under conscious control. These two processes differ in one important respect. In the automatic, unconscious channel, information builds up steadily, without interference from other mental activity that may be going on at the same time. The conscious control channel is limited in its capacity, and thus its commitment to any one operation reduces its availability for any other operation. Many puzzling phenomena can be explained by postulating these two kinds of cognitive process that occur almost simultaneously.

Broadbent (1977) has synthesized the results of a great many investigations, his own and those of other people, on what he calls "hidden preattentive processes." He distinguishes between two kinds of process. The first, *filtering,* means segregating a collection of stimuli into regions, one of which can then be selected for detailed attention. The second, *pigeonholing,* involves the classification of multiple stimuli into coherent sets on the basis of some aspect of meaning. In experiments, filtering is demonstrated by a person's response speeds and pattern of errors when asked after a very brief presentation of twelve words to report which one was in capital rather than lowercase letters. Pigeonholing shows up when subjects are asked to report which of the twelve words was the name of an animal. The second task requires more information processing than the first. When subjects pigeonhole they seem to alternate between a passive, global phase and an active search or inquiry. In Broadbent's words, "There is an early and relatively passive stage in which evidence arrives from the senses and suggests certain possible interpretations of the situation" (1977, p. 115). What makes this line of research particularly interesting in the present context is that a theory of this sort gives promise of accounting for perceptual individuality. This is one of its most appealing aspects for Broadbent himself. His 1977 paper begins with a practical research situation in which groups are asked to represent the current British government trying to make a decision about economic variables. Looking at the same computer printout of economic statistics, one person comes out with a statement of purpose, another with an evaluation of some part of the data. A third makes a statement of fact, a fourth a suggested decision. Where do these marked differences in response to the same information come from? "To understand, assist, and improve human decision, we need to know the causes of these strange selections and jumps of topic, which do not themselves appear in consciousness" (1977, p. 109). Broadbent considers that the experiments on attention have taken only a first step toward understanding the ways individuals construe the environment. "It will be a long haul; but the progress is steady, and so is the dependence of each worker's advance upon the findings of the others" (p. 118).

Early psychologists were much interested in the part mental imagery plays in thinking, as indeed the philosophers who preceded them had always been. Research on imagery declined during the decades when behaviorism dominated psychological thinking, but it is flourishing again in the 1970s with the shift to models based on information processing. There are two kinds of questions that can be asked about the imagery of individuals: "What *kind* of images do different persons experience, visual, auditory, tactual, kinesthetic, gustatory, or olfactory?" and "How *vivid* are the person's images?" In the early days, attempts were made to delineate imagery types and to relate differences in imagery to various criteria, such as school or occupational success. Nothing of importance came out of these attempts. But along the way a somewhat different concept emerged as to what the important aspects of imagery were. This was a distinction between *visualizers* and *verbalizers*. Sir Francis Galton himself, who in 1883 reported on his famous "breakfast table" test of imagery, in which individuals tried to visualize as many details as they could of their morning meal, was surprised to find that most scientists were poor visualizers (Galton, 1883). The things they remembered were words symbolizing what had been perceived, rather than the visual scenes themselves. Intelligence tests that were produced over the years used mainly verbal material, although special tests requiring the mental manipulation of visual forms were also constructed and used mainly as indicators of mechanical ability.

The information-processing approach has led to a resurgence of interest in this visualizer-verbalizer distinction. Marks (1973) has carried out a series of experiments in which he uses a brief questionnaire to identify visualizers, the Vividness of Visual Imagery Questionnaire (VVIQ). Subjects rate on a seven-point scale how vivid their images are of a relative or friend, the rising sun, the front of a shop, and a country scene. Ratings are summed for a total score. Marks then compares the top 25 percent with the bottom 25 percent on various tasks. One of these was to answer questions about a picture of a scene, briefly presented. Whether the subjects were college students or grade school children, the good visualizers were clearly superior in reporting on the picture. In subsequent experiments (1973), Marks recorded the eye movements of subjects as they scanned the picture. The vivid imagers used fewer eye movements and a different scanning pattern, in comparison with the subjects low on the VVIQ.

A book by Paivio (1971) summarizes a large amount of research pointing to a conclusion that there are two independent processes which may be used to encode information, visual and verbal, and that most individuals make use of both, depending on the nature of the task. For tasks in which either system would work, individuals differ in their preference. Not all psychologists accept Paivio's dual-process theory (Pylyshyn, 1973), and it may be modified as time passes, but it provides a framework for investigating the imagery of individuals. Some developmental research suggests that encoding through images occurs somewhat earlier than encoding through words. Bruner (1964, 1966) proposed that there are really three processes which develop sequentially, namely enactive (coding through action), ikonic (coding through images), and symbolic (coding through verbal symbols).

One research lead that is generating considerable interest, on which Paivio comments briefly, is the evidence that different halves of the brain are involved in visual and verbal information processing. Some kinds of individual differences that may be based on physiological differences are being explored in a research program at the University of Oregon. Snyder (1972) investigated the visual side of the typology in his dissertation. He gave his subjects tests designed to measure the controllability as well as the vividness of imagery, along with a test of space relations. He then tried them out in several experiments where the task was always to report whether two drawings of three-dimensional forms were the same or different. Clear evidence emerged that persons classified as "strong imagers" were superior to the "weak imagers" on many variations of the experimental task. It was the test for controllability of images rather than the test for vividness that indicated which persons would show this superiority.

Snyder's research had nothing to say about the persons whose coding is verbal rather than visual, but Keele and Lyons (1975) are working on a variant of this distinction. They are examining differences in word fusion, which Day (1968) has proposed as a means of classifying persons as "language bound" or "stimulus bound." In these ingenious experiments, two slightly different stimuli are briefly presented to the two ears, stimuli such as "lanket" and "banket." Some persons fuse the two and report that they heard the word *blanket.* Others keep them separate and report one or both exactly as presented. The variations on this experiment Keele and Lyons (1975) carried out showed that the dichotomy between fusers and nonfusers is not so clear-cut as Day believed it to be. What each person did depended on various features of the experimental situation. Since Day's work linking the distinction to a number of other aspects of individuality has not been published, and this newer work casts doubt on the usefulness of the typology, the question of whether there are "verbalizers" or "language-bound" persons is still an open one. Keele and Lyons suggest that there may be real differences in how heavily language influences sensory discriminations and that they may have important correlates even if verbal types cannot be identified.

What now seems important to some investigators is to link up what we know about human cognition from mental testing with what we have learned from experiments on information processing. In a volume titled *The Nature of Intelligence* (Resnick, 1976), many aspects of this challenging task are explored by specialists in testing, cognitive psychology, linguistics, and cross-cultural research. A leader in this movement has been Earl Hunt, the author of one of the chapters. Hunt, Lunneborg, and Lewis (1975) had compared university students who scored in the top quarter of the college aptitude distribution with those who scored in the bottom quarter on a number of information-processing variables. The ones that differentiated most clearly were (1) name accessing and code arousal, (2) sensitivity to order, and (3) speed of processing. They concluded that intelligence test scores identify persons who can code and manipulate stimuli rapidly in situations where knowledge per se is not a factor. Carroll (1976), another contributor to the volume, has undertaken the ambitious task of classifying all the principal abilities identified through factor analysis according to a coding system based on the information-processing model. The system is too complex for detailed consideration here, but it constitutes an impressive achievement. Carroll has succeeded in describing in one condensed table the aspects of the information-processing sequence involved in each of twenty-four mental ability factors. As an example, we can look at the description of the N factor, number facility. Principally, it involves long-term memory. The operations it requires are retrieving number associations and algorithms and performing serial operations with algorithms. The strategies required are the chunking and recording of intermediate results. What Carroll is aiming at is a new "structure of intellect" system couched in the language of cognitive psychology. The end result could be a complete overhauling of the technology of mental testing.

With all its uncertainties and incompleteness, research on information processing is important in two ways to a psychology of individuality. First, it has pointed to concepts and principles that help us understand how individuality arises and why each person is unique. Second, it promises to revitalize the whole field of measured individual differences and to enable us to devise new tests sounder and more useful than those of the past.

The first value is probably the more important. All of us are the products of our information-processing history. No two histories are identical. Neisser (1976, p. 187) expresses this truth very vividly:

> Schemata are developed by experience; everyone's experiences are different; therefore we must all be very different from one another. Since every person's perceptual history is unique, we should all have unique cognitive structures, and the differences between us can only increase as we grow older and become more individualized. Indeed, we did not even start out alike: Unless you are an identical twin, you were born different from anyone else who ever lived. While not much is known about *how* genetic differences affect behavior

> . . . it is clear *that* they affect behavior. Infants are
> differently active, mobile, and responsive from birth; it
> is more than likely that they start with different percep-
> tual schemata as well.
>   This is true as far as it goes, and it poses another
> formidable obstacle to the fine-grained prediction of
> perception or behavior.

Neisser goes on to explain why our perceptions of the physical world are as similar as they are, given the fact that information about the properties of things has adaptive significance, and why our perceptions of people and the social world, although less similar, are shaped by the culture to become enough like those of other people to enable us to anticipate others' behavior as well as we need to to function in society. The significant thing here is that Neisser recognizes it is the likenesses, rather than the differences, which require explanations. Individuality is fundamental.

Many of the concepts and principles we have met in previous chapters of this book have been stressed in discussions of information processing. It is an *active* process, and people develop *strategies* to use in carrying it on. It is a *selective* process, with a far greater amount of information entering the system than can be processed. It involves *organization* at every stage, from the initial chunking to the storage in long-term memory.

The second kind of importance this research has for the student of individuality is that it tells us what characteristics may be worth observing and measuring. It has redirected our efforts to attention and imagery. It has suggested the breakdown of intelligence into more specific skills and competencies. It is replacing the idea of capacity or amount of some hypothetical entity with the idea of *repertoires* of strategies and skills, some more easily modified than others through experience and training. These are some of the features that make research on information processing encouraging and exciting.

∽∽ 13 ∽∽

Creativity: The
Recognition of
Possibilities

Over the centuries, millions of words have been written about creative persons, their work, their lives, their personalities. It has been a recurrent challenge to psychologists to explain creative thinking. Research on creativity is very diverse and not well integrated. Investigators flying this flag often seem to be speaking different languages. One thread does, however, run through all the discussions. Whatever else it means, creativity involves the exploitation of possibilities—in materials, in situations, in people. Creative artists, musicians, scientists, and philosophers serve to remind us in each generation how broad the scope of human potentialities really is.

Early efforts to study creativity grew out of interest in the nature of genius. Like their predecessors in philosophy, psychologists were curious about those landmark figures in every generation on whose achievements civilization rests. The idea that such figures are qualitatively different from the rest of humanity has had considerable currency. The idea that genius is akin to madness goes back to the times when madness was much more of a mystery than it is now, and considerable biographical evidence for a relationship has accumulated, although other biographies prove that a genius can be perfectly sane. What biographies do show clearly is that great artists, writers, musicians, scientists, and others possess not only an awesome degree of talent of some sort but also an overriding motivation to express it.

After intelligence tests were invented, psychologists set up the hypothesis that genius represented the high end of the intelligence distribution and that the great creators were only quantitatively different from other people. Besides high intelligence, it was assumed that people of genius possessed some outstanding special talent and exceptional motivation. It seemed feasible to measure all these essentials. In the early 1920s, Terman initiated a large-scale research project to test these assumptions. One thrust of the program was to examine in detail the biographies of outstanding persons, writers, artists, statesmen, and others to find out whether they were exceptionally high in general intelligence. Cox (1926) was able to dig out evidence that this was indeed true by assigning mental age (MA) equivalents to accomplishments their biographers reported for these persons at specified ages during childhood. All the eminent individuals, without exception, had shown unusual mental ability at an early age. For the group as a whole, the average IQ was estimated to be 140. For some of the subgroups, the average was as high as 160. Another thrust of Terman's research was a longitudinal developmental project. About 1,300 bright children with IQs of 140 or above were studied intensively in 1922 and have now been followed up for more than fifty years. At each successive stage of their lives, they have been retested and interviewed. The findings have been reported in detail in several volumes (Terman, 1925; Terman and Oden, 1947, 1959; Oden, 1968; Sears, 1977). The great majority of these high-IQ children became strikingly successful people and lived useful, productive lives. However, it seems clear now that only a small minority deserve the "genius" designation. High intelligence does not guarantee outstanding creativity. Some very intelligent persons are creative; others are not.

In accordance with this conclusion, psychologists since about 1950 have focused their efforts on the measurement of creativity as distinguished from intelligence. Guilford (1950) began this research trend with an idea that has turned out to be very fruitful, the distinction between *divergent* and *convergent* thinking. One carries on convergent thinking when solving a problem for which there is only one right answer. One carries on divergent thinking in dealing with problems that have no single right answer, problems for which a variety of solutions can be formulated. Standard intelligence tests are made up almost exclusively of the convergent type of task. It appears plausible that divergent tasks might be better indicators of creativity. Several separate aspects of divergent thinking have been differentiated: fluency, flexibility, originality, sensitivity to problems, redefinition, and elaboration (Dellas and Gaier, 1970). Tests for all these aspects have been devised, calling for the production of a large and diverse assortment of ideas and their combination into new structures and patterns. Divergent thinking means becoming aware of and dealing with a great many possibilities.

In one important branch of creativity research, the focus has been on outstandingly creative people, their backgrounds, their motives, and their ways of working, as well as their abilities. The Institute of Personality Assessment Research (IPAR) carried out a series of such studies. MacKinnon's (1962) work on architects is one outstanding example. First a panel of experts in the profession was asked to nominate the persons they considered to be its most creative members. For comparison purposes, two other groups of architects were selected. One was made up of persons of the same age and geographical location who had worked with the architects in the creative group but had not themselves been nominated for creativity. The other group was made up of nonchosen architects who had not worked with those in the creative group. All of them were invited to spend a weekend at IPAR, taking tests, being interviewed, and being observed in a variety of situations. The investigators found that for these generally high-level people what most clearly separated the creative from the noncreative was not abilities of any kind, but rather motivation, self-image, and style. The same finding emerged from other studies of professional persons, such as writers and mathematicians. Creative architects described themselves as inventive, determined, independent, individualistic, enthusiastic, and industrious. Noncreative architects described themselves as responsible, sincere, reliable, and tolerant. The same sort of differences showed up on tests of personality, interests, and values. Creative persons were more open to experience, more aware of their own feelings, wider in their interests, and more vulnerable to some sorts of psychopathology. However, they also possessed strong ego controls that served to keep inner turbulence from erupting.

In an attempt to synthesize the findings from this and many other creativity studies, Dellas and Gaier (1970) classify the characteristics of creative people under three main headings. The first, *cognitive preferences and style,* covers the preferences for complex rather than simple pictures, the occurrence of primitive along with highly sophisticated mental processes, and the perceptual openness arising from the repudiation of repression as a defense mechanism. The second, *personality,* covers characteristics discussed in the preceding paragraph, self-descriptions, evidence of inner turbulence governed by a strong ego, and also the fact that interest patterns are not restricted by sex roles. Creative men tend to score more "feminine" than noncreative men; creative women tend to score more "masculine" than noncreative women. The third heading, *motivation,* has to do with willingness to take risks and the need to impose order on chaotic situations. Thus it appears that creative people are sensitive to more possibilities than other people are and are strong and independent enough to deal with the complexity and disorder such sensitivity brings, able to choose, reject, organize.

Another offshoot of the movement to analyze and measure creativity that began with Guilford's 1950 paper was research comparing groups of children who scored differently on the so-called creativity tests, using test scores rather than achievements as the basis for selecting groups to be compared. The first step in a project of this sort is to administer a standard intelligence test along with one or more creativity tests. Those who score above the average of the group in "intelligence" but below average in "creativity" are classified as "high intelligents." Those who score above the group average in "creativity" but below in "intelligence" are classified as "high creatives." There are, of course, some children who score high on both or low on both. (Quotation marks are used in this discussion as a reminder that test-defined intelligence and creativity are not necessarily the same qualities as intelligence and creativity judged from outstanding achievements, as in the research discussed in previous pages.)

Most commonly used as "creativity" measures are tests of divergent thinking. One frequently included is to ask the subject to think of as many uses as possible for some common object, such as a brick or a newspaper. Another is to look at abstract line drawings and think of a number of things each might represent. Others involve making up stories to go with pictures, producing clever titles for pictures, or elaborating simple line figures into pictures of something. The one quality all these tests have in common is open-endedness. The person taking them must produce responses, not just choose the best answer among those provided. They can be scored for several characteristics: *ideational fluency,* based on the sheer number of responses produced; *originality,* based on how rare the responses are; and *flexibility,* based on the number of shifts of concept or direction the responses show. The quality of the responses can also be evaluated by judges.

Major investigations designed in this way have been reported by Getzels and Jackson (1962), Wallach and Kogan (1965), and Hudson (1966, 1968). Hudson's designation of the types being compared as "divergers" and "convergers" is probably more suitable then the "creativity versus intelligence" label. Many interesting differences between the two types of children have turned up. Divergers are less interested in success, more interested in self-expression. They choose unusual occupations, such as inventor or entertainer, rather than the more conventional lawyer or doctor. In England, where secondary school students must choose to major in either arts or science, divergers choose arts, convergers science. In the stories and pictures they produce, divergers show more fantasy, more humor, more violence and obscenity than do convergers. In school, divergers are less docile and more troublesome than convergers, but their level of achievement does not differ. Where home backgrounds have been looked into, it has been found that divergers have been less closely supervised than convergers and less shaped by their parents' expectations. Many other differences have been reported, but these will perhaps suffice for a rough sketch.

The most recent study built on this pattern (Welsh, 1975) used a different sort of creativity test, one that has differentiated better than the divergent thinking tests have in comparisons of creative with noncreative people. It is an art scale made up of paired figures, one simple in design, one complex. Artists and other creative persons prefer the complex alternatives, and scores for the number of complex figures preferred clearly differentiate between creative and noncreative adults. Welsh administered the art scale and a high-level test of intelligence to adolescents attending a summer school for talented and gifted students. Using the terms "origence" and "intellectence" rather than "creativity" and "intelligence," he compared four groups: (1) high origence, low intellectence; (2) high origence, high intellectence; (3) low origence, low intellectence; and (4) low origence, high intellectence, showing that the four groups differed significantly in their self-descriptions, their scores on the Minnesota Multiphasic Personality Inventory, and their Strong Vocational Interest profiles. The group high on both measures and the group low on both were just as distinctive as the two groups in which one characteristic predominated over the other. In fact, the group showing most promise for creative achievement consisted of persons who scored high on both tests. (It must be remembered that all these subjects were highly intelligent by ordinary school standards, so that labeling some of them "low" was a relative matter.) Like the previous "creativity-intelligence" studies, this one clearly demonstrated that there are differences in personality, style, and outlook related to whatever it is so-called creativity tests measure.

Another research direction has involved attempts to develop "creativity" in adults or children. "Creativity" is one of our good words. Whatever their actual accomplishments, people like to think of themselves as creative and would like to have their children described in this way. What research of this kind has actually focused on is divergent thinking. It can be stimulated and facilitated in a number of ways. Some of this work has been done in business and industry (Stein, 1974, 1975). Individual procedures have been designed with the purpose of changing personality characteristics limiting the "creativity" of executives and scientists and teaching them cognitive skills, such as hypothesis formation and testing. Group procedures are often used, including brainstorming, creative problem solving, and synectics (use of metaphor and analogy). Stein's volumes provide a useful compendium.

Torrance (1962, 1963) has been a prime mover in the attempts to stimulate "creativity" in children. He constructed a battery of verbal and nonverbal divergent thinking tests suitable for children, by means of which each child's performance could be scored for fluency, flexibility, originality, and elaboration and the composite could be considered to be an index of the child's creative ability. Validity studies have left some doubt as to whether what is measured is really creativeness, as explained before, but there are large individual differences in children, and the use of such tests has led to a greater appreciation of qualities of mind not revealed by intelligence tests. The principal use of the Torrance tests has been to evaluate procedures designed to teach or to stimulate these qualities. In one such project, for example, Torrance and others (1960) taught ten grade school teachers how to stimulate divergent thinking in the children they taught. The methods are rather obvious ones, such as treating pupils' questions with respect and allowing them to do things without the threat of critical evaluation. Torrance and his coworkers compared classes taught in this way with those taught in the customary way after four weeks. Results were mixed. In four of the six grades, the experimental groups showed larger gains than the others in scores for originality and elaboration; in three of the six, experimental groups gained more in fluency. One difficulty was that about a third of the teachers failed to understand the principles. Their own personalities stood in their way. Since Torrance's initial work, however, there has been enough other research to remove any doubt about the fact that divergent thinking can be stimulated by appropriate classroom procedures (Guilford, 1967, chap. 14). Ward, Kogan, and Pankove (1972) showed that monetary incentives worked with children from low socioeconomic levels, as they had been shown to work for middle-class children. Giving a penny for each successive idea generated led to more ideas and thus higher fluency scores. Stratton and Brown

(1972) trained children to produce and evaluate solutions to problems, improving both the quantity and the quality of their divergent
production. Even more striking is a report by Ford and Renzulli
(1976) showing that the fluency of mentally retarded children in
the "educable" range could be markedly increased through training. Renzulli's New Directions in Creativity Program has been made
available to teachers of the retarded. In the study reported, the program was tried out in eighteen experimental classrooms and twelve
control classrooms. Large and significant differences appeared on
tests of the Torrance type, such as alternate uses of objects, ideational and verbal fluency, and consequences of actions and situational changes.

Flowing in a completely separate channel from the divergent-
thinking investigations has been a stream of psychological research
and theorizing about what goes on in the minds of creative persons
while they are creating. And in a still different channel has been
research and theorizing about what goes on in the mind of anybody
who is trying to find a solution to a complex problem. One of Guilford's major contributions (Guilford, 1967, chap. 14) was to recognize that these two lines of research had much in common with
each other and with his factor-analytic research on divergent
production.

John Dewey (1910) was perhaps the first psychologist to
analyze the steps in the problem-solving process: (1) a difficulty is
felt, (2) the difficulty is located and defined, (3) possible solutions
are suggested, (4) consequences are considered, and (5) a solution
is accepted. Merrifield and others (1962) updated these steps and
brought them into relationship with the work the Guilford group
had been doing on the structure of intellect. Merrifield's five steps
were preparation, analysis, production, verification, and reapplica-
tion. An early and influential analysis of the creative process was
that of Wallas (1926). The similarity to the analysis of problem
solving is apparent. Wallas's four steps were: (1) preparation (information is gathered), (2) incubation (unconscious work is going
on), (3) illumination (an "inspired" synthesis emerges), and (4)
verification (the new idea is tried out and elaborated). Later writers
and researchers have usually accepted the Wallas framework and
attempted to fill it in. The relevance of the divergent thinking we

have been considering in earlier sections to the problem-solving or creative process can readily be seen. Persons who generate a large number of ideas have an advantage over those who do not. However, what the problem-solving or creative process starts with is not just disconnected words or phrases but structures, schemata, possibilities for action. The Alternate Uses test seems closer to this requirement than simple fluency tests such as "Think of all the words you can that begin with the letter *P*."

The most mysterious part of the creative sequence has been the incubation period. But it is generally agreed that an interlude in which no active effort occurs is an indispensable stage. Patrick (1938), for example, whose subjects had been assigned the task of planning a laboratory experiment on heredity and environment, arranged for half of them to do the whole thing in a single session and the other half to spend two or three weeks at home not working on the task, before presenting their final plans. There was evidence for an incubation process in both groups, but experts who judged the plans gave higher ratings to those produced after the longer interval. Guilford (1967) suggests that what happens during the incubation period is a transformation of the ideas similar to the transformations that have been shown to occur in all sorts of memory traces. The transformed schemata can then be combined in new ways.

The illumination step, the "intuitive leap" or "Eureka" phenomenon, is a dramatic occurrence. It has been described in artists, mathematicians, scientists, writers, and many other kinds of creative persons. It also occurs frequently enough in the lives of ordinary people so that we can all understand what is meant by it. Whether or not individuals serving as subjects in problem-solving experiments arrive at this moment of insight depends on their personality characteristics, on how rigid or flexible they are, and on situational factors and chance happenings that provide clues. In one of Maier's (1931) experiments, for example, the subject was supposed to tie together the ends of two strings, both hanging from the ceiling but too far apart for him to reach both at the same time. If the experimenter walked past one of the strings and apparently by accident set it in motion, this slight clue was enough to enable many subjects to see that a swinging pendulum might be the answer. They would then proceed to attach a pair of pliers to one string, set it in motion, and grasp it when it approached the other string. Only one out of seventeen subjects who took this "hint" had any awareness that a hint had been given. For Koestler (1964), whose book on the creative process brings together a vast amount of material from artists, writers, and philosophers, as well as psychologists, the essence of the creative act is a sudden fusion of two or more schemata (Koestler calls them "matrices") that one has never brought together before. He calls this "bisociation." "The creative act is not an act of creation in the sense of the Old Testament. It does not create something out of nothing; it uncovers, selects, reshuffles, combines, synthesizes already existing facts, ideas, faculties, skills. The more familiar the parts, the more striking the new whole" (Koestler, 1964, p. 120).

All these accounts of the creative process have been descriptive rather than explanatory. They tell what happens, but not how or why it happens. Arieti (1976), after reviewing former discussions, attempts to build a more adequate theory on the formulations of Freud and later psychoanalysts. An important distinction in psychoanalysis is that between *primary process,* the archaic, unconscious mental functioning we see in dreams and in mental illness, and *secondary process,* the logical, adaptive mental functioning characteristic of normal adults in the waking state. Primary-process thinking develops very early and never completely disappears. Psychoanalytic theories about the creative process make much of the observation that creative persons are able to revert to primary-process thinking much more easily than noncreative persons, fusing images and symbols without regard for logic, undergoing states of mind similar to those of psychotic persons but maintaining ego control. Kris (1952) called this aspect of creativity "regression in the service of the ego." For Arieti, the essence of creativity is the matching of primary-process and secondary-process mechanisms. He uses the term *tertiary process* for this combination and shows how it operates in the ordinary person's use of wit and humor as well as in the creation of masterpieces of painting, music, and literature. Whether one considers psychoanalytic concepts to be explanatory or simply descriptive, Arieti's theory constitutes one way of accounting for the aspects of creativity that are most difficult to explain. Perhaps a more adequate explanation will eventually arise from research on the more subtle aspects of information processing. Broadbent's (1977) investigations of "hidden preattentive processes," discussed in Chapter Twelve, begin to elucidate the unconscious work of incubation that produces sudden illumination. The hardheaded experimental psychologists and the psychoanalysts may now be closer together than they realize.

The facts and findings we have been considering in this chapter make up a very mixed bag of some of the most intriguing ideas psychologists have generated. The trouble with them is that they do not answer the research questions they were intended to answer. Those who, like Terman, set out to study genius accumulated a vast amount of highly interesting material about what happens to able people as life proceeds, but we know little or nothing more about the development of genius than we did before the research began. Those who, like the IPAR group, focused their spotlight on creative persons identified a considerable number of ability, personality, and motivational variables with regard to which creative people average higher than noncreative people. But we still do not know how these originated or whether the creators could have been spotted at an earlier stage of their lives. Those who began with children, contrasting intellectual styles thought to have some relevance to creativity, discovered that there were dimensions of individual differences which we had not been taking into consideration. But they have not demonstrated clearly that these are what count in creative achievement. Those who analyzed the creative process found that it was not very different from the process by means of which ordinary people solve day-to-day problems. Parts of the process, especially the incubation stage, are obscure and lend themselves to a variety of theoretical explanations.

Gradually it is dawning on psychologists that our difficulties may have to do with the questions we are asking, the assumptions we are making. Perhaps we should be studying individuality rather than creativity. Perhaps the achievements that cause us to designate certain individuals as creative are not a good basis for differentiating individuals. Albert (1975) has suggested that we may be clinging to an outmoded concept of genius. He proposes that we cease to try to define it in terms of psychological traits possessed by individuals and move to a behavioral definition. We would define a genius as one who produces a large body of work that has a significant influence for many years, requiring people to assimilate new attitudes, ideas, viewpoints, or techniques. High productivity is necessary but not sufficient. There are no "mute, inglorious Miltons." Genius grows out of society's needs and attitudes as well as the talents of individuals, and thus it is unlikely that we shall ever be able to identify early the persons who eventually will be labeled *geniuses*. Another searching analysis of concepts we have been taking for granted is that of Nicholls (1972). He recommends that we abandon the assumption that creativity is a normally distributed trait or a combination of several normally distributed traits. Although it is true that people who produce things judged to be creative contributions differ from those who do not in scores for divergent thinking, intelligence, intrinsic task involvement, and preference for complexity, there is no solid evidence that these traits necessarily converge in children. To single out one of them and label it "creativity" as has been done in the case of divergent thinking makes for confusion, not clarity.

As has been stated, efforts to predict, on the basis of tests, which individuals will do creative things at a later time have not been very successful. Vernon (1972) did find that divergent thinking tests given to 400 eighth-graders correlated positively with a composite criterion of creative achievement based on information obtained concurrently. Intelligence also played a part in these achievements. But when the relationship with verbal intelligence was partialed out by a statistical technique, there was still a correlation of .29 for boys and .42 for girls. This is, of course, evidence of concurrent, not predictive validity. What one can conclude is that children high in divergent thinking are somewhat more likely to be doing things that observers in the school situation consider to be creative. One unexplained finding in this and other studies is that creativity, as measured by tests of divergent thinking, is linked to other characteristics differently for boys and girls. Hetherington and McIntyre (1975) have reviewed some of these differences. It seems, for example, that for children between the ages of seven and ten creativity is correlated with IQ for boys but not for girls. At the kindergarten age, IQ and creativity are not correlated for either sex, but boys and girls differ with regard to the relationships between personality characteristics and creativity. Boys high on the tests are more open, expressive, exploratory, and playful than their less creative classmates. For girls, groups high on both creativity and IQ or low on both kinds of tests are handicapped in several social ways. They are more inhibited, less effective with peers, less self-confident than the others. One can only speculate about what such differences mean. They are not the only research results to suggest that females view too much "giftedness" as a disability.

Wallach and Wing (1969) found similar evidence for the concurrent validity of tests labeled "creativity" at the college level. Comparing the third of the student group who scored highest with the third who scored lowest, they found that nonacademic productivity was somewhat higher in the upper third. Numbers, however, were small, and differences were not large. For example, 7 percent of the students in the highest third had won art competitions, as compared with 2 percent of the students in the lowest third. Differences of the same order were found for other kinds of accomplishments. Rossman and Horn (1972) reported similar results for the art and engineering students they studied. The concurrent validity coefficients of the tests ranged from .26 to .37. Results such as these do not justify the selection of children or college students who score high as "gifted" or "potential creators."

But if the efforts that have been made to analyze individual differences in creativity and to dissect the creative process have not produced the results hoped for, they have accomplished something that may turn out to be even more important. They have made us aware that people do deal actively with possibilities, recognizing, selecting, combining, organizing the voluminous raw material of experience and incorporating the patterns they construct into their own distinctive patterns of individuality. Whether we conclude that everyone is creative or define creativity more narrowly so that only high achievements are classified under the label, the process occurs in all of us.

≫≫ 14 ≪≪

Choices and Decisions

More than on anything else, one's individuality depends on the choices one makes. These need not be conscious or deliberate. Many of them are completely automatic, regulated by the kinds of cognitive structures discussed in earlier chapters. Many are made hastily and impulsively. Many are trivial. The green dress or the brown dress? A Toyota or a Datsun? A game or a movie? But others have serious implications, usually recognized at the time one faces them. There may be careful, sometimes agonizing soul searching over the choice of a mate or a career. The words *choice* and *decision* are more or less synonymous, with *choice* used for the less important and unconscious process more often and *decision* used for the serious deliberations. But there is no uniformity about this. We shall use the terms more or less interchangeably.

All of them, little or big, influence the development of individuality in at least three ways. First, they determine what will be learned, what cognitive structures will take shape. For example, the seventh-grade boy who goes out for band rather than basketball will learn to read music and to produce the indicated sounds on his instrument. Along with these skills, he will be acquiring listening skills, social skills of particular kinds, and attitudes different from those he would have developed on the playing field. And, since by his choice he commits a sizable fraction of his time to band practice, he must necessarily forgo the learning of other things in which he is interested, such as cryptography or the building of model airplanes. The second way in which choices affect the development of individuality is by determining what situations will be included in one's personal world. Life on a college campus is considerably different from life on a farm or in a factory. Whether one's environment is quiet or noisy, crowded or uncrowded, simple or complex, stable or in constant flux is a matter of choice. Related to this kind of effect choices have is the third kind, that choices determine the people with whom one's lot will be cast. Will they be predominantly children or adults, intellectuals or nonintellectuals, diverse in background and values or much alike? Will the structure of the social situation leave room for independent action, or will one's opinions and judgments be constrained to match those of the others in the group? Persons making important life decisions may or may not consider all these aspects, but they are sure to meet up with them as time passes. A girl who decides to marry the man she loves and settle down to life as a housewife may discover that she is not satisfied to spend most of her time within the four walls of a suburban house, no matter how comfortable, and to associate mainly with young children and housewives like herself. She did not realize when she made her decision that these limitations went with it.

As society has become more and more complex and the number of alternative ways to live has multiplied, human problems related to choices and decisions have become acute. Toffler (1970), in his best-selling book *Future Shock,* was one of the first to recognize that the sheer number of products, organizations, causes, recreational activities, travel opportunities, and other bids for one's time and resources are making it harder and harder for the individual to establish a clear sense of personal identity. One still has only a limited life span made up of days of fixed length. To be greedy for all sorts of experience is to set oneself up for frustration and failure. To refuse to make decisions is to hand over the direction of one's life to other people or to chance circumstances.

Psychologists have no monopoly on decision-making research. It is being carried on in economics, medicine, political

science, business marketing and management, and various other
academic disciplines. However, during the 1950s, 1960s, and
1970s it has become an increasingly important concern of psychologists. Slovic, Fischhoff, and Lichtenstein (1977), reviewing work
published from 1971 through 1975, included 319 references in their
bibliography, and these were selected from more than a thousand
that they considered. As these reviewers explain, the research has
had two main facets: normative and descriptive. Normative research is directed to the question: How *should* people make decisions? How would one go about it to make the best possible decision
in a given set of circumstances? Descriptive research is directed to
the questions "How *do* people make decisions? How do they combine their beliefs and values with their perceptions of alternative
courses of action into a unity?" Frequently researchers deal with
both facets, describing how actual decision processes deviate from
a normative model.

The dominant set of ideas has been *utility theory*. According to this theory, what the decision maker does is to multiply a
weight representing the *utility* each alternative he is considering has
for him by another weight representing the *probability* of obtaining
or carrying out that alternative. This gives rise to a simple equation
indicating that one's choice is the alternative for which the product
of the two weights is highest. Betting behavior is a favorite vehicle
for such research. If a person knows that there is a 10 percent probability of winning $50 and a 90 percent probability of winning $5,
he should choose the first alternative, according to the normative
utility model, because the product is $5, and the product for the
second alternative is $4.50. The basic equation has been elaborated
and complicated to include other variables, but the skeleton has
remained the same. In a recent version, Multi-Attribute Utility
Theory (MAUT), each differentiable attribute of each alternative
is separately weighted for utility and for importance of this attribute
in one's total evaluation of such alternatives. To illustrate MAUT,
Slovic, Fischhoff, and Lichtenstein (1977) give the example of a
person's choice of a car. One attribute might be beauty of design.
The weight for this attribute would be a quantification of how good
the design of, say, a Toyota is in comparison with its competitors.
The second weight for this attribute would be a quantification of the

importance of design in one's value system for judging cars, as compared with other attributes, such as durability or engine power of a car.

Although utility theory can get very complicated mathematically, it also has a commonsense appeal. This sounds like what people might be doing when they choose between alternatives. But actually it has not contributed as much as was hoped to the practical analysis and improvement of decision making. For one thing, what people do spontaneously is much more varied and diverse than the theory predicts. People have all sorts of strategies and decision rules that they employ. A choice may be accomplished in several stages, applying different rules at each stage. Studies of career development, for example, show that for most people final choices of occupation are the end result of a period of "floundering" (Super, 1957), in which the person changes jobs frequently, often for trivial reasons. Recent follow-up data on a large number of men and women who were tested in 1960 as subjects in Project TALENT show the same phenomenon very clearly. Choices of marriage partners are also often made hastily, without any of the kind of reasoned consideration the utility model presupposes. Research has also made it clear that even if one attempts to follow this model, there are numerous sorts of errors and biases which can make the final decision unsound. Probabilities are very difficult to estimate, and people make many kinds of errors in estimating them, especially in life circumstances much more complicated than the experimental situations psychologists use in the laboratory. Each of us has biases that interfere with objective judgments. For example, overconfidence has been found to be common among bankers and stock market experts, and jurors find it difficult to ignore first impressions of the accused. These and many other examples are cited in the review by Slovic, Fischhoff, and Lichtenstein (1977).

The process of making the major life decisions on which one's individuality depends often suffers from another defect perhaps even more important than these. The person tends to consider too few alternatives. Creativity research has shown us that under special instructions individuals can identify many more possibilities in a situation than they were initially aware of. But when facing an important decision one seldom takes time to generate nonobvious alternatives. Spivack, Platt, and Shure (1976), in their research on interpersonal problem solving as carried on by children and adults, have pointed to the skill of generating alternative solutions as the first essential, even in preschool children. Generally speaking, the experimental research on decision making has not told us anything about this. In the usual experimental design, the experimenter provides the alternatives to be considered by the subject. No room is left for others, especially alternatives that the experimenter might not have thought of. What we need if we are to understand how individuals create themselves through their decisions is a theory broad enough to cover the perception of possibilities as well as choices between them. We do not as yet have such a theory.

In the early 1960s, Tyler, Sundberg, and various associates and students initiated an exploratory investigation of the cognitive structures and processes underlying the choices being made by early adolescent boys and girls that would have a bearing on their own future development as individuals. The general plan was to select roughly comparable groups of young people (about fifteen years of age) from schools in the United States, Holland, and India and to try out with them a variety of techniques designed to reveal the sorts of thinking they were doing about their own futures. It was thought that the three national settings might constitute a sort of natural experiment to show how such thinking is related to cultural and social influences. Two of the assessment procedures devised for this study are relevant to the questions under consideration in this chapter, namely the Listing Questionnaire and the Choice Pattern Procedure.

The purpose of the Listing Questionnaire was to find out how extensive and varied each person's world of perceived possibilities was. On the occupational section, subjects were first asked to write down all the job titles they could think of. Then they were asked to go over the list and indicate which ones they saw as possibilities for themselves. Other sections followed the same plan for leisure time activity, places to live, and people they knew. The analysis and comparison of the three national groups were carried out mainly on the occupations and leisure activities lists. Results showed striking individual differences both in total number listed and number viewed as personal possibilities. Dutch subjects produced significantly longer lists of occupations than their American and Indian counterparts, probably reflecting the differentiation of secondary schools in Holland according to abilities and occupational plans. American subjects, on the other hand, listed significantly more leisure activities than did the subjects from the other two countries, perhaps as a result of American affluence and of the pleasure-seeking attitude television programs portray. But the differences between individuals in the same country were even more extreme. One boy might check only one or two occupations as possibilities for him; another might check twenty. The averages indicated, however, that boys and girls are aware of various possible directions their lives might take, even in a country such as India, where opportunities are more limited than they are in the United States.

The Choice Pattern Procedure is essentially an interview aid rather than a standardized test. Its purpose is to reveal the psychological structures underlying the choices and rejections an individual makes in important areas of life. Several kinds of items have been tried out, but only the occupational items have been thoroughly analyzed. In the Dutch-American comparison, the first step was to print on separate cards the names of fifty occupations that had appeared on at least 10 percent of the free lists described earlier in both countries. (For the comparisons involving India, some substitutes were made in the list of fifty titles, because the subjects there were not familiar with all the occupations the Dutch and American young people listed.) The person being interviewed was handed this set of fifty cards and asked to sort them into two groups, those considered to be "possibilities for a person like you" and those considered to be "out of the question for a person like you." (A "no opinion" response was permitted but not encouraged.) After this preliminary sorting, the subject was then asked to break down the choice and rejection groups into subgroups of occupations that "go together in your mind," or "you would choose for the same reason," or "you would rule out for the same reason." The interviewer then questioned the person about the reasons for the groupings. Comparisons of objective indices such as "number of positive items," "number of negative groups," and the like revealed some statistically significant differences between boys and girls and between nationalities (Tyler and others, 1968), but the most interesting aspect of the protocols was the wide variety of qualitative individual differences that turned up in the reasons subjects gave for their groupings. It was difficult to classify and organize these in any systematic way. A system proposed by Robert Ellis that he called "morphology of occupational choice" (personal communication) was finally employed to code the diverse responses. Its three sets of categories covered (1) intrinsic features of the work task, including self-fulfillment, social fulfillment, power considerations, stimulation, work conditions, and institutional locus; (2) extrinsic features of the work task, including status, respectability, money, and security; (3) feasibility considerations, including self-appraisal and appraisal of opportunities. There were some interesting and statistically significant differences in the extent to which particular categories characterized the two sexes and the three nationalities, but what is more relevant here is the fact that each individual used only *some* of these standards for judging occupations. One might explain her groupings on the basis of creativity, work with people, and appraisal of her own talents. Another might explain them in terms of a preference for head work over hand work, and a desire for travel and adventure. Furthermore, individuals show very different strategies or patterns of behavior as they carry out the assigned task. Some rule out many things immediately; others initially classify most of the occupations as possibilities. Some organize them into broad categories; others make fine distinctions; still others produce one large group and a lot of singles. Some use familiar concepts about kinds of work to be sought or avoided; others are highly idiosyncratic. Some come out with hierarchies of groups within groups, distinctions within distinctions; others arrange their groups in an end-to-end fashion. This profusion of differences raises the question with which this book is attempting to deal. (In fact, the ideas discussed here arose mainly from the findings of this exploratory study and others using the Choice Pattern Procedure.) It makes no sense to try to scale these choices and rejections along some standard dimensions of values or needs. Shall we attempt to reduce this multiplicity to an order that makes statistical analysis possible but loses sight of salient aspects of individuality, or shall we accept idiosyncracy and attempt to deal with it even if it does not fit our established assumptions about the nature of science? And if so, how?

The most completely elaborated theory of decision making to date is the one proposed by Janis and Mann (1977). Its principal advantage over previous formulations is that it takes into consideration the psychological side effects of the emotional stress which accompanies the struggle to make a difficult decision and commit oneself to a particular course of action. It is a theory designed to facilitate effective intervention as well as continuing research. The authors begin by listing seven criteria (1977, p. 11) by which the quality of a decision-making process can be evaluated. They call this ideal process *vigilant* decision making.

The decision maker, to the best of his ability and within his information-processing capabilities,

1. Thoroughly canvasses a wide range of alternative courses of action.
2. Surveys the full range of objectives to be fulfilled and the values implicated by the choice.
3. Carefully weighs whatever he knows about the costs and risks of negative consequences, as well as the positive consequences, that could flow from each alternative.
4. Intensively searches for new information relevant to further evaluation of the alternatives.
5. Correctly assimilates and takes account of any new information or expert judgment to which he is exposed, even when the information or judgment does not support the course of action he initially prefers.
6. Reexamines the positive and negative consequences of all known alternatives, including those originally regarded as unacceptable, before making a final choice.
7. Makes detailed provisions for implementing or executing the chosen course of action, with special attention to contingency plans that might be required if various known risks were to materialize.

They then formulate, in the terminology of general systems theory, a model of the process complex and versatile enough to account for many different outcomes. Figure 4 is their graphic representation of this model.

As can be seen from the figure, what happens depends on

Figure 4. A Conflict-Theory Model of Decision Making Applicable to All Consequential Decisions.

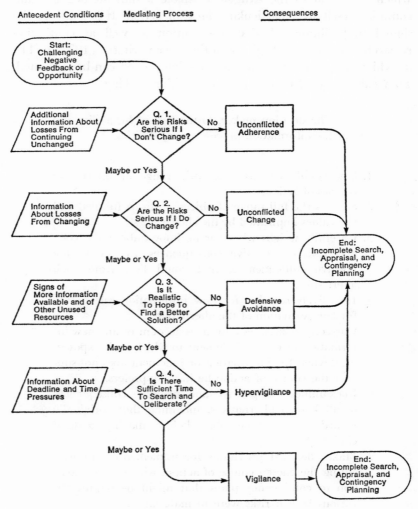

the answers the person gives to four basic questions. The first is "Are the risks serious if I don't change?" If the answer is positive, one will continue the process to the next stage. If the answer is negative, one will go on with the present state of affairs and drop any consideration of other alternatives. The second question, answered separately for each alternative for change being considered, is "Are the risks serious if I do change to this alternative course of action?" If the answer is positive, one will go on to consider other alternatives and continue the decision-making process to the next stage. If the answer is negative, one will adopt the alternative and cease to concern oneself about other possibilities. The third question is "Is it reasonable to hope for a better solution?" If the answer is positive, one will continue to search for alternatives. If the answer is negative, one will react to the situation with some sort of defensive avoidance to reduce the emotional stress. The fourth question is "Is there sufficient time to search and deliberate?" If the answer is positive, one will continue to search and deliberate. If the answer is negative, a pattern of what the authors call "hypervigilance" will become evident, the kind of panic behavior that occurs during fires, earthquakes, and other sudden catastrophes. The person who answers the four successive questions yes or maybe is likely to come out with a good or "vigilant" decision.

Within this basic structure, Janis and Mann find places for results that have been obtained in a great many laboratory and field experiments as well as for detailed case studies based on biographical information. The type of outcome labeled *defensive avoidance* is discussed in considerable detail. It has been much studied by social psychologists. Three subcategories are differentiated here on the basis of additional questions that the person who has decided it is not reasonable to hope for a better solution asks himself or herself. "Are the risks serious if I postpone the decision?" If the answer is no, the probable outcome will be *procrastination* and refusal to think about the problem. If the risks of postponement are serious, the next question arises: "Can I turn the decision over to somebody else?" If it is possible to *let someone else decide,* this is probably what one will do. If not, one will probably adopt the least objectionable solution and *bolster* the decision with biased arguments and selective perceptions of consequences.

Sometimes the stages in the decision-making process are run

through rapidly, with the person unaware of the questions. At other times, the whole sequence may take years. One of the most interesting biographical examples cited is the case of Louis Fischer's decision to break with the Communist Party. The process began in 1928 when he first realized that a police state had been created in the Soviet Union. For years he kept up his search for a better alternative but repeatedly reverted to an earlier stage of the decision-making process instead of following it through. It was not until 1939 and the signing of the Hitler-Stalin nonaggression pact that he made the final commitment to sever his ties with Communism completely and publicly. Janis and Mann suggest that what appears to be a sudden decision to get a divorce after many years of marriage or to change one's career or life-style in some drastic way may well be the outcome of one of these "slow burn" processes.

The most useful thing about this new formulation is that it suggests techniques one can employ to help people avoid unsatisfactory outcomes. Counselors, consultants to industry and government, and people needing to improve their own decision making can apply these. One is the *decisional balance sheet,* which summarizes relevant considerations a person might not think of spontaneously. Others make use of psychodrama and role playing to head off postdecisional regrets and setbacks. The authors provide numerous examples of the sorts of interview questions that help or hinder a client's search for a satisfactory alternative. The discussion should stimulate productive research, innovative assessment techniques, and more emphasis on choices and decisions in counseling and psychotherapy.

The nature of the decisions and choices individuals are called on to make changes as life progresses. Only recently has there been enough research attention to the process of development during the adult years so that we can begin to understand these changes, although research on life stages actually began in Vienna in the 1930s. Charlotte Bühler's book, *Der Menschliche Lebenslauf als Psychologische Problem,* published in 1933 and revised in 1959, divided the whole course of life into five periods. Frenkel (1936) reviewed in English the ideas of the Vienna researchers based on biographical studies. The five periods are

1. *Childhood,* during which period the child lives at home and is dependent on his or her family.
2. *Self-determination,* a period extending from about seventeen to twenty-one, during which the person establishes his or her independence and discovers what he or she wants to do with life.
3. *Stabilization,* a period extending from about twenty-eight to fifty, during which a person does important work and carries major responsibilities.
4. *Decline,* a period extending from about fifty to sixty-five, during which a person evaluates what has been accomplished and comes to terms with the fact that life is limited.
5. *Retirement,* beginning at about sixty-five, during which a person gradually restricts activities, accepts his past life, and comes to terms with the inevitability of death.

Since this initial formulation, all sorts of variations on the "life stage" idea have been proposed, but the general pattern has persisted. One important variation was the idea that each stage constitutes a particular kind of crisis and presents the person with a particular kind of challenge. Erikson (1950) has been the most influential exponent of this theory. In place of the undifferentiated childhood stage, Erikson differentiates four successive stages, labeled according to the developmental challenge they present: (1) trust versus mistrust, (2) autonomy versus shame and doubt, (3) initiative versus guilt, and (4) industry versus inferiority. The fifth stage is the challenge of adolescence, which has interested Erikson most, identity versus identity diffusion. The sixth stage, the challenge of young adulthood, is intimacy versus isolation. The seventh, faced by adults of intermediate age, is generativity versus stagnation. The eighth and last is integrity versus despair. According to Erikson's theory, it is especially important that the dilemma central to a particular stage be resolved in a satisfactory way if the person is to meet the challenges of later stages constructively. An adolescent who never achieves a clear sense of identity is not able to enter into the intimate relationships of the next stage wholeheartedly. A person who has not achieved intimacy will find it difficult or impossible to develop the concern for others, especially those in the next generation, that Erikson calls *generativity.*

Several large-scale research efforts are now being made to obtain detailed information about how individuals meet the challenges of successive life stages. A best-selling book, Gail Sheehy's *Passages* (1976), contains vivid case descriptions of individuals confronting crises, and Chew (1976) has turned a similar journalistic spotlight on the midlife crisis many men go through. To date, complete reports on most of the research investigations to which these popular books refer have not been published, but there have been brief reports indicating that the psychological world of the individual does change rather drastically at certain ages. Gould (1972) sent out a questionnaire to identify the major concerns of male respondents from sixteen to sixty. Comparing the responses of successive age groups, he found that there were major shifts in the thirties, the forties, and the fifties. In the mid thirties, there was a "peeling away of magical illusions" and an identification of self with family. The major decisions to be made concerned one's children and one's marriage. In the early forties, an unstable period of great personal discomfort was often reported. Once this crisis was resolved, personality stabilized, and there was greater marital happiness and more interest in friends and social activities. The fifties were characterized by a decrease in responsibility and concern about children, an increase in concern about health, and a certainty that life is running out. One of the subjects in a longitudinal study quoted in a report by Vaillant and McArthur (1972, p. 419) put the difference succinctly: "At twenty to thirty, I think I learned how to get along with my wife. From thirty to forty, I learned how to be a success at my job. At forty to fifty, I worried less about myself and more about the children." Levinson (1974) is making an intensive study of men in the age group from thirty-five to forty-five, using interview techniques. The periods that these men recognize in their own adult lives are similar to those which others have mentioned, although in each study the age boundaries demarcating stages are set somewhat differently from the others. Levinson calls the stages (1) leaving the family, (2) getting into the adult world through exploration and choice, (3) settling down at forty after a crisis beginning at about thirty, (4) becoming one's own man, and (5) midlife transition.

There are several longitudinal studies covering a long period of years which do not support the idea that a crisis marks each stage. Neugarten (1970), reporting on the lives of 100 middle-aged women, finds that the majority were not disturbed by menopause or by the departure of the youngest child, the "empty nest" phenomenon. She concludes that events occurring at anticipated times are not disturbing. It is the unexpected that leads to a crisis. Reports of longitudinal research by Crandall (1972), Haan (1972), and Maas and Kuypers (1974) have also emphasized continuities or the relationships between life-style and environmental and personality factors rather than crises and decisions. Some of the results in the Maas and Kuypers book do suggest, however, that choice is important. For example, among the men in the study, most of whom were over seventy, whether they were working or retired seemed not to be related to their satisfaction or involvement in life. Most of them were well satisfied, whichever they were doing. But these were all fairly affluent men who had been free to continue working or retire as they wished. The authors concluded: "Freedom to choose whether to work full-time, part-time, or not at all seems crucial" (p. 79). Among the women, one of the most satisfying lifestyles was the work-centered pattern. All the twelve women in this group had been housewives at the time of the first assessment, when they were about thirty, and at that time they seemed to be in less favorable circumstances and to possess fewer assets of ability and personality than did other subjects. But divorce or the husband's death faced them with the challenge of what to do with the rest of their lives. They met the challenge, with the result that in their sixties not only the work they were doing but also their relationships to family members and friends were very satisfying.

During the 1960s, social and personality psychologists became increasingly interested in a variable labeled *locus of control*. It was a spin-off from Rotter's social learning theory (Rotter, 1954), with its basic premise that the likelihood that behavior satisfying a need will occur is a function of two variables, the *expectancy* that the behavior will lead to reinforcements or rewards, and the *strength* or *value* of these reinforcements. Rotter noticed that the expectancy that one's own actions would lead to rewards seemed to be a general attitude rather than one specific to a particular situation. He called this general expectancy "freedom of movement," and he and his

coworkers initiated research into its origins, concomitants, and consequences. To identify contrasting expectations about the efficacy
of one's own actions, he constructed a simple inventory, in which
each item asked the respondent to indicate which of two statements
he or she believed to be more nearly true. The statements making
up one of these items, for example, were

1. "Many of the unhappy things in people's lives are partly due to
   bad luck."
2. "People's misfortunes result from the mistakes they make."

The more often one chooses statements saying that what happens is
a result of chance or luck, the higher is one's score for external locus
of control or *externality*. The more often one chooses statements
saying that one is responsible for the things which happen in one's
own life, the higher the score for internal locus of control or *internality* is. A similar distinction is the one made by De Charms
(1968) between people who are *pawns* and people who are *origins*.

Since the distinction was first proposed, there have been
hundreds of research investigations in which it has figured. Lefcourt's (1976) book provides an excellent compendium and synthesis of findings. Generally speaking, *internals* or *origins* have a
considerable advantage over *externals* or *pawns*. They achieve more
in schools and in many other situations, they are more resistant to
influence, more able to defer gratification. People from less privileged sectors of the population, who in fact do have less control over
their destinies than people from more privileged sectors, consistently
score in the external direction. But research has also demonstrated
that one's orientation can be shifted toward internality by appropriate educational procedures. As usually happens with personality
variables, this one has turned out to be multidimensional. Special
testing instruments have been constructed to distinguish, for example, between expectations about success and expectations about
failure and between assumptions that success and failure depend
on good or bad luck and assumptions that one is controlled by
powerful others.

The portion of this body of research findings most closely
related to decision making consists of evidence that persons with a

predominantly internal orientation avail themselves of more information, make better use of the information they have, and devote
more attention to information considered to be relevant to a decision. However, this depends partly on what the instructions tell them
about the decisions to be made. Lefcourt, Lewis, and Silverman
(1968) had their subjects work with a Level of Aspiration Board,
which requires that they state before each trial the score they expect
to make on the next trial. Under one condition, instructions indicated that this was a game of skill, under the other condition that it
was a game of chance. Clear differences showed up in the behavior
of externals and internals in response to these differing instructions.
Internals who believed that skill was involved set higher aspiration
levels, took more time to make their decisions, and kept their attention more closely focused on the task than did internals who believed only chance was involved. For externals, differences in
instructions seemed not to matter very much. Differences between
the two conditions were smaller and in the opposite direction; that
is, they paid more attention to the task when they thought it was a
game of chance than when they thought it was a game of skill.

Decisions are important in people's lives. Some persons are
better at making them than others are. Probably everybody could
make better ones than they usually do. These are the implications
of the psychological research done so far. There will undoubtedly
be more as time passes.

~~ 15 ~~

The Plural Individual

For many people, the phenomenon of multiple personality is one of the most mystifying to be encountered in all of human experience. How can two or more very different personalities coexist in the same body, using in turn the same sensory apparatus, the same muscles and nerves, the same respiratory and digestive systems? Most of our friends and acquaintances appear to be fairly consistent. We think we know what to expect of them when a car breaks down, a child gets sick, or an unexpected check arrives. It is frightening to contemplate what life would be like if there were not a fair amount of consistency and predictability in the behavior of individuals.

Each generation, however, has its universally known example of multiple personality. Familiar to all of us is Robert Louis Stevenson's fictional case, Dr. Jekyll and Mr. Hyde. During the twentieth century, the three faces of Eve held center stage (Thigpen and Cleckley, 1957). In 1976 another striking example turned up, reported by the team of psychiatrists and psychologists who studied her (Osgood and others, 1976). Jeans, the psychiatrist, encountered the first of the "three faces of Evelyn" in the person of a patient, Gina. The symptom for which she sought treatment was somnambulism. She would walk in her sleep, retaining no memory of the experience when she awoke. Otherwise she was an attractive, competent, somewhat masculine young woman, doing well at an important job. During the course of the psychotherapy, another quite different personality emerged, called Mary Sunshine or simply Mary, a very feminine, almost silly girl who resented the psychiatrist's efforts to draw her out and who recognized no need for treatment. The third personality, whom the doctor considered more promising for mature growth and integration, was Evelyn, a sort of composite of Gina and Mary. The psychologists on the team, without knowing anything about the content of the psychiatrist's interviews, studied protocols of tests and other information obtained from the patient while each personality was in the ascendant. This blind analysis of what the three personalities were like agreed in almost all respects with Jeans' description, and the psychologists' hypotheses about how the personalities had originated were generally borne out by the biographical data. As usual in such cases, traumatic childhood experiences had played a part. The loss of an important figure caused the child to shift allegiance to someone else in her surroundings, and with the shift to a different model she acquired a whole different set of behaviors and attitudes. The painfulness of the experiences necessitating these shifts was responsible for the repression that kept the personalities separate.

Some features of this case, with its unusually thorough description and analysis, are of particular interest as we consider individuality. For one thing, the two principal contrasting selves do not represent a "good" self and a "bad" self, as with Eve White and Eve Black. The difference is instead a matter of masculinity versus femininity, or at least the commonly understood stereotypes these labels designate. Furthermore, the three principal personalities described were not the only ones that turned up during the course of the therapy. Jeans encountered seven other selves, temporary but distinguishable. It requires no great leap of the imagination to hypothesize that multiple personalities may not be so rare and abnormal as we have been assuming them to be. It was not the multiplicity of personalities that moved Gina to enter psychiatric treatment. Had she not suffered from somnambulism, the dissociated selves might not have been discovered by herself or by others. For every plural individual who becomes a psychiatric case, there may be hundreds of others who do not. Multiple personalities may be common, perhaps even universal.

Suspending judgment for the time being on this question, let us turn to another kind of psychological research. Ever since mental tests were invented early in this century, much of the technology has been focused on the goal of making them "reliable." Over the years, the reliability concept has split into two parts: consistency (the relationship of parts of a test to one another), and stability (the relationship between a set of scores obtained at one time and those obtained on a later occasion). Looking first at the stability aspect, we recognize that no test ever produces a correlation across occasions of 1.00, even when the interval is very short and the testing conditions very carefully controlled. Individuals always change some of their responses, and some individuals change many of them. This is particularly true for the tests we label *personality* rather than *ability* tests. In following up this clue, one direction research has taken is to analyze data from longitudinal investigations to locate consistencies over successive periods of life, to compare various traits with regard to stability, and to discover differences in environments that lead to differences in scores over time. Bloom (1964) brought together all available information about physical characteristics, intelligence, achievement, interests, attitudes, and personality. Most of the data are for the age period from preschool to adulthood. It appears that physical characteristics, such as height, are fairly stable even over long periods of time. Tall children become tall adults. For intelligence, the correlations between scores at successive age levels are also fairly high (.65 to .90) after the school age of six or seven is reached. Scores on school achievement tests fluctuate more, but correlations are still moderately high. The least stable scores are for measures of personality and motivation, and for them there is also much more variation in what is reported by different investigators. However, for adults, measured vocational interests tend to be stable even over long intervals, with correlations of .60 or higher. Correlations for values and attitudes also tend to be fairly high, but there are not as many studies on which to base the conclusion.

Psychologists have concentrated mainly on two kinds of question about the meaning of stability coefficients. One major consideration has been prediction. How well can we predict how individuals will respond to test questions in the future from the ways they have responded in the past? The other question has to do with the relationships between environmental influences and changes in test scores over the years. In neither case has the harvest of usable information been very impressive. Predictions are probabilistic and not very accurate. Environmental influences do seem to affect the upward and downward movement of test scores but not uniformly. In general, the conclusion seems to be warranted that just correlating sets of test scores over various time intervals is not going to tell us much of interest about individuals.

There is another way of looking at the data, and from time to time it has been tried. One can analyze which individuals change most over time and which change least and can then attempt to find out in what ways the changers and nonchangers differ. Dunkleberger and Tyler (1961) carried out one such study using scores obtained from students tested in the eleventh and again in the twelfth grade with the Strong Vocational Interest Blank. The differences between the changers and the nonchangers on personality tests were not large, but they generally favored the changers. On the California Psychological Inventory, differences on almost all scales suggested that the less stable individuals were more mature and better adjusted than the more stable. Results such as this suggest that the emphasis psychologists place on reliability of tests may be an obstacle to the understanding of important aspects of individuality.

Research on the other kind of reliability, namely consistency, which is indicated by high correlations between different measures of the same trait, have also led to conclusions many psychologists find disappointing. Evidence that individuals are not very consistent in their expression of what we single out as important personality characteristics has been coming in for a long time. As early as 1928, Hartshorne and May showed that children are not consistent in behavior we classify under the labels of *honesty, generosity,* and *self-control.* One child may cheat but not lie. Another may cheat on examinations but be honest about money. A boy who gets an average score for generosity may be generous to his playmates but not to his brother, or he may give away candy but not toys. Newcomb (1929) showed that evidences of what we call *introversion-extraversion* were not consistent in a group of problem boys. Dudycha (1936) demonstrated the same lack of consistency with regard to punctuality in college students.

What may be at fault with our concepts is the way we label traits, assuming that they are "nomothetic" and apply in the same way to everybody. Bem and Allen (1974) have produced some evidence that individuals will be more consistent if we allow them to tell us which of their traits are consistent and how they should be scaled. They tried these hypotheses on two personality characteristics: friendliness and conscientiousness. Students who said that they were consistently friendly did in fact show higher correlations between different indicators of the quality than students who said that their consistency for friendliness was low. (The indicators were self-reports, mother's report, father's report, and rating of behavior during discussions.) For conscientiousness, there were similar findings, with an extra little idiographic detail. Some students included neatness in their concept of conscientiousness; others did not. These results point once more to what has been emphasized in previous sections of this book, that progress toward understanding individuality requires the abandonment of the concept that all traits are nomothetic. Besides its contribution to this conclusion, the Bem and Allen report also provides an ingenious new research technique for dealing with partially idiographic data.

Another attempt to make sense of the inconsistencies as well as the consistencies revealed by mental test data was launched by Berdie (1961, 1969a, 1969b), using scores on ability rather than personality tests. His basic hypothesis was that some individuals are inherently more variable than others. He set out to measure this trait of intra-individual variability and find out what it was related to. In the largest of several studies, 100 college students took twenty alternate forms of six "factorially pure" tests designed to measure aiming, flexibility of closure, number facility, perceptual speed, speed of closure, and visualization. (These names may sound strange to the general reader, but persons who have been involved in the long search for primary mental abilities will find them quite familiar. It is not necessary to know what the tests are like to understand the Berdie results.) The resulting plethora of data allowed him to compute several variability indices. The variance of an individual's scores over the twenty parallel tests of the same ability served as an index of his or her temporal variability (what we were calling *stability* in our earlier discussion). The variance of an individual's scores over the six ability factors tested on each occasion served as an index of his or her consistency in overall mental ability. The results of this investigation were very complex and could not be accounted for on the basis of the initial hypothesis that intra-individual variability is a single unitary trait. Persons rated as highly variable on aiming, for example, might receive low variability ratings for speed of closure. Persons showing a great deal of temporal variability may or may not be consistent over content domains. Viewed from the perspective of trait psychology, the results were discouraging. But here again, what may be most significant about this line of research is the fact that it leads to recognition of the inadequacies of the trait concept. We might speculate that, if even with highly standardized ability tests individuals vary their performance in so many ways, perhaps they have at their disposal more alternative ways of dealing with the demands situations make than we have assumed they have. Perhaps a closer look at just what they are doing on successive occasions would be useful. Perhaps each person has several strategies appropriate for most situations and uses sometimes one, sometimes another.

Some fundamental questioning of the trait concept has revolved around situational differences and the effects they have on behavior. Until fairly recently, for example, it was assumed that a man scoring high on an anxiety scale would be an anxious person at home, at work, and at social affairs. A woman scoring high on talkativeness would be expected to strike up acquaintanceships with strangers, to enjoy cocktail parties, and to carry on long telephone conversations with friends and neighbors. Research on situational differences took shape as a corrective measure to check out these assumptions and to throw light on a number of problems that have plagued personality assessment.

Personality tests have had serious validation problems. Do they really measure what their titles indicate? Does a high score for anxiety designate a chronically anxious person? If an anxious man reveals the characteristic only in some situations, the one the psychologist chooses in developing a criterion for the trait may be one in which this particular person is free from anxiety. Close scrutiny of the behavior of a woman rated very sociable on the basis of a high test score may show that she talks animatedly with her neighbors and close friends but clams up in a large group, especially if it is made up mostly of strangers. So what does her high score for sociability mean? After hundreds, perhaps even thousands, of disappointing attempts to predict behavior from personality test scores (correlations between tests and criteria seldom exceed .30), some psychologists are now swinging to the opposite viewpoint and placing the burden of prediction on situations. Situationism assumes that behavior is not determined by personal dispositions but by the situations in which it occurs. This is what experimental psychologists generally assume, and the increasing emphasis on behavioral therapies in clinical psychology has made it attractive to professional psychologists as well. Behavior is made up of responses to stimuli. Which responses will be made and become habitual depends on the contingencies of reinforcement. Actions producing rewarding consequences will be repeated. Actions producing punishing consequences or no consequences at all will be discontinued and will disappear.

Early in the 1960s, Endler, Hunt, and Rosenstein (1962) came out with a report that seemed to show that differences between situations were responsible for a much larger proportion of variance in behavior than were personality differences. The conclusion was based on answers subjects gave to questions on a specially designed inventory of "anxiousness," in which ratings of the degree of anxiety one felt were made separately for a number of situations. This made it possible to compute separate variances for subjects and for situations. The conclusion has been widely quoted: "The fact that a sampling of situations can contribute over eleven times the amount of variance contributed by individual differences among a sample of S's [subjects] should give pause to clinicians, personologists, and psychometricians in general" (Endler, Hunt, and Rosenstein, 1962, p. 12). And so it did. The trait versus situation controversy organized a great deal of the research of the 1960s and 1970s on personality assessment. This emphasis on assessment fit in with the increasing preference for behavioral therapy over the formerly preferred "talking" therapies. Psychologists treating phobias, hyperactivity, or stuttering by setting up situations in which the desired behavior would be reinforced and the unwanted behavior extinguished saw little use for personality tests. Instead, they worked out ad hoc ways of measuring how much of a particular kind of behavior a particular person emitted in a particular situation. General traits, such as anxiety, aggressiveness, or persistence, did not need to be considered. The clearest and most comprehensive account of this orientation to personality and assessment was Mischel's (1968) book. The last paragraph expresses the promise it seemed to offer:

> Global traits and states are excessively crude, gross units to encompass adequately the extraordinary complexity and subtlety of the discriminations that people constantly make. . . . The traditional trait-state conceptualization of personality, while often paying lip-service to man's complexity and to the uniqueness of each person, in fact led to a grossly oversimplified view that misses both the richness and the uniqueness of individual lives. A more adequate conceptualization must take full account of man's extraordinary adaptiveness and capacities for discrimination, awareness, and self-regulation; it must also recognize that men can and do reconceptualize themselves and change and that an understanding of how humans can constructively modify their behavior in systematic ways is the core of a truly dynamic personality psychology [Mischel, 1968, p. 301].

As time passed and research findings accumulated, the enthusiasm for situationism as contrasted with the trait approach to personality was toned down somewhat. It was pointed out that the conclusion drawn by Endler, Hunt, and Rosenstein (1962)—that situational variance was eleven times the variance arising from individual differences—was certainly not generalizable to all groups and situations. Golding (1975) analyzed methodological problems, making it impossible to draw conclusions about the relative importance of traits and situations from the kinds of data and data analysis that investigators had been reporting. Bowers (1973) brought together the results of eleven studies in which variance had been partitioned between persons, situations, and the interaction between them. He showed that there is a great deal of variation from study to study. Proportions of the variance attributed to situations range from less than 1 percent to almost 44 percent. Proportions attributed to individual differences range from 2 to 30 percent. Interaction proportions range from 9 to 29 percent. In seven out of the eleven reports, interaction accounted for more variance than did either situations or persons. This suggests that what one must observe is the relationship between differences in individuals and differences in the situations in which they operate.

The most articulate and knowledgeable critic of the extreme situationist position over the years has been Jack Block (1968). In his 1971 book *Lives through Time,* his analysis of data from the Berkeley longitudinal studies demonstrated that there is indeed continuity of personality characteristics over the years. In a 1977 preliminary draft of a paper called "Recognizing the Coherence of Personality" (personal communication), he points out flaws in the evidence on which most of the criticism of personality assessment rests and shows that research based on ratings or self-reports demonstrates a fair amount of personality consistency over time. It is the behavioral tests used in laboratory investigations that show subjects to be most inconsistent, and they are of questionable validity as measures of the qualities they are taken to represent. A current longitudinal study (Block and Block, 1977) of young children shows moderately high correlations over ages three, four, and five for the composite scores on ego control and ego resiliency, the two characteristics in which the Blocks are most interested. Our thinking about the way individuality develops over time must take into account both consistency and variability over time and situations.

One main reason why it has been difficult to fuse research on traits with research on situations is that real-life situations are so numerous and so diverse that it is almost impossible to devise a research plan which takes even a sizable proportion of them into consideration. What seems to be needed is a reasonable taxonomy or classification of situations according to their psychological similarity. There has been considerable interest and some preliminary research on this problem during the 1970s, but so far no consensus has emerged about how situations should be classified (Frederiksen, 1972; Pervin, 1975b). The most fundamental issue is whether the taxonomy should rest on external, observable aspects of situations or on internal perceptions of them. Those who favor the external approach believe that it will generate more productive research than will the other. The independent and dependent variables do not become confounded so easily if concepts of situations are anchored to realities outside the responding person. Those who favor the internal approach are impressed by the discrepancies that have shown up again and again in psychotherapy between what a situation looks like to an outsider and what it looks like to the troubled client. And it is the perceived situation that generates the feelings and behavior. A position intermediate between the external and the internal has been proposed. "A situation is a set of circumstances that is likely to influence the behavior of at least some individuals and that is likely to recur repeatedly in the same form" (Frederiksen, Jensen, and Beaton, 1972, p. 22).

Some research has resulted from each of these approaches. Barker and Wright (1954) identified and classified objective behavior settings in the little town of Midwest and described the rather consistent behavior of children and adults occurring in these places. During the year of the survey, they were able to differentiate 2,030 behavior settings—1,445 within homes and 585 in public areas. For children, the number of settings entered increased with age, but even at the earliest ages a large proportion of them were accessible. One of the most striking things the ecological research of the Barker group has shown is how very numerous identifiable behavior settings are, even in a very small town. The subjective or internal approach to the classification of situations is exemplified in the Endler and Hunt research on anxiousness mentioned earlier. Subjects responded to questions on an inventory, rating their anxiety level in various situations (Endler and Hunt, 1966). Although this constituted an interesting classification of situations in which anxiety may occur, it does not carry us very far toward a general taxonomy of situations related to all sorts of feelings.

An ambitious attempt to combine a taxonomy of situations with test and background information to predict the behavior of men in management positions was made by Frederiksen, Jensen, and Beaton (1972). The subjects were 260 administrators from California government departments. An experiment was designed to simulate closely the work in which men in such positions are engaged. Each man was sent a set of materials about a hypothetical department of commerce. These materials were of four varieties, differentiated according to two aspects of organizational climate: innovation versus rules and global versus detailed supervision. At an institute to which the men were invited, they took a number of tests and personality inventories and completed an in-basket test, consisting of problems, challenges, and demands such as those an executive faces. Each person's responses to these items were listed and rated for adequacy. The in-basket scores were used as the criteria to be predicted, the dependent variables in the experiment on organizational climates.

An example of what one in-basket item is like is a memo from Ray Loupe stating that an Illinois company is considering two sites for a new manufacturing plant, one of them in California. The administrator is asked to authorize an expenditure of $250 to get a printout of information to be sent to the manufacturer. Along with the request is a handwritten note from Loupe suggesting that Jay Capitola, Loupe's superior in the organization but the manager's subordinate, has been bypassed because he is not likely to act quickly. What actions might be taken? Eleven different ones were mentioned by men responding to the item, including referral to Capitola, with or without special instructions, approval of the expenditure after discussing the matter with Loupe, and several others. On the basis of about sixty of such in-basket items, rating scales were developed for a considerable number of characteristics reflecting both style and content of decisions. Factor analysis was then used to reduce the complexity of the data that had been generated.

The evidence was brought to bear on two fundamental questions: "Did the four groups of managers, differentiated by the material they had received about organizational climates, perform differently on the in-basket test? Were the correlations of background and personality characteristics with in-basket performance different from groups assigned to the four organizational climates?" The answer to both questions was a qualified yes. There were some differences, but they were not very striking. For example, one performance factor, "thoughtful analysis of problems," was negatively correlated with "interacts with superiors" and positively correlated with "interacts with peers" in the "innovation" and "global" climates, not in the "rules" and "detailed supervision" climates. This sort of difference makes sense. But all correlations were low, warranting no practical predictions about the performance of individuals in this simulated work situation. Results such as these dampen one's hopes for the practical utility of a taxonomy of situations.

Contrasting with this large-scale nomothetic project is a small but intensive idiographic study by Pervin (1975a). Pervin approached the question of how situations should be classified by obtaining from five college students their free responses to several questions. First the person was asked to list situations in his or her current life. Sample answers obtained were "presenting my ideas before a class," "arguing with my mother," and "studying alone." Second, the person described the situations listed. Third, the person described his or her feelings in each situation. Fourth, the person described the behavior likely to occur in each situation. At the completion of the four steps, the subject had four lists: situations, situational characteristics, feelings, and behaviors. He or she was then asked to rate the applicability of each characteristic, feeling, and behavior to each situation on the first list. The ratings provided numerical data to which correlational and factor analytical procedures could be applied to obtain a unique taxonomy of situations for each individual. There was a great deal of diversity on all the lists and ratings, but the results of the factor analysis suggested that the number of categories any one person uses to classify situations is fairly limited—about four or five. For example, Jennifer's twenty-three situations boiled down to four categories: home-volatile, schoolwork-pressure to perform, friends versus alone, and uncertain. Ben's twenty-eight situations were sorted into five categories: social-friends, work-nonstimulating conditions, family, army, and band-conflict. The results of this idiographic investigation make it appear improbable that a single taxonomy will serve for everybody. Inconvenient as it is for psychologists to deal with data different for each subject, they may have to do so if they expect to comprehend the complexities of individual structure. This ingenious study shows how such research can be designed. Perhaps methods derived from personal construct theory may also be applicable here.

In summing up, it can be said that the attempts to take situations as well as personal characteristics into consideration in predicting behavior have not turned out to be the breakthrough some psychologists had hoped they would be. There are levels of complexity not conquered by the use of techniques presently available. As suggested in the title of Bem and Allen's (1974) paper ("On Predicting Some of the People Some of the Time: The Search for Cross-Situational Consistencies in Behavior"), people do not do what we expect them to a great deal of the time. It would seem that the time has come to examine one unstated assumption, that behavior is in principle completely predictable. Possibility thinking based on Whitehead's philosophical system assumes that the future is not completely determined by the past and that any person in any situation has more than one alternative for taking action.

The diverse research results brought together in this chapter—multiple personality, intra-individual variability, analysis and classification of situations—have in common this one theme, that an individual is not limited to one way of dealing with any of life's demands. Through encounters with a very large number of situations and persons exemplifying different possibilities for structuring reality, one puts together one's own repertoire of possibility-processing structures. If we need to predict a person's behavior in some situation and we are familiar with his or her repertoire, we can predict with some certainty what he or she will *not* do, but with much less certainty what he or she *will* do. The more extensive the person's repertoire, the more uncertainty there is about which of the available structures will control the behavior in any one "actual occasion." People are less limited and more versatile than our dominant psychological theories have led us to assume. Individuality is plural, not singular.

❧ 16 ❧

Implications
and Applications

The purpose of this book has been to construct a framework to be used in thinking about individuals and how they differ from one another. The core idea is that each individual represents a different sequence of selective acts by means of which only some of the developmental possibilities are chosen and organized. No one individual can ever be considered typical of the human race. People complement one another. Individual uniqueness is what makes full humanity possible. As Whitehead pointed out, the fundamental realities are actual occasions in which indeterminate possibilities are transformed into determinate actualities. The individual is a unique sequence of such actual occasions. As Jordan puts it, "The identity of the person consists of living occasions extended in time: a man plus a history and a future" (Jordan, 1968, p. 119). Individuals create themselves. To understand a person completely, we would need to trace the road he or she has taken on one occasion after another. It is development we must study, but the development of the shaper rather than the

233

shaped. Obviously such complete understanding of an individual, especially of oneself, is impossible, but it is not unrealistic to hope that an expanded theory and technology for studying individuality will enable us to assess more accurately what has been created in an individual so far through the endless process of becoming what one is, to appreciate more deeply the value of human diversity, and to utilize the unique contributions of individuals to enrich the pattern of our common social fabric.

The material brought together in the foregoing chapters is the result of a systematic search through psychological books and journals for concepts and techniques that fit in with this general view. Many lines of research point to the active participation of individuals in their own development. The existence of different patterns of mental organization, different repertoires of competencies, and different strategies and styles has been well documented. What we have not done so far is to incorporate these new insights into the research we do on all psychological problems and the applications of psychological knowledge we make in the world at large.

The adoption of the viewpoint espoused here has implications for the conduct of psychological research, especially in the areas of social psychology, development, personality, and individual differences. The first and most important is that we cannot expect to draw general conclusions about human nature unless we analyze what individuals in experimental situations actually do, observing qualitative as well as quantitative aspects of the behavior. The people in our experiments are not inert, interchangeable units such as the materials physicists and chemists use in their experiments. Psychology must necessarily be a different sort of science from physics. What a subject does in an experiment depends on what he or she thinks the purpose of the experiment is as well as on the experimenter's intentions. No matter how carefully we equate groups of subjects for age, sex, social class, education, and other characteristics, each of them has unique ways of handling situations, unique concepts, strategies, and values, and these are partial determiners of the behavior being studied. Psychologists must learn to look separately at what each individual does and says and to rest their conclusions and generalizations not just on group averages but on their own creative syntheses of what the individual responses show. A related implication is that the whole concept of experimenters and subjects is not really appropriate for psychological research. Whether the psychologist recognizes it or not, the subject is really a collaborator in the important undertaking of increasing our knowledge of human nature. The word *participant* fits this role better than does *subject*.

In some instances it will turn out that participants behave in very similar ways in experiments. Sometimes they will fall into classes or types, as happened with field dependence and independence. As Kluckhohn, Murray, and Schneider (1953) observed many years ago: Every man is in certain respects (1) like all other men, (2) like some other men, and (3) like no other men. It is up to the investigator to find out which phrase applies to the characteristic being studied. At least a beginning has been made in the devising of research designs adapted to whatever the findings about similarities and differences are. The point is that what individuals do should not be ignored. The behavior of one extreme exception to a group trend may be as significant for an understanding of some psychological phenomenon as the average of the group is.

Research on individuals has always had a focus on applications. Its social purpose is to help individuals find places in our complex social order. Techniques have been elaborated to enable organizations to select the most suitable people to play particular roles and to enable individuals to discover what roles they are suited for and wish to play. The technology of mental testing has been designed to serve these purposes. What we are beginning to recognize now, however, is that in the years since World War II accelerating social changes have been making our present approaches to the study and utilization of individual differences increasingly obsolete. Our technology of mental testing began in a society where roles to be played by individuals could be graded along a single scale of desirability or status. Intelligence tests were a useful tool schools could use to facilitate the sorting process through which people found their proper places. Fifty years ago, when these tests came into widespread use, such sorting by successive screening for higher levels was one main function of the school system. Everybody went to elementary school, because it was agreed that everybody needed the basic skills of reading, writing, and arithmetic. But only those who showed some aptitude for "bookish" activities continued into secondary school, and only a fraction of these students, the brightest fraction, went to college. Intelligence tests were welcomed because they provided an index of brightness more accurate than the un-aided judgment of teachers. They often served to identify bright in-dividuals from the lower classes who might not have been selected for advanced education otherwise.

As other kinds of ability and achievement tests were devel-oped for use in employment situations, they also served to screen and sort. High scorers were selected for the most desirable jobs and training programs. Low scorers could always get unskilled labor jobs. There were always plenty of places at the bottom of the occu-pational pyramid. It was assumed that each person would thus end up at the level where he or she was capable of functioning success-fully, and thus the social order was maintained.

What we have not sufficiently taken into account, in psy-chology as in other fields of specialized knowledge, is the almost complete collapse of the social system in which these concepts were embedded. We have shifted in education to a way of thinking based on the assumption that everybody, regardless of ability level, must continue through the secondary level in school, whether they wish to or not, and that everybody who wishes to has a right to go to col-lege. The task of the educational system is no longer one of screen-ing and sorting; what it is expected to do is to stimulate maximum learning in persons of all ability levels, a much more difficult task. With the advent of automation and power machinery, the insatiable demand for unskilled workers no longer exists. Persons who fall through the successive screens have nowhere to go. Bulldozers have replaced ditchdiggers; computers have replaced bookkeepers and typists. The system that worked reasonably well a generation ago to sort individuals into suitable slots is now producing a vast layer of unemployed workers at the bottom, a vast number of alienated and dissatisfied workers at all levels.

This analysis is obviously an oversimplification of our cur-rent personnel problems, but it is at least suggestive of directions in which we might move and ways in which psychology might encour-age such movement. The measurements of individual differences we have been making down through the years are primarily *vertical*. The techniques we use show us how high a level an individual has attained or should be able to attain, but they tell us much less about exactly what he or she might do at that level. Our whole system of test standardization produces vertical differentiations: scores are high, moderate, or low; they tell us how much above or below average each person is. Mental measurement is a competitive undertaking, tied in with the competitive aspects of our social order. There are winners and losers; half of the group tested is below average.

It is true that competition is a salient aspect of our society and that individuals must adapt themselves to it. But it is not the *only* aspect. A psychology of individual differences should recognize *complementarity* as well as competition. It is necessary that individuals play different roles, do different things, and these differences need not be scaled or graded. In schools, teachers are being challenged to find out how each individual learns most readily rather than just how much he or she learns in a standard situation. In work places, new systems of organization are being explored, systems in which individual workers contribute in different ways to the functioning of work groups rather than acting as competitive units in an impersonal machine. Colleges that practice open enrollment must find for each individual who enters some fraction of the world's vast store of knowledge which will contribute to his or her intellectual development. Whatever one's occupation, one encounters opportunities for volunteer work and recreational activities from which choices can be made. Americans are coming to appreciate human diversity, to welcome the rich qualitative variety manifested in our population.

The search through psychological writings for promising ways to identify horizontal rather than vertical differences between individuals has turned up several promising approaches. These have been discussed in some detail in previous chapters. For some purposes, what is needed is an inventory of the person's unique assortment of competencies. These may be work skills such as cake baking or television repairing, recreational skills such as swimming or playing the guitar, or social skills such as starting conversations or soothing an irate customer. For other purposes, what we need to analyze are the individual's psychological structures through which experience is processed. What concepts are used? What persons, jobs, virtues, or political labels are classified together and dealt with in the same way? In other contexts, it is the individual's styles or strategies that seem most important—cognitive styles, life-styles, strategies for decision making. In any of these approaches to the assessment of individuals, we must examine repertoires and priorities rather than single types or variables. An individual is characterized by his or her total assortment of competencies, structures, styles, and strategies as well as by the amount of specified traits he or she possesses.

In the foregoing chapters we looked at specific techniques for assessing aspects of individuality that are seldom if ever used in the schoolroom, the clinic, or the personnel office. There are the instruments used in personal construct research, for example, the REP test with its many variations. There are the many kinds of sorting procedures, for example, objects sorts, Q-sorts of value statements or personality descriptions, choice pattern sorts for occupations and other activities. There are apparatus situations, such as the Rod and Frame test. There are inventories and checklists of competencies. There are the aids to decision making that Janis and Mann (1977) employ. There are probably others that would be turned up in a more comprehensive search. The foundation has been laid for a new technology of psychological assessment, different from and supplementary to the prevailing psychometric technology.

Individuality does not mean self-sufficiency, and equality does not mean sameness. Because the development of an individual involves the actualization of only a small fraction of human potentialities, each of us is incomplete without other human beings. Our incompletenesses complement one another, and our uniqueness contributes to the richness of the total pattern. The ideal for society is one expressed with great vividness by St. Paul in the early days of the Christian church: "For the body is not one member, but many. If the foot shall say, Because I am not the hand, I am not of the body; is it therefore not of the body? And if the ear shall say, Because I am not the eye, I am not of the body; is it therefore not of the body? If the whole body were an eye, where were the hearing? If the whole were hearing, where were the smelling? But now hath God set the members every one of them in the body, as it hath pleased him. And if they were all one member, where were the body? But now are they many members, yet but one body" (1 Corinthians 12:14–20).

References

ADORNO, T. W., and others. *The Authoritarian Personality.* New York: Harper & Row, 1950.

ALBERT, R. S. "Toward a Behavioral Definition of Genius." *American Psychologist,* 1975, *30,* 140–151.

ALLPORT, G. W. *Personality: A Psychological Interpretation.* New York: Holt, Rinehart and Winston, 1937.

ALLPORT, G. W. *The Use of Personal Documents in Psychological Science.* Bulletin 49. New York: Social Science Research Council, 1942.

ALLPORT, G. W. *Personality and Social Encounter.* Boston: Beacon Press, 1960.

ALLPORT, G. W. *Letters from Jenny.* New York: Harcourt Brace Jovanovich, 1965.

ALLPORT, G. W. *Pattern and Growth in Personality.* New York: Holt, Rinehart and Winston, 1961.

ALLPORT, G. W., and VERNON, P. E. *A Study of Values.* Boston: Houghton Mifflin, 1931.

ALLPORT, G. W., VERNON, P. E., and LINDZEY, G. *A Study of Values.* Boston: Houghton Mifflin, 1951.

239

ANDERSON, J. R., and BOWER, G. H. *Human Associative Memory.* Washington, D.C.: Winston, 1973.

ARIETI, S. *Creativity: The Magic Synthesis.* New York: Basic Books, 1976.

ARONSON, L. R., and others (Eds.). *Development and Evolution of Behavior.* San Francisco: W. H. Freeman, 1970.

AUSTIN, J. "The Roots of Serendipity." *Saturday Review World,* November 2, 1974, pp. 60–64.

BAIRD, R. R., and BEE, H. L. "Modification of Conceptual Style Preference by Differential Reinforcement." *Child Development,* 1969, *40,* 903–910.

BALLER, W. R. "A Study of the Present Social Status of a Group of Adults Who, When They Were in the Elementary Schools, Were Classified Mentally Deficient." *Genetic Psychology Monographs,* 1936, *18,* 165–244.

BALTES, P. B., and NESSELROADE, J. R. "The Developmental Analysis of Individual Differences on Multiple Measures." In J. R. Nesselroade and H. W. Reese (Eds.), *Life-Span Developmental Psychology: Methodological Issues.* New York: Academic Press, 1973.

BANNISTER, D., and FRANSELLA, F. "A Grid Test of Schizophrenic Thought Disorder." *British Journal of Social and Clinical Psychology,* 1955, *5,* 95.

BANNISTER, D., and MAIR, J. M. M. *The Evaluation of Personal Constructs.* New York: Academic Press, 1968.

BANNISTER, D., and SALMON, P. "Schizophrenic Thought Disorder: Specific or Diffuse?" *British Journal of Medical Psychology,* 1966, *39,* 215

BARKER, R. G., and WRIGHT, H. F. *Midwest and Its Children.* Evanston, Ill.: Row, Peterson, 1954.

BARTLETT, F. C. *Remembering.* Cambridge, England: Cambridge University Press, 1932.

BAYLEY, N., and ODEN, M. H. "The Maintenance of Intellectual Ability in Gifted Adults." *Journal of Gerontology,* 1955, *10,* 91–107.

BAYLEY, N., and SCHAEFER, E. S. "Correlations of Material and Child Behaviors with the Development of Mental Abilities: Data from the Berkeley Growth Study." *Monographs of the*

Society for Research on Child Development, 1964, *29* (6, serial no. 97).

BELMONT, J. M., and BUTTERFIELD, E. C. "What the Development of Short-Term Memory Is." *Human Development,* 1971, *14,* 236–248.

BEM, D. J., and ALLEN, A. "On Predicting Some of the People Some of the Time: The Search for Cross-Situational Consistencies in Behavior." *Psychological Review,* 1974, *81,* 506–520.

BENTLER, P. M. "Assessment of Developmental Factor Change at the Individual and Group Level." In J. R. Nesselroade and H. W. Reese (Eds.), *Life-Span Developmental Psychology: Methodological Issues.* New York: Academic Press, 1973.

BENTZ, V. J. "A Test-Retest Experiment on the Relationship Between Age and Mental Ability." *American Psychologist,* 1953, *8,* 319–320.

BERDIE, R. F. "Intra-Individual Variability and Predictability." *Educational and Psychological Measurement,* 1961, *21,* 663–676.

BERDIE, R. F. "Intra-Individual Temporal Variability and Predictability." *Educational and Psychological Measurement,* 1969a, *29,* 235–257.

BERDIE, R. F. "Consistency and Generalizability of Intraindividual Variability." *Journal of Applied Psychology,* 1969b, *53,* 35–41.

BERRY, J. W. *Human Ecology and Cognitive Style.* New York: Halsted Press, 1976.

BERTALANFFY, L. VON. *General System Theory.* New York: Braziller, 1968.

BIERI, J. "Complexity-Simplicity as a Personality Variable in Cognitive and Preferential Behavior." In D. W. Fiske and S. Maddie (Eds.), *Functions of Varied Experience.* Homewood, Ill.: Dorsey, 1961.

BINET, A., and SIMON, T. "Le développement de l'intelligence chez les enfants" [The Development of Intelligence in Children]. *Année Psychologique [Psychology Annual],* 1908, *14,* 1–94.

BLOCK, J. *The Q-Sort Method in Personality Assessment and Psychiatric Research.* Springfield, Ill.: Thomas, 1961.

BLOCK, J. "Some Reasons for the Apparent Inconsistency of Personality." *Psychological Bulletin,* 1968, *70,* 210–212.

BLOCK, J. *Lives Through Time.* Berkeley, Calif.: Bancroft, 1971.

BLOCK, J., and BLOCK, J. H. "The Developmental Continuity of Ego Control and Ego Resiliency: Some Accomplishments." Paper presented at the meeting of the Society for Research in Child Development, New Orleans, March 1977.

BLOCK, N. J., and DWORKIN, G. (Eds.). *The IQ Controversy: Critical Readings.* New York: Pantheon, 1976.

BLOOM, B. S. *Stability and Change in Human Characteristics.* New York: Wiley, 1964.

BOLLES, R. N. *The Quick Job-Hunting Map.* Berkeley, Calif.: Ten Speed Press, 1975.

BOLLES, R. N. *What Color Is Your Parachute?* Berkeley, Calif.: Ten Speed Press, 1976.

BONARIUS, H. "The Interaction Model of Communication: Through Experimental Research Toward Existential Relevance." In A. W. Landfield (Ed.), *1976 Nebraska Symposium on Motivation: Personal Construct Psychology.* Lincoln: University of Nebraska Press, 1977.

BORNSTEIN, M. H., KESSEN, W., and WEISSKOPF, S. A. "The Categories of Hue in Infancy." *Science,* 1976, *191,* 201–202.

BOWER, G. H. "Cognitive Psychology: An Introduction." In W. K. Estes, *Handbook of Learning and Cognitive Processes.* Vol. 1. Hillsdale, N.J.: Erlbaum, 1975.

BOWERS, K. S. "Situationism in Psychology: An Analysis and a Critique." *Psychological Review,* 1973, *80,* 307–336.

BRADWAY, K. P., and THOMPSON, C. W. "Intelligence at Adulthood: A Twenty-Five Year Follow-Up." *Journal of Educational Psychology,* 1962, *53,* 1–14.

BRAY, D. W., and MOSES, J. L. "Personnel Selection." *Annual Review of Psychology,* 1972, *23,* 545–576.

BROADBENT, D. E. "The Hidden Preattentive Process." *American Psychologist,* 1977, *32,* 109–118.

BROWN, A., CAMPIONE, J. C., and MURPHY, M. "Keeping Track of Changing Variables: Long-Term Retention of a Trained Rehearsal Strategy by Retarded Adolescents." *American Journal of Mental Deficiency,* 1974, *78,* 446–453.

BROWN, A., and others. "Keeping Track of Changing Variables: Effect of Rehearsal Training and Rehearsal Prevention in Normal and Retarded Adolescents." *Journal of Experimental Psychology*, 1973, *101*, 123–131.

BRUNER, J. S. *On Knowing: Essays for the Left Hand*. Cambridge, Mass.: Harvard University Press, 1963.

BRUNER, J. S. "The Course of Cognitive Growth." *American Psychologist*, 1964, *19*, 1–15.

BRUNER, J. S. "On Cognitive Growth," chapters 1 and 2. In J. S. Bruner and others, *Studies in Cognitive Growth*. New York: Wiley, 1966.

BRUNER, J. S., GOODNOW, J., and AUSTIN, G. A. *A Study of Thinking*. New York: Wiley, 1956.

BÜHLER, C. *Der Menschliche Lebenslauf als Psychologische Problem* [*The Human Life Cycle as a Psychological Problem*]. Göttingen, Germany: Verlag für Psychologie, 1959. (Originally published 1933.)

BURKS, B. S., JENSEN, D. W., and TERMAN, L. M. *Genetic Studies of Genius*. Vol. 3: *The Promise of Youth: Follow-Up Studies of a Thousand Gifted Children*. Stanford, Calif.: Stanford University Press, 1930.

BUROS, O. K. (Ed.). *The Seventh Mental Measurement Yearbook*. Highland Park, N.J.: Gryphon Press, 1972.

CAMPBELL, D. P. "A Cross-Sectional and Longitudinal Study of Scholastic Abilities over Twenty-Five Years." *Journal of Counseling Psychology*, 1965, *12*, 55–61.

CAMPBELL, D. P. *Handbook for the Strong Vocational Interest Blank*. Stanford, Calif.: Stanford University Press, 1971.

CARROLL, J. B. "Psychometric Tests as Cognitive Tasks: A New 'Structure of Intellect.' " In L. B. Resnick (Ed.), *The Nature of Intelligence*. Hillsdale, N.J.: Erlbaum, 1976.

CASSIRER, E. *The Philosophy of Symbolic Forms*. Vol. 1: *Language*. New Haven, Conn.: Yale University Press, 1953.

CASSIRER, E. *The Philosophy of Symbolic Forms*. Vol. 2: *Mythical Thought*. New Haven, Conn.: Yale University Press, 1955.

CASSIRER, E. *The Philosophy of Symbolic Forms*. Vol. 3: *The Phenomenology of Knowledge*. New Haven, Conn.: Yale University Press, 1957.

CATTELL, R. B. *Abilities: Their Structure, Growth, and Action.* Boston: Houghton Mifflin, 1971.

CHARLES, D. C. "Ability and Accomplishment of Persons Earlier Judged Mentally Deficient." *Genetic Psychology Monographs,* 1953, *47,* 3–71.

CHEW, P. *The Inner World of the Middle-Aged Man.* New York: Macmillan, 1976.

CHOMSKY, N. *Syntactic Structures.* The Hague: Mouton, 1957.

CHOMSKY, N. *Aspects of the Theory of Syntax.* Cambridge, Mass.: MIT Press, 1965.

CLEARY, T. A., and others. "Educational Uses of Tests with Disadvantaged Students." *American Psychologist,* 1975, *30,* 15–41.

CONNOLLY, K. J., and BRUNER, J. (Eds.). *The Growth of Competence.* New York: Academic Press, 1974.

CONRAD, H., and JONES, H. E. "A Second Study of Familial Resemblances in Intelligence, Environmental and Genetic Implications of Parent-Child and Sibling Correlations in the Total Sample." *Yearbook of the National Society for the Study of Education,* 1940, *39* (2), 97–141.

COOLEY, W. W. "Who Needs General Intelligence?" In L. B. Resnick (Ed.), *The Nature of Intelligence.* Hillsdale, N.J.: Erlbaum, 1976.

COX, C. M. *Genetic Studies of Genius.* Vol. 2: *The Early Mental Traits of Three Hundred Geniuses.* Stanford, Calif.: Stanford University Press, 1926.

CRANDALL, V. C. "The Fels Study: Some Contributions to Personality Development and Achievement in Childhood and Adulthood." *Seminars in Psychiatry,* 1972, *4,* 383–397.

CRANO, W. D. "What Do Infant Mental Tests Test? A Cross Lagged Panel Analysis of Selected Data from the Berkeley Growth Study." *Child Development,* 1977, *48,* 144–151.

CROCKETT, W. H. "Cognitive Complexity and Impression Formation." In B. Maher (Ed.), *Progress in Experimental Personality Research.* Vol. 2. New York: Academic Press, 1965.

CRONBACH, L. J. "The Two Disciplines of Scientific Psychology." *American Psychologist,* 1957, *12,* 671–684.

CUNNINGHAM, J. W. " 'Ergometrics': A Systematic Approach to

Some Educational Problems." Center for Occupational Education Monograph, 1971, No. 7. *JSAS Catalog of Selected Documents in Psychology*, 1974, *4*, 144–145. Ms. No. 804.

DAVIDSON, P. O., and COSTELLO, C. G. (Eds.). *N = 1: Experimental Studies of Single Cases*. New York: Van Nostrand, 1969.

DAVIS, A. J. "Cognitive Styles: Methodological and Developmental Considerations." *Child Development*, 1971, *42*, 1447–1459.

DAY, R. W. "Fusion in Dichotic Listening." Unpublished doctoral dissertation, Stanford University, 1968.

DE CHARMS, R. *Personal Causation: The Internal Affective Determinants of Behavior*. New York: Academic Press, 1968.

DELLAS, M., and GAIER, E. S. "Identification of Creativity: The Individual." *Psychological Bulletin*, 1970, *73*, 55–73.

DENNEY, D. R. "Modeling Effects upon Conceptual Style and Cognitive Tempo." *Child Development*, 1972, *43*, 105–119.

DENNEY, D. R., and DENNEY, N. W. "The Use of Classification for Problem Solving: A Comparison of Middle and Old Age." *Developmental Psychology*, 1973, *9*, 275–278.

DENNEY, N. W. "A Developmental Study of Free Classification in Children." *Child Development*, 1972a, *43*, 221–232.

DENNEY, N. W. "Free Classification in Preschool Children." *Child Development*, 1972b, *43*, 1161–1170.

DENNEY, N. W., and ACITO, M. A. "Classification Training in Two- and Three-Year-Old Children." *Journal of Experimental Child Psychology*, 1974, *17*, 37–48.

DEWEY, J. *How We Think*. Boston: Heath, 1910.

DUBOWITZ, L. M. S., DUBOWITZ, V., and GOLDBERG, C. "Clinical Assessment of Gestational Age in the Newborn Infant." *Journal of Pediatrics*, 1970, *77*, 1–10.

DUDYCHA, G. J. "An Objective Study of Punctuality in Relation to Personality and Achievement." *Archives of Psychology*, 1936, *204*, 1–319.

DUNKLEBERGER, C. J., and TYLER, L. E. "Interest Stability and Personality Traits." *Journal of Counseling Psychology*, 1961, *8*, 70–74.

DVORAK, B. *Differential Occupational Ability Patterns*. Minneapolis: University of Minnesota Press, 1935.

DYK, R. B. "An Exploratory Study of Mother-Child Interaction in

Infancy as Related to the Development of Differentiation." *Journal of the American Academy of Child Psychiatry,* 1969, *8,* 657–691.

DYK, R. B., and WITKIN, H. A. "Family Experiences Related to the Development of Differentiation in Children." *Child Development,* 1965, *30,* 21–55.

ELLIS, M. J. *Why People Play.* Englewood Cliffs, N.J.: Prentice-Hall, 1973.

ENDLER, N. S., and HUNT, J. M. "Sources of Behavioral Variance as Measured by the S-R Inventory of Anxiousness." *Psychological Bulletin,* 1966, *65,* 336–346.

ENDLER, N. S., HUNT, J. M., and ROSENSTEIN, A. J. "An A-S Inventory of Anxiousness." *Psychological Monographs,* 1962, *76* (entire issue no. 536), 1–33.

ERIKSON, E. *Childhood and Society.* New York: Norton, 1950.

ESCALONA, S. K. *The Roots of Individuality.* Chicago: Aldine, 1968.

ESCALONA, S. K., and HEIDER, G. *Prediction and Outcome: A Study of Child Development.* New York: Basic Books, 1959.

ESCALONA, S. K., and others. "Early Phases of Personality Development: A Nonnormative Study of Infant Behavior." *Monographs of the Society for Research in Child Development,* 1953, *17* (1).

FAIRBANKS, D. W., and HATHAWAY, W. E. *Competency-Based Education in Oregon (Product 1).* Salem, Ore.: Northwest Regional Educational Laboratory, 1975.

FATERSON, H. F., and WITKIN, H. A. "Longitudinal Study of Development of the Body Concept." *Developmental Psychology,* 1970, *2,* 429–438.

FINE, S. A., and WILEY, W. W. *An Introduction to Functional Job Analysis: A Scaling of Selected Tasks from the Social Welfare Field.* Kalamazoo, Mich.: Upjohn Institute, 1971.

FLEISHMAN, E. A. "The Description and Prediction of Perceptual-Motor Skill Learning." In R. Glaser (Ed.), *Training Research and Education.* Pittsburgh: University of Pittsburgh Press, 1962.

FLEISHMAN, E. A. "Development of a Behavior Taxonomy for Describing Human Tasks: A Correlational-Experimental Approach." *Journal of Applied Psychology,* 1967, *51,* 1–10.

FLEISHMAN, E. A., and PARKER, J. F. "Factors in the Retention and Relearning of Perceptual-Motor Skill Learning." *Journal of Experimental Psychology*, 1962, *64*, 215–226.

FLORES, M. B., and EVANS, G. T. "Some Differences in Cognitive Abilities Between Selected Canadian and Filipino Students." *Multivariate Behavioral Research*, 1972, *7*, 175–191.

FORD, B. G., and RENZULLI, J. W. "Developing the Creative Potential of Educable Mentally Retarded Students." *Journal of Creative Behavior*, 1976, *10*, 210–218.

FOULDS, G. A., and RAVEN, J. C. "Normal Changes in the Mental Abilities of Adults as Age Advances." *Journal of Mental Science*, 1948, *94*, 133–142.

FRANSELLA, F., and ADAMS, B. "An Illustration of the Use of Repertory Grid Technique in a Clinical Setting." *British Journal of Social and Clinical Psychology*, 1966, *5*, 51–62.

FREDERIKSEN, N. "Toward a Taxonomy of Situations." *American Psychologist*, 1972, *27*, 114–123.

FREDERIKSEN, N., JENSEN, O., and BEATON, A. E. *Prediction of Organizational Behavior*. New York: Pergamon, 1972.

FREEDMAN, D. G. "Heredity Control of Early Social Behavior." In B. M. Foss (Ed.), *Determinants of Infant Behavior*. Vol. 3. New York: Wiley, 1965.

FRENKEL, E. "Studies in Biographical Psychology." *Character and Personality*, 1936, *5*, 1–34.

GALLUP, G. H. "Seventh Annual Gallup Poll of Public Attitudes Toward Education." *Phi Delta Kappan*, 1975, *57*, 227–241.

GALTON, F. *Inquiries into Human Faculty and Its Development*. London: Macmillan, 1883.

GARDNER, R. W. "The Development of Cognitive Structures." In C. Sheerer (Ed.), *Cognition: Theory, Research, Promise*. New York: Harper & Row, 1964.

GARDNER, R. W., and SCHOEN, R. A. "Differentiation and Abstraction in Concept Formation." *Psychological Monographs*, 1962, *76* (41; entire issue no. 560), 1–21.

GETZELS, J. W., and JACKSON, P. W. *Creativity and Intelligence*. New York: Wiley, 1962.

GHISELLI, E. E. *The Validity of Occupational Aptitude Tests*. New York: Wiley, 1966.

GOLDFARB, W. "Effects of Early Institutional Care on Adolescent Personality." *Journal of Experimental Education,* 1943, *12,* 106–129.

GOLDFRIED, M. R., and D'ZURILLA, T. J. "A Behavioral-Analytic Model for Assessing Competence." In C. D. Spielberger (Ed.), *Current Topics in Clinical and Community Psychology.* Vol. 1. New York: Academic Press, 1969.

GOLDFRIED, M. R., and KENT, R. N. "Traditional Versus Behavioral Personality Assessment: A Comparison of Methodological and Theoretical Assumptions." *Psychological Bulletin,* 1972, *77,* 409–420.

GOLDING, S. L. "Flies in the Ointment: Methodological Problems in the Analysis of the Percentage of Variance Due to Persons and Situations." *Psychological Bulletin,* 1975, *82,* 278–288.

GOODENOUGH, D. R. "The Role of Individual Differences in Field Dependence as a Factor in Learning and Memory." *Psychological Bulletin,* 1976, *83,* 675–694.

GOODENOUGH, D. R., and others. "Repression, Interference, and Field Dependence as Factors in Dream Forgetting." *Journal of Abnormal Psychology,* 1974, *83,* 32–44.

GOTTESMAN, I. I. "Developmental Genetics and Ontogenetic Psychology: Overdue Detente and Propositions from a Matchmaker." In A. D. Pick (Ed.), *Minnesota Symposium on Child Psychology.* Vol. 8. Minneapolis: University of Minnesota Press, 1974.

GOULD, R. "The Phases of Adult Life: A Study in Developmental Psychology." *American Journal of Psychiatry,* 1972, *129,* 521–531.

GRAY, S. W., and KLAUS, R. A. "The Early Training Project: A Seventh-Year Report." *Child Development,* 1970, *41,* 909–924.

GUILFORD, J. P. "Creativity." *American Psychologist,* 1950, *14,* 469–479.

GUILFORD, J. P. *The Nature of Human Intelligence.* New York: McGraw-Hill, 1967.

HAAN, N. "Personality Development From Adolescence to Adulthood in the Oakland Growth and Guidance Studies." *Seminars in Psychiatry,* 1972, *4,* 399–414.

HAGEN, J. W. "Some Thoughts on How Children Learn to Remember." *Human Development,* 1971, *14,* 262–271.

HAITH, M. M. "Developmental Changes in Visual Information Processing and Short-Term Visual Memory." *Human Development,* 1971, *14,* 249–261.

HALPERN, A., and others. *Social and Prevocational Information Battery.* Monterey, Calif.: CTB/McGraw-Hill, 1975.

HARRELL, R. "Further Effects of Added Thiamin on Learning and Other Processes." In *Teachers College Contributions to Education,* no. 928. New York: Teachers College, Columbia University, 1947.

HARRELL, T. W., and HARRELL, M. S. "Army General Classification Test Scores for Civilian Occupations." *Educational and Psychological Measurement,* 1945, *5,* 229–239.

HARTSHORNE, H., and MAY, M. A. *Studies in Deceit.* New York: Macmillan, 1928.

HARTSHORNE, H., MAY, M. A., and MALLER, J. B. *Studies in Service and Self-Control.* New York: Macmillan, 1929.

HARTSHORNE, H., MAY, M. A., and SHUTTLEWORTH, F. K. *Studies in the Organization of Character.* New York: Macmillan, 1930.

HATHAWAY, W. E. *Plan for OCBE Program Research Activities.* Salem, Ore.: Northwest Regional Educational Laboratory, 1976.

HERRNSTEIN, R. J. *IQ in the Meritocracy.* Boston: Little, Brown, 1973.

HETHERINGTON, E. M., and MC INTYRE, C. W. "Developmental Psychology." *Annual Review of Psychology,* 1975, *26,* 97–136.

HIRSCHMAN, R., and KATIN, E. S. "Psychophysiological Functioning, Arousal, Attention, and Learning During the First Year of Life." In H. W. Reese (Ed.), *Advances in Child Development and Behavior.* Vol. 9. New York: Academic Press, 1974.

HOLTZMAN, W. H., and others. *Personality Development in Two Cultures: A Cross-Cultural Longitudinal Study of School Children in Mexico and the United States.* Austin: University of Texas Press, 1975.

HOLZMAN, P. S., and KLEIN, G. S. "Cognitive System-Principles of

Leveling and Sharpening: Individual Differences in Visual Time-Error Assimilation Effects." *Journal of Psychology,* 1954, *37,* 105–122.

HONIKMAN, B. "Construct Theory as an Approach to Architectural and Environmental Design." In P. Slater (Ed.), *Explorations of Intrapersonal Space.* New York: Wiley, 1976, pp. 167–182.

HONZIK, M. P. "Developmental Studies of Parent-Child Resemblance in Intelligence." *Child Development,* 1957, *28,* 215–228.

HORN, J. L. "Organization of Abilities and the Development of Intelligence." *Psychological Review,* 1968, *75,* 242–259.

HORN, J. L. "Human Abilities: A Review of Research and Theory in the Early 1970s." *Annual Review of Psychology,* 1976, *27,* 437–485.

HOROWITZ, F. D. "Infant Attention and Discrimination: Methodological and Substantive Issues." *Monographs of the Society for Research in Child Development,* 1974, *39* (serial nos. 5 and 6), 1–15.

HOYT, D. P. "The Relationship Between College Grades and Adult Achievement: A Review of the Literature." Research Report no. 7. Iowa City: American College Testing Program, 1965.

HUDSON, L. *Contrary Imaginations: A Psychological Study of the English Schoolboy.* London: Methuen, 1966.

HUDSON, L. *Frames of Mind.* London: Methuen, 1968.

HUNT, E. "Varieties of Cognitive Power." In L. B. Resnick (Ed.), *The Nature of Intelligence.* Hillsdale, N.J.: Erlbaum, 1976.

HUNT, E., and LANSMAN, M. "Cognitive Theory Applied to Individual Differences." In N. K. Estes (Ed.), *Handbook of Learning and Cognitive Processes.* Vol. 1. Hillsdale, N.J.: Erlbaum, 1975.

HUNT, E., and LOVE, L. T. "How Good Can Memory Be?" In A. Melton and E. Margin (Eds.), *Coding Processes in Human Memory.* Washington, D.C.: Winston, 1972.

HUNT, E., LUNNEBORG, C., and LEWIS, J. "What Does it Mean to be High Verbal?" *Cognitive Psychology,* 1975, *7,* 194–227.

HUTTENLOCHER, J., and BURKE, D. "Why Does Memory Span Increase with Age?" *Cognitive Psychology,* 1976, *8,* 1–31.

IRVIN, L. K., HALPERN, A., and REYNOLDS, W. M. *Social and Prevocational Information Battery—Form T*. Eugene: Research and Training Center in Mental Retardation, University of Oregon, 1977.

JACOB, F. *The Logic of Life*. New York: Random House, 1973.

JACOB, F., and MONOD, J. "Genetic Regulatory Mechanisms in the Synthesis of Proteins." *Journal of Molecular Biology*, 1961, *3*, 318–356.

JANIS, I. L., and MANN, L. *Decision Making*. New York: Free Press, 1977.

JARVIK, L. F., and BLUM, J. E. "Cognitive Declines as Predictors of Mortality in Discordant Twin Pairs—A Twenty-Year Longitudinal Study." In E. Palmore and F. C. Jeffers (Eds.), *Prediction of Life Span*. Lexington, Mass.: Heath Lexington Books, 1971, pp. 199–211.

JENSEN, A. R. *Genetics and Education*. New York: Harper & Row, 1972.

JONES, H. E., and CONRAD, H. "The Growth and Decline of Intelligence." *Genetic Psychology Monographs*, 1933, *13*, 223–298.

JORDAN, M. *New Shapes of Reality*. London: Allen & Unwin, 1968.

JUNG, C. G. *Psychological Types*. London: Routledge & Kegan Paul, 1923.

KAGAN, J. *Change and Continuity in Infancy*. New York: Wiley, 1971.

KAGAN, J. "Do Infants Think?" *Scientific American*, 1972, *226*, 74–82.

KAGAN, J., and MOSS, H. A. *Birth to Maturity*. New York: Wiley, 1962.

KAGAN, J., MOSS, H. A., and SIGEL, I. E. "Psychological Significance of Styles of Conceptualization." *Monographs of the Society for Research in Child Development*, 1963, *28* (2), 73–112.

KAGAN, J., and others. "Information Processing in the Child: Significance of Analytic and Reflective Attitudes." *Psychological Monographs*, 1964, *78* (1, entire issue no. 568), 1–37.

KAHNEMAN, D., BEN-ISHAI, R., and LOTAN, M. "Relation of a Test of

Attention to Road Accidents." *Journal of Applied Psychology*, 1973, *58*, 113–115.

KAUFMAN, A. S., and DOPPELT, J. E. "Analysis of the WISC-R Standardization Data in Terms of the Stratification Variables." *Child Development*, 1976, *47*, 165–171.

KEELE, S. W., and LYONS, D. R. *Individual Differences in Word Fusion*. ONR and ARPA Technical Report 2. Eugene: University of Oregon, 1975.

KELLY, G. S. *The Psychology of Personal Constructs*. New York: Norton, 1955.

KELLY, G. S. "Behaviour Is an Experiment." In D. Bannister (Ed.), *Perspectives in Personal Construct Theory*. New York: Academic Press, 1970.

KLUCKHOHN, C., MURRAY, H. A., and SCHNEIDER, D. M. *Personality in Nature, Society, and Culture*. New York: Knopf, 1953.

KLUCKHOHN, F. R., and STRODTBECK, F. L. *Variations in Value Orientations*. Evanston, Ill.: Row, Peterson, 1961.

KOESTLER, A. *The Act of Creation*. New York: Macmillan, 1964.

KOGAN, N. "Creativity and Cognitive Style: A Life-Span Perspective." In P. B. Baltes and K. W. Schaie, *Life-Span Developmental Psychology: Personality and Socialization*. New York: Academic Press, 1973.

KOGAN, N. "Categorizing and Conceptualizing Styles in Younger and Older Adults." *Human Development*, 1974, *17*, 218–230.

KOGAN, N. *Cognitive Styles in Infancy and Early Childhood*. New York: Wiley, 1976.

KOGAN, N., and PANKOVE, E. "Creative Ability over a Five-Year Span." *Child Development*, 1972, *43*, 427–442.

KOGAN, N., and WALLACH, M. A. *Risk Taking: A Study in Cognition and Personality*. New York: Holt, Rinehart and Winston, 1964.

KORNER, A. F. "The Effect of the Infant's State, Level of Arousal, Sex, and Ontogenetic Stage on the Caregiver." In M. Lewis and L. A. Rosenbloom (Eds.), *The Effect of the Infant on the Caregiver*. New York: Wiley, 1974.

KRETSCHMER, E. *Physique and Character*. New York: Harcourt Brace Jovanovich, 1925.

KRIS, E. *Psychoanalytic Explorations in Art.* New York: International Universities Press, 1952.

KUO, Z.-Y. *The Dynamics of Behavior Development: An Epigenetic View.* New York: Random House, 1967.

KUO, Z.-Y. "The Need for Coordinated Efforts in Developmental Studies." In L. R. Aronson and others (Eds.), *Development and Evaluation of Behavior.* San Francisco: W. H. Freeman, 1970.

LANDFIELD, A. W. (Ed.). *1976 Nebraska Symposium on Motivation.* Lincoln: University of Nebraska Press, 1977.

LANGER, S. *Mind: An Essay on Human Feeling.* Vol. 1. Baltimore, Md.: Johns Hopkins University Press, 1967.

LANGER, S. *Mind: An Essay on Human Feeling.* Vol. 2. Baltimore, Md.: Johns Hopkins University Press, 1972.

LEFCOURT, H. M. *Locus of Control.* Hillsdale, N.J.: Erlbaum, 1976.

LEFCOURT, H. M., LEWIS, L., and SILVERMAN, I. W. "Internal Versus External Control of Reinforcement and Attention in Decision-Making Tasks." *Journal of Personality,* 1968, *36,* 663–682.

LEVINSON, D. "The Psychosocial Development of Men in Early Adulthood and the Mid-Life Transition." Minneapolis: University of Minnesota Press, 1974.

LEWIN, K. *A Dynamic Theory of Personality.* New York: McGraw-Hill, 1935.

LEWIN, K. *Principles of Topological Psychology.* New York: McGraw-Hill, 1936.

LEWIS, H. B. *Shame and Guilt in Neurosis.* New York: International Universities Press, 1971.

LEWIS, M., and LEE-PAINTER, S. "An Interactional Approach to the Mother-Infant Dyad." In M. Lewis and L. A. Rosenbloom (Eds.), *The Effect of the Infant on Its Caregiver.* New York: Wiley, 1974.

LEWIS, M., and MC GURK, H. "Evaluation of Infant Intelligence: Infant Intelligence Scores—True or False?" *Science,* 1972, *178,* 1174–1177.

LEWIS, M., and ROSENBLOOM, L. A. (Eds.), *The Effect of the Infant on Its Caregiver.* New York: Wiley, 1974.

LEWIS, P. S. "The Prisoner's Perception of Himself and of His

World." Unpublished doctoral dissertation, University of London, 1973.

LOEHLIN, J. C., LINDZEY, G., and SPUHLER, J. N. *Race Differences in Intelligence.* San Francisco: W. H. Freeman, 1975.

LOFTUS, G. R., and LOFTUS, E. F. *Human Memory: The Processing of Information.* Hillsdale, N.J.: Erlbaum, 1976.

LORENZ, K. Z. "Eighth Discussion." In J. M. Tanner and B. Inhelder (Eds.), *Discussions on Child Development.* London: Tavistock, 1956.

LOWE, V. *Understanding Whitehead.* Baltimore, Md.: Johns Hopkins University Press, 1962.

LYONS, D. R. "Source of Individual Differences in Digit Span." Unpublished doctoral dissertation, University of Oregon, 1975.

MAAS, H. S., and KUYPERS, J. A. *From Thirty to Seventy: A Forty-Year Longitudinal Study of Adult Life Styles and Personality.* San Francisco: Jossey-Bass, 1974.

MC CALL, R. B., HOGARTY, P. S., and HURLBURT, N. "Transitions in Infant Sensorimotor Development and the Prediction of Childhood IQ." *American Psychologist,* 1972, *27,* 728–748.

MC CLELLAND, D. C. "Testing for Competence Rather Than for Intelligence." *American Psychologist,* 1973, *28,* 1–14.

MAC KINNON, D. W. "The Nature and Nurture of Creative Talent." *American Psychologist,* 1962, *17,* 484–495.

MAIER, N. R. F. "Reasoning in Humans: The Solution of a Problem and Its Appearance in Consciousness." *Journal of Comparative and Physiological Psychology,* 1931, *12,* 181–194.

MAIR, J. M. M. "Metaphors for Living." In A. W. Landfield (Ed.), *1976 Nebraska Symposium on Motivation: Personal Construct Psychology.* Vol. 24. Lincoln: University of Nebraska Press, 1977.

MANCUSO, J. C. "Current Motivational Models in the Elaboration of Personal Construct Psychology." In A. W. Landfield (Ed.), *1976 Nebraska Symposium on Motivation: Personal Construct Psychology.* Vol. 24. Lincoln: University of Nebraska Press, 1977.

MARKS, D. F. "Visual Imagery Differences in Recall of Pictures." *British Journal of Psychology,* 1973, *64,* 17–24.

MEACHAM, J. A. "The Development of Memory Abilities in the Individual and Society." *Human Development,* 1972, *15,* 205–228.

MEICHENBAUM, D. H., and GOODMAN, J. "Reflection-Impulsivity and Verbal Control of Motor Behavior." *Child Development,* 1969, *40,* 785–797.

MERRIFIELD, P. R., and others. "The Role of Intellectual Factors in Problem Solving." *Psychological Monographs,* 1962, *76* (10, entire issue no. 529), 1–21.

MESSER, S. "The Effect of Anxiety Over Intellectual Performance on Reflection-Impulsivity in Children." *Child Development,* 1970, *41,* 723–735.

MESSER, S. "Reflection-Impulsivity: A Review." *Psychological Bulletin,* 1976, *83,* 1026–1052.

MESSICK, S. (Ed.). *Individuality in Learning: Implications of Cognitive Styles and Creativity for Human Development.* San Francisco: Jossey-Bass, 1976.

MILES, C. C., and MILES, W. R. "The Correlation of Intelligence Scores and Chronological Age From Early to Late Maturity." *American Journal of Psychology,* 1932, *44,* 44–78.

MILLER, G. A. "The Magical Number Seven, Plus or Minus Two. Some Limits on Our Capacity to Process Information." *Psychological Review,* 1956, *63,* 81–97.

MILLER, G. A., GALANTER, E., and PRIBRAM, K. H. *Plans and the Structure of Behavior.* New York: Holt, Rinehart and Winston, 1960.

MISCHEL, W. *Personality and Assessment.* New York: Wiley, 1968.

MISCHEL, W. "Toward a Cognitive Social Learning Reconceptualization of Personality." *Psychological Review,* 1973, *80,* 252–283.

MONOD, J. *Chance and Necessity.* New York: Knopf, 1971.

MORRIS, C. *Paths of Life.* New York: Harper & Row, 1942.

MORRIS, C. *Varieties of Human Value.* Chicago: University of Chicago Press, 1956.

MUCCHIELLI, R. *Introduction to Structural Psychology.* New York: Avon Books, 1970.

MYERS, I. B. *The Myers-Briggs Type Indicator, Manual.* Princeton, N.J.: Educational Testing Service, 1962.

NEIMARK, E. D. "Natural Language Concepts: Additional Evidence." *Child Development,* 1974, *45,* 508–511.

NEISSER, U. *Cognition and Reality.* San Francisco: W. H. Freeman, 1976.

NELSON, K. "Some Evidence for the Cognitive Primacy of Categorization and Its Functional Basis." *Merrill-Palmer Quarterly,* 1973, *19,* 21–30.

NEUGARTEN, B. L. "Dynamics of Transition of Middle Age to Old Age." *Journal of Geriatric Psychiatry,* 1970, *4,* 71–87.

NEWCOMB, T. M. *Consistency of Certain Extrovert-Introvert Behavior Patterns in 51 Problem Boys.* New York: Teachers College, Columbia University, 1929.

NEWELL, A., and SIMON, H. A. *Human Problem Solving.* Englewood Cliffs, N.J.: Prentice-Hall, 1972.

NICHOLLS, J. G. "Creativity in the Person Who Will Never Produce Anything Original and Useful: The Concept of Creativity as a Normally Distributed Trait." *American Psychologist,* 1972, *27,* 717–727.

NISBET, J. D. "Symposium: Contributions to Intelligence Testing and the Theory of Intelligence. Part 4: Intelligence and Age: Retesting with Twenty-Four Years Interval." *British Journal of Educational Psychology,* 1957, *27,* 190–198.

NUNNALLY, J. C. "Research Strategies and Measurement Methods for Investigating Human Development." In J. R. Nesselroade and H. W. Reese (Eds.), *Life-Span Developmental Psychology: Methodological Issues.* New York: Academic Press, 1973.

ODEN, M. H. "The Fulfillment of Promise: 40-Year Follow-Up of the Terman Gifted Group." *Genetic Psychology Monographs,* 1968, *77,* 3–93.

OLTMAN, P. K., and others. "Psychological Differentiation as a Factor in Conflict Resolution." *Journal of Personality and Social Psychology,* 1975, *32,* 730–736.

OSGOOD, C. E., and others. "The Three Faces of Evelyn: A Case Report." *Journal of Abnormal Psychology,* 1976, *85,* 247–286.

OVERTON, W. F., and REESE, H. W. "Models of Development: Methodological Implications." In J. R. Nesselroade and

H. W. Reese (Eds.), *Life-Span Developmental Psychology: Methodological Issues.* New York: Academic Press, 1973.

OWENS, W. A., JR. "Age and Mental Abilities: A Longitudinal Study." *Genetic Psychology Monographs,* 1953, *48,* 3–54.

PAIVIO, A. *Imagery and Verbal Processes.* New York: Holt, Rinehart and Winston, 1971.

PATRICK, C. "Scientific Thought." *Journal of Psychology,* 1938, *5,* 55–83.

PEASE, D., WOLINS, L., and STOCKDALE, D. F. "Relationship and Predictions of Infant Tests." *Journal of Genetic Psychology,* 1973, *122,* 31–35.

PEIRCE, C. S. *Values in a Universe of Chance.* Garden City, N.Y.: Doubleday, 1958. (Originally published 1892.)

PEPPER, S. *World Hypotheses.* Berkeley, Calif.: University of California Press, 1942.

PERVIN, L. A. "A Free-Response Description Approach to the Analysis of Person-Situation Interaction." RB-75-22. Princeton, N.J.: Educational Testing Service, 1975a.

PERVIN, L. A. "Definitions, Measurements, and Classifications of Stimuli, Situations, and Environments." RB-75-23. Princeton, N.J.: Educational Testing Service, 1975b.

PETTIGREW, T. F. "The Measurement and Correlation of Category Width as a Cognitive Variable." *Journal of Personality,* 1958, *26,* 532–544.

PIAGET, J. *The Origins of Intelligence in Children.* New York: International Universities Press, 1952.

PIAGET, J. *Structuralism.* New York: Basic Books, 1970.

POPPER, K. R. *Objective Knowledge.* Oxford: Clarendon, 1972.

POSNER, M. I., and BOIES, S. J. "Components of Attention." *Psychological Review,* 1971, *78,* 391–408.

POSNER, M. I., and ROGERS, M. G. K. "Chronometric Analysis of Abstraction and Recognition." In W. K. Estes (Ed.), *Handbook of Learning and Cognitive Processes.* Vol. 6. Hillsdale, N.J.: Erlbaum, 1977.

POSNER, M. I., and SNYDER, C. R. R. "Attention and Cognitive Control." In R. L. Solso (Ed.), *Information Processing and Cognition: The Loyola Symposium.* Hillsdale, N.J.: Erlbaum, 1974.

PRICE, P. B., and others. "Measurement of Physician Performance."
Report presented at American Association of Medical Col-
leges, Second Annual Conference on Research in Medical
Education, October 30, 1963.

PROTHRO, E. T. "Arab Students' Choices of Ways to Live." *Journal
of Social Psychology*, 1958, *47*, 3–7.

PYLYSHYN, Z. W. "What the Mind's Eye Tells the Mind's Brain: A
Critique of Mental Imagery." *Psychological Bulletin*, 1973,
80, 1–24.

RESNICK, L. B. (Ed.). *The Nature of Intelligence.* Hillsdale, N.J.:
Erlbaum, 1976.

RICCIUTI, H. N. "Object Grouping and Selective Ordering Behavior
in Infants 12–24 Months Old." *Merrill-Palmer Quarterly*,
1965, *11*, 129–148.

RICCIUTI, H. N., and PORESKY, R. H. "Emotional Behavior and De-
velopment in the First Year of Life: An Analysis of Arousal,
Approach-Withdrawal and Affective Responses." In A. D.
Pick (Ed.), *Minnesota Symposium on Child Psychology.*
Vol. 6. Minneapolis: University of Minnesota Press, 1972.

RICHARDS, R. L. "A Comparison of Selected Guilford and Wallach-
Kogan Creative Thinking Tests in Conjunction with Measures of Intelligence." *Journal of Creative Behavior*, 1976,
10, 151–164.

RIEGEL, K. F. "Toward a Dialectical Theory of Development." *Human Development*, 1975, *18*, 50–64.

RIEGEL, K. F., and ROSENWALD, G. C. (Eds.). *Structure and Transformation.* New York: Wiley, 1975.

ROKEACH, M. *Beliefs, Attitudes, and Values: A Theory of Organization and Change.* San Francisco: Jossey-Bass, 1968.

ROKEACH, M. *The Nature of Human Values.* New York: Free Press,
1973.

ROSENBERG, S. "New Approaches to the Analysis of Personal Constructs in Person Perception." In A. W. Landfield (Ed.),
*1976 Nebraska Symposium on Motivation: Personal Con-
struct Psychology.* Vol. 24. Lincoln: University of Nebraska
Press, 1977.

ROSSMAN, B. B., and HORN, J. L. "Cognitive, Motivational, and
Temperamental Indicants of Creativity and Intelligence."
Journal of Educational Measurement, 1972, *9*, 256–286.

ROTTER, J. B. *Social Learning and Clinical Psychology.* Englewood Cliffs, N.J.: Prentice-Hall, 1954.

ROWE, D. "Grid Techniques in the Conversation Between Patient and Therapist.'" In P. Slater (Ed.), *Explorations of Intrapersonal Space.* New York: Wiley, 1976.

SALMON, P. "Grid Measures with Child Subjects." In P. Slater (Ed.), *Explorations of Intrapersonal Space.* Vol. 1. New York: Wiley, 1976, pp. 15–46.

SALTZ, E., SOLLER, E., and SIGEL, I. E. "The Development of Natural Language Concepts." *Child Development,* 1972, *43,* 1191–1202.

SARBIN, T. R. "Contextualism: A World View For Modern Psychology." In A. W. Landfield (Ed.), *1976 Nebraska Symposium on Motivation: Personal Construct Psychology.* Vol. 24. Lincoln: University of Nebraska Press, 1977.

SCARR, S., and WEINBERG, R. A. "IQ Test Performance of Black Children Adopted by White Families." *American Psychologist,* 1976, *31,* 726–739.

SCHAEFER, E. S., and BAYLEY, N. "Maternal Behavior, Child Behavior, and Their Intercorrelations from Infancy Through Adolescence." *Monographs of the Society for Research on Child Development,* 1963, *28* (3), 1–127.

SCHAFFER, H. R., and EMERSON, P. E. "Patterns of Response to Physical Contact in Early Human Development." *Journal of Child Psychology and Psychiatry,* 1964, *5,* 1–13.

SCHAIE, K. W. "Translations in Gerontology—From Lab to Life." *American Psychologist,* 1974, *29,* 802–807.

SCHAIE, K. W., LABOUVIE, G. V., and BUECH, B. U. "Generational and Cohort Specific Differences in Adult Cognitive Functioning: A Fourteen-Year Study of Independent Samples." *Developmental Psychology,* 1973, *9,* 151–166.

SEARS, R. R. "Sources of Life Satisfactions of the Terman Gifted Men." *American Psychologist,* 1977, *32,* 119–128.

SELF, P. A. "Control of Infant Visual Attending by Auditory and Interspersed Stimulation." *Monographs of the Society for Research in Child Development,* 1974, *39* (5 and 6, serial 158), 16–28.

SHEEHY, G. *Passages.* New York: Dutton, 1976.

SHELDON, W. H. *The Varieties of Human Physique.* New York: Harper & Row, 1940.

SHERBURNE, D. W. (Ed.). *A Key to Whitehead's Process and Reality.* Bloomington: Indiana University Press, 1966.

SIGEL, I. E., and OLMSTED, P. "Modification of Cognitive Skills Among Lower-Class Black Children." In J. Hellmuth (Ed.), *The Disadvantaged Child.* Vol. 3. New York: Brunner-Mazel, 1970.

SIGEL, I., JARMAN, P., and HANESIAN, H. "Styles of Categorization and Their Intellectual and Personality Correlates in Young Children." *Human Development,* 1967, *10,* 1–17.

SIMON, H. A. "Identifying Basic Abilities Underlying Intelligent Performance of Complex Tasks." In L. B. Resnick (Ed.), *The Nature of Intelligence.* Hillsdale, N.J.: Erlbaum, 1976.

SIMONS, J. "Measuring the Meaning of Fertility Control." In P. Slater (Ed.), *Explorations in Intrapersonal Space.* New York: Wiley, 1976.

SKODAK, M., and SKEELS, H. M. "A Final Follow-Up Study of One Hundred Adopted Children." *Journal of Genetic Psychology,* 1949, *75,* 85–125.

SLATER, P. (Ed.). *Explorations of Intrapersonal Space.* Vol. 1. New York: Wiley, 1976.

SLOVIC, P., FISCHHOFF, B., and LICHTENSTEIN, S. "Behavioral Decision Theory." *Annual Review of Psychology,* 1977, *28,* 1–39.

SMITH, M. B. "Personal Values in the Study of Lives." In R. W. White (Ed.), *The Study of Lives.* New York: Atherton, 1963.

SMITH, M. B., BRUNER, J. S., and WHITE, R. W. *Opinions and Personality.* New York: Wiley, 1956.

SNYDER, C. R. R. "Individual Differences in Imagery and Thought." Unpublished doctoral dissertation, University of Oregon, 1972.

SPEARMAN, C. E. *The Abilities of Man.* New York: Macmillan, 1927.

SPERLING, G. "The Information Available in Brief Visual Presentations." *Psychological Monographs,* 1960, *74,* 1–29.

SPIVACK, G., PLATT, J. J., and SHURE, M. B. *The Problem-Solving*

Approach to Adjustment: A Guide to Research and Intervention. San Francisco: Jossey-Bass, 1976.

SPRANGER, E. *Types of Men.* Halle, German Democratic Republic: Niemeyer, 1928.

STEIN, M. I. *Stimulating Creativity.* Vol. 1: *Individual Procedures.* New York: Academic Press, 1974.

STEIN, M. I. *Stimulating Creativity.* Vol. 2: *Group Procedures.* New York: Academic Press, 1975.

STEPHENSON, W. *The Study of Behavior.* Chicago: University of Chicago Press, 1953.

STERN, D. N. "Mother and Infant at Play: The Dyadic Interaction Involving Facial, Vocal, and Gaze Behaviors." In M. Lewis and L. A. Rosenbloom (Eds.), *The Effect of the Infant on the Caregiver.* New York: Wiley, 1974.

STEWART, R. A., TUTTON, S. J., and STEELE, R. E. "Stereotyping and Personality: 1. Sex Differences in Perception of Female Physiques." *Perception and Motor Skills,* 1973, *36,* 811–814.

STRATTON, P. R., and BROWN, R. V. "Improving Creative Thinking by Training in the Production and/or Judgment of Solutions." *Journal of Educational Psychology,* 1972, *63,* 390–397.

STRONG, E. K., JR. "Interests and Sales Ability." *Personnel Journal,* 1934, *13,* 204–216.

STRONG, E. K., JR. "Nineteen-Year Follow-Up of Engineer Interests." *Journal of Applied Psychology,* 1952a, *36,* 65–74.

STRONG, E. K., JR. "Twenty-Year Follow-Up of Medical Interests." In L. L. Thurstone (Ed.), *Applications of Psychology.* New York: Harper & Row, 1952b.

SUNDBERG, N. D., and TYLER, L. E. "Awareness of Action Possibilities in Indian, Dutch, and American Adolescents." *Journal of Cross-Cultural Psychology,* 1970, *1,* 153–157.

SUNDBERG, N. D., ROHILA, P. K., and TYLER, L. E. "Values of Indian and American Adolescents." *Journal of Personality and Social Psychology,* 1970, *16,* 374–397.

SUNDBERG, N. D., SNOWDEN, L. R., and REYNOLDS, W. M. "Toward Assessment of Personal Competence and Incompetence in

Life Situations." *Annual Review of Psychology,* 1978, *29* (in press).

SUPER, D. E. *The Psychology of Careers.* New York: Harper & Row, 1957.

TANNER, J. M. "Variability of Growth and Maturity in Newborn Infants." In M. Lewis and L. A. Rosenbloom (Eds.), *The Effect of the Infant on the Caregiver.* New York: Wiley, 1974.

TERMAN, L. M. *Genetic Studies of Genius.* Vol. 1: *Mental and Physical Traits of a Thousand Gifted Children.* Stanford, Calif.: Stanford University Press, 1925.

TERMAN, L. M., and ODEN, M. *The Gifted Child Grows Up.* Stanford, Calif.: Stanford University Press, 1947.

TERMAN, L. M., and ODEN, M. *The Gifted Group at Mid-Life.* Stanford, Calif.: Stanford University Press, 1959.

THIGPEN, C. H., and CLECKLEY, H. M. *The Three Faces of Eve.* New York: McGraw-Hill, 1957.

THOMAS, A., CHESS, S., and BIRCH, H. B. *Temperament and Behavior Disorders in Children.* New York: New York University Press, 1968.

THOMAS, A., and others. *Behavioral Individuality in Early Childhood.* New York: New York University Press, 1963.

THORNDIKE, E. L. *The Measurement of Intelligence.* New York: Teachers College, Columbia University, 1926.

THORNDIKE, R. L., and HAGEN, E. *10,000 Careers.* New York: Wiley, 1959.

THURSTONE, L. L. *Primary Mental Abilities.* Psychometric Monograph No. 1. Chicago: University of Chicago Press, 1938.

TOFFLER, A. *Future Shock.* New York: Random House, 1970.

TORRANCE, E. P. *Guiding Creative Talent.* Englewood Cliffs, N.J.: Prentice-Hall, 1962.

TORRANCE, E. P. *Education and the Creative Potential.* Minneapolis: University of Minnesota Press, 1963.

TORRANCE, E. P., and others. *Rewarding Creative Thinking.* Minneapolis: University of Minnesota Press, 1960.

TYLER, L. E. "Toward a Workable Psychology of Individuality." *American Psychologist,* 1959, *14,* 75–81.

TYLER, L. E. (Ed.). *Intelligence: Some Recurring Issues.* New York: Van Nostrand Reinhold, 1969.

TYLER, L. E., and others. "Patterns of Choices in Dutch, American, and Indian Adolescents." *Journal of Counseling Psychology,* 1968, *15,* 522–529.

VAILLANT, G. E., and MC ARTHUR, C. C. "Natural History of Male Psychological Health. 1. The Adult Life Cycle from 18 to 50." *Seminars in Psychiatry,* 1972, *4,* 415–427.

VANDENBERG, S. C. "What Do We Know Today About the Inheritance of Intelligence and How Do We Know It?" In R. Cancro (Ed.), *Intelligence: Genetic and Environmental Influences.* New York: Grune & Stratton, 1971.

VERNON, P. E. "The Validity of Divergent Thinking Tests." *Alberta Journal of Educational Research,* 1972, *18,* 249–258.

VINCENT, D. F. "The Linear Relationship Between Age and Score of Adults in Intelligence Tests." *Occupational Psychology* (London), 1952, *26,* 243–249.

WADDINGTON, C. H. *Principles of Development and Differentiation.* New York: Macmillan, 1966.

WADDINGTON, C. H. "The Theory of Evolution Today." In A. Koestler and J. R. Smithies (Eds.), *Beyond Reductionism.* Boston: Beason Press, 1971.

WALLACH, M. A., and KOGAN, N. *Modes of Thinking in Young Children.* New York: Holt, Rinehart and Winston, 1965.

WALLACH, M. A., and WING, C. W., JR. *The Talented Student.* New York: Holt, Rinehart and Winston, 1969.

WALLAS, G. *The Art of Thought.* London: Watts, 1926.

WALLER, J. H. "Achievement and Social Mobility: Relationships Among IQ Score, Education and Occupation in Two Generations." *Social Biology,* 1971, *18,* 252–259.

WARD, W. C., KOGAN, N., and PANKOVE, E. "Incentive Effects in Children's Creativity." *Child Development,* 1972, *43,* 669–676.

WATSON, J. P., GUNN, J. C., and GRISTWOOD, J. "A Grid Investigation of Long-Term Prisoners." In P. Slater (Ed.), *Explorations in Intrapersonal Space.* Vol. 1. New York: Wiley, 1976.

WAUGH, H. C., and others. "Effects of Age and Stimulus Repetition on Two-Choice Reaction Time." *Journal of Gerontology,* 1973, *28,* 466–470.

WECHSLER, D. *The Measurement of Adult Intelligence.* Baltimore, Md.: Williams & Wilkins, 1941.

WEISLER, A., and MC CALL, R. B. "Exploration and Play Résumé and Redirection." *American Psychologist,* 1976, *31,* 492–508.

WELSH, G. S. *Creativity and Intelligence: A Personality Approach.* Chapel Hill, N.C.: Institute for Research in Social Science, University of North Carolina, 1975.

WHITE, R. W. "Motivation Reconsidered: The Concept of Competence." *Psychological Review,* 1959, *66,* 297–333.

WHITEHEAD, A. N. *Adventures of Ideas.* New York: Macmillan, 1933.

WHITEHEAD, A. N. *Modes of Thought,* New York: Macmillan, 1938.

WHITEHEAD, A. N. *Process and Reality.* New York: Free Press, 1969. (Originally published 1929.)

WILDEN, A. "Piaget and Structure as Law and Order." In K. F. Riegel and G. C. Rosenwald (Eds.), *Structure and Transformation.* New York: Wiley, 1975.

WILLIAMS, R. J. *Biochemical Individuality.* New York: Wiley, 1956.

WILSON, R. S. "Twins: Early Mental Development." *Science,* 1972, *175,* 914–917.

WITKIN, H. A. "Psychological Differentiation and Forms of Pathology." *Journal of Abnormal Psychology,* 1965, *70,* 317–336.

WITKIN, H. A. "Social Influences in the Development of Cognitive Style." In D. A. Goslin (Ed.), *Handbook of Socialization Theories and Research.* Chicago: Rand McNally, 1969.

WITKIN, H. A. "Individual Differences and Dreaming." *International Psychiatry Clinics.* Vol. 7, No. 2. Boston: Little, Brown, 1970.

WITKIN, H. A. "Cognitive Styles in Learning and Teaching." In S. Messick (Ed.), *Individuality in Learning: Implications of Cognitive Styles and Creativity for Human Development.* San Francisco: Jossey-Bass, 1976.

WITKIN, H. A., and BERRY, J. W. "Psychological Differentiation in

Cross-Cultural Perspective." *Journal of Cross-Cultural Psychology,* 1975, *6,* 4–87.

WITKIN, H. A., and GOODENOUGH, D. R. *Field Dependence Revisited.* Research Bulletin 76-39. Princeton, N.J.: Educational Testing Service, 1976.

WITKIN, H. A., and GOODENOUGH, D. R. "Field Dependence and Interpersonal Behavior." *Psychological Bulletin,* 1977, *84,* 661–689.

WITKIN, H. A., GOODENOUGH, D. R., and KARP, S. A. "Stability of Cognitive Style From Childhood to Young Adulthood." *Journal of Personality and Social Psychology,* 1967, *7,* 219–300.

WITKIN, H. A., LEWIS, H. B., and WEIL, E. "Affective Reactions and Patient-Therapist Interactions Among More Differentiated and Less Differentiated Patients Early in Therapy." *Journal of Nervous and Mental Diseases,* 1968, *146,* 193–208.

WITKIN, H. A., and others. *Personality Through Perception.* New York: Harper & Row, 1954.

WITKIN, H. A., and others. *Psychological Differentiation.* New York: Wiley, 1962.

WITKIN, H. A., and others. "Social Conformity and Psychological Differentiation." *International Journal of Psychology,* 1974, *9,* 11–29.

WITKIN, H. A., and others. "Field-Dependent and Field-Independent Cognitive Styles and Their Educational Implications." *Review of Educational Research,* 1977a, *47,* 1–64.

WITKIN, H. A., and others. "The Role of the Field-Dependent and Field-Independent Cognitive Styles in Adolescent Development: A Longitudinal Study." *Journal of Educational Psychology,* 1977b, *69,* 197–211.

WOHLWILL, J. F. "The Age Variable in Psychological Research." *Psychological Review,* 1970, *77,* 49–64.

WOODROW, H. "The Ability to Learn." *Psychological Review,* 1946, *53,* 147–158.

WOODWORTH, R. S. *First Course in Psychology.* New York: Holt, Rinehart and Winston, 1944.

WOZNIAK, R. H. "Dialecticism and Structuralism: The Philosophical Foundation of Soviet Psychology and Piagetian Cognitive

Development Theory." In K. F. Riegel and G. C. Rosenwald (Eds.), *Structure and Transformation*. New York: Wiley, 1975.

YERKES, R. M. (Ed.). *Memoirs of the National Academy of Sciences*. Vol. 15: *Psychological Examining in the U.S. Army*. Washington, D.C.: National Academy of Sciences, 1921.

Index

A

Abilities: competencies related to, 91–105; concept of, 91–92; testing of, 93–97

ACITO, M. A., 158, 245

ADAMS, B., 122, 247

ADLER, A., 6, 17

ADORNO, T. W., 145, 239

ALBERT, R. S., 201–202, 239

ALLEN, A., 224, 232, 241

ALLPORT, G. W., 17, 20, 33–34, 131, 133–134, 142, 239

ANDERSON, J. R., 79, 240

Aptitude testing, 93–95

ARIETI, S., 200, 240

ARONSON, L. R., 53, 240

Attention: in infancy, 58–59, 67–68; research on, 184–186

Attitudes, research on, 144–145

AUSTIN, G. A., 160, 243

AUSTIN, J., 15, 240

Autoregulation, and prenatal development, 51

B

BAIRD, R. R., 156, 240

BALLER, W. R., 88, 240

BALTES, P. B., 27–28, 240

BANNISTER, D., x, 117n, 118, 120, 121–122, 240

BARKER, R. G., 229, 240

BARTLETT, F. C., 112, 240

BAYLEY, N., 64, 86, 240–241, 259

BEATON, A. E., 229–230, 247

BEE, H. L., 156, 240

Behavior modification: and competence, 102; in research on individuals, 34

Behavior potentials, 52–53

Behavioral gradient, 52

BELMONT, J. M., 182, 241

BEM, D. J., 224, 232, 241

BEN-ISHAI, R., 180–181, 251–252

BENTLER, P. M., 31, 241

BENTZ, V. J., 86, 241

BERDIE, R. F., 224–225, 241

Berkeley Growth Study, 62

BERRY, J. W., 171, 241, 264–265